WOLF KINDERMANN; GISEL[A ...]

ECHOES IN A MIRROR:
THE ENGLISH INSTITUTE AFTER 125 YEARS

Hallenser Studien zur Anglistik und Amerikanistik

Veröffentlichungen des Hallenser Forums für Fremdsprachenforschung (HFF)

Herausgegeben am

Institut für Anglistik und Amerikanistik

Martin-Luther-Universität Halle-Wittenberg

HSAA = Band 9

LIT

WOLF KINDERMANN; GISELA HERMANN-BRENNECKE
(EDS.)

ECHOES IN A MIRROR: THE ENGLISH INSTITUTE AFTER 125 YEARS

LIT

Die Deutsche Bibliothek – CIP-Einheitsaufnahme

Echoes in a Mirror: The English Institute after 125 Years / Wolf Kindermann; Gisela Hermann-Brennecke (eds.). – Münster : LIT, 2001
(Hallenser Studien zur Anglistik und Amerikanistik ; 9.)
ISBN 3-8258-5675-5

© LIT VERLAG Münster – Hamburg – Berlin – London
Grevener Str. 179   48159 Münster   Tel. 0251-23 50 91   Fax 0251-23 19 72
e-Mail: lit@lit-verlag.de   http://www.lit-verlag.de

Distributed in North America by:

Transaction Publishers
New Brunswick (U.S.A.) and London (U.K.)

Transaction Publishers
Rutgers University
35 Berrue Circle
Piscataway, NJ 08854

Tel.: (732) 445 - 2280
Fax: (732) 445 - 3138
for orders (U. S. only):
toll free (888) 999 - 6778

Contents

WOLF KINDERMANN
The Slumber of Reason: Poe's 'The Pit and the Pendulum'   7

ANGELA SENST
Regional Aspects in T.S. Eliot's Poetry   37

EVA BOESENBERG
Interrogating Whiteness: Perspectives on 'Race' in Texts
by James McBride, Shirlee Taylor Haizlip, and Edward Ball   49

SABINE VOLK-BIRKE
Romance, Madness, and Woman's History:
Charlotte Lennox's *The Female Quixote* Revisited   63

JÜRGEN MEYER
Games With/Out Frontiers: A Ludic Analysis of Salman Rushdie's *Grimus*   85

HANS-DIETER METZGER/DIETMAR SCHNEIDER
Social Competence and Linguistic Performance in Elizabethan Parliaments   100

ANNEMARIE HINDORF
Man's View of His World in *Beowulf*   126

WERNER PLEHN
Black Vernacular English and the Feature of Ethnicity   139

OLAF JÄKEL
Denotational Incongruencies: A Very Short Introduction and Typology   156

HANS-DIETER SCHÖNE/DIETMAR SCHNEIDER
Expressive Adjectives and Their Semantic-Syntactic Patterning:
A Corpus-Linguistic Study of Newspaper English   170

ANDREAS MARSCHOLLEK
Pupils Reflecting on Languages, Cultures, and Perception:
An Account of a Teaching Programme at Primary Level   191

JULIA SEMMER/DIRK THORMANN
"I Want to Become a Teacher Because ...":
Future Teachers Between School and University   216

GISELA HERMANN-BRENNECKE
"Every Decoding Is Another Encoding":
A Didactic Discovery of David Lodge's *Small World*   231

Contributors   259

The Slumber of Reason: Poe's "The Pit and the Pendulum"

Wolf Kindermann

"If popularity be a test of merit," Mabbott writes, "'The Pit and the Pendulum' must rank high among its author's works. [...] The central idea is that the fear of the unknown exceeds the fear of anything known" (678-679). Like a number of Poe's tales and *Pym* "Pit" is a story of ordeal told by a survivor who, however, no longer shares the heroic qualities of many of his predecessors in this genre. The narrator is shrunk to anonymity and only has a presence through his *anamnesis*, the telling of his story of suffering and deliverance. If this is also an reenactment of the parable of Lazarus (cf. Hirsch 635), it leaves the reader with the question as to how Poe's "resurrected" narrator-protagonist will be able to go on living with - not only the memory of the tortures he underwent, but also - the haunting vision of the pit:

> I threw my straining vision below. The glare from the enkindled roof illuminated its innermost recesses. Yet, for a wild moment, did my spirit refuse to comprehend the meaning of what I saw. At length it forced - it wrestled its way into my soul - it burned itself in upon my shuddering reason. Oh! for a voice to speak! oh! horror! - oh! any horror but this! With a shriek, I rushed from the margin, and buried my face in my hands - weeping bitterly. (Mabbott 696)

The whole inquisitorial procedure and machinery seems to only be an accessory to the "revelation" with which Poe's narrator will have to live ever after his rescue by Lasalle's soldiers. There is not a salvation in a vision of the immortality of the soul that Link implies in his thesis of a *Gnadenakt*, an act of divine redemption (259). On the contrary, Poe presents a vision of omnipresent cosmic terror that remains forever burned upon the narrator's "shuddering reason." The revelation offered to Poe's narrator is the total obverse of that which guides

Christian theology: The "blackness of darkness" (Mabbott 682) is omnipresent, the short life span meted out to human beings in this world is the only "gift of grace" granted to them and *angst*, not hope, is all there is to define man's expectation of what lies beyond this world. Poe, however, skilfully defuses this implication by putting the reader on a totally different track through his "Jacobin" motto, prefixed to the second version of the tale (*Broadway Journal*, May 1845):

> Impia tortorum longas hic turba furores
> Sanguinis innocui, non satiata, aluit.
> Sospite nunc patriâ, fracto nunc funeris antro,
> Mors ubi dira fuit, vita salusque patent.

If one tries to relate this motto to the "meaning" of the tale, one has to take into account Poe's propensity of choosing mottoes from recondite or unreliable sources (such as the reference to Glanvill in "Ligeia"), or of cutting them out of whole cloth. This implies - contrary to the practice of "authenticating" the respective tale or chapter by giving it a mooring in a familiar literary context - a strategy of defamiliarization and obfuscation, and in the last resort, of arcane self-reference. Thus the spurious motto in "Pit" (cf. Mabbott 697) was deliberately made up in Latin in order to establish a connection between the French Jacobins and the Inquisition, the symbolic affinity between the "pendulum" as an instrument of torture and the guillotine of the French Terror. Poe wanted his readers to interpret "Pit" as a "moral" tale which warns against fanaticism and extols the virtues of a civil society based on free economic enterprise, as insinuated in his reference to the market (Marché St. Honoré) erected on the former site of the Jacobin club. Poe by implication celebrates the Napoleonic system of order, which did away with the "unsavory" elements of the French Revolution, refining its republican achievements, as well as Bonaparte's attempts to destroy the old feudal order and replace it with a republican society all over Europe (on the "Napoleonic legend" in contemporary literature cf. Wülfing 200-201).

Poe and Nativism

This "political" commitment seems strange in an avowedly non-political writer like Poe. "Pit" was written and finished in the summer of 1842 when Poe nourished a desperate hope of getting an appointment to the Philadelphia Custom House through his - rather distant - connections with the Tyler administration (cf. Quinn 321-325; 359-363; 368-369; 378-381). Poe's Whig sympathies and anti-Jacksonian leanings may well have influenced his writing of "Pit" - especially his references to the "wicked mob" and its "unappeased, long cherished [...] hatred of innocent blood" (Mabbott 697). Reynolds argues that Poe's fiction has to be interpreted in the context of the "emerging forms of popular literature" in his day and that "The Cask of Amontillado" (1846) should be read as an "enactment of the historical conflict between Catholics and Masons" ("Poe's Art of Transformation", 100-101). Anti-Masonic sentiment, had been stirred up by the Morgan case in 1826 and subsequently influenced the opposition to President Jackson, a Mason. The Anti-Masonic party eventually merged with the Whig party. Poe may well have intended to warn against the Masons as a subversive group that endangered the republican fabric of the nation. He certainly was aware of the Nativist scare that shaped the public sentiment in the 1840s. At the same time there were growing fears that the ongoing crisis of the liberal government in Spain might result in a re-establishment of the Inquisition in that country, which had been restored by Ferdinand VII in 1814 until it was again abolished by the regent Maria Christina in July 1834. (cf. Peters 103-104; cf. Esdaile 63-97).

Besides echoing contemporary political concerns, Poe did not only tap Gothic classics such as Matthew Gregory Lewis's *The Monk* (1796), Ann Radcliffe's *The Italian* (1797), Scott's *Anne of Geierstein* (1829) [cf. Ringe] or more recent variants in *Blackwood Gentleman's Magazine* (cf. Clark), he also seems to have been aware of contemporary Romantic interest in Spain. This was evident in the recent success of Irving's *Tales of the Alhambra* (1832) and Prescott's *History of the Reign of Ferdinand and Isabella the Catholic* (1837) as well as a number of illustrated travel books about Spain. In the context of the Nativist scare a spate of "hue and cry"-tracts and lurid "true stories" whipped up current prejudices and guaranteed a nice profit to their publishers. Rebecca Reed's *Six*

Months in a Convent (1835) and especially Maria Monk's *Awful Disclosure* (1836) became bestsellers which catered to contemporary pornographic phantasies in the guise of moralist anti-Catholic exposure (cf. Reynolds, *Renaissance* 64-65; cf. Billington 90-92, 99-108). The fervent anti-Catholic rhetoric of the "Protestant Crusade" in the 1840s continued the lurid tales of the Gothic novel as well as the tradition of the anti-Spanish and anti-Catholic "Black Legend" whose origins can be traced back to the Age of Reformation (cf. Maltby 29-43; cf. Peters 122-154).

During the Jacksonian Age the anti-Catholic hysteria reached its first peak in the burning of the Boston Ursuline Convent on August 11, 1834 which had been fuelled by Lyman Beecher's rabid anti-catholic sermons (cf. Billington 73-75). Beecher's xenophobic theory of a "papal plot" to impose a Catholic counter-reformation upon the American Republic (published in *A Plea for the West* in 1835) was seconded by Samuel F.B. Morse – painter, inventor of the telegraph, and in 1836 candidate for the office of mayor of New York - in a series of anti-Catholic letters, published under the title *Foreign Conspiracy* late in 1834, and B.F. Ellis in his *History of the Romish Inquisition Compiled from Various Authors* (Hanover, IN 1835). Ellis claimed that the Catholics were secretly building inquisitorial chambers under their churches and storing arms in preparation for an impending revolution (cf. Billington 122-127). Anti-Catholic propaganda was also spread through sensationalist and crypto-pornographic novels, popular gift books and almanacs which "were as essential to the pre-Civil War generation as the Bible" (Billington 350). When "Pit" first appeared in the *Gift: A Christmas and New Year's Present* for 1843 (on sale by the end of 1842) Poe must have been well aware of the context in which he was publishing his "Spanish tale." When in 1842 Poe was writing the story he may have visited the New York exhibition of a "model Inquisitorial building depicting the tortures commonly employed," with which a New York businessman tried to cash in on the Nativist hysteria (Billington 375).

As early as in 1933 Alterton argued that Poe's major source was Juan Antonio Llorente's *Historia Critica de la Inquisición en Espana*, which had been published in an abridged English translation in London and Philadelphia in 1826 and then again in Philadelphia in 1843, simultaneously with Poe's tale.

Alterton also discovered the original source for the "pendulum" as an instrument of torture in a note appended to the preface to the 1826 English edition of Llorente's book, from where it made its way into the contemporary British and American reviews (Alterton 350-352; cf. Mabbott 699). In his original text Llorente only briefly mentions the use and methods of torture (*Critical History*, Chapter IX, 64-65). Historians now agree that the facts do not bear out the tales about the horrible tortures invented and practiced by the Spanish Inquisition (cf. Kamen 174-176; cf. Monter 74-75). Poe may also have used John Joseph Stockdale's *History of the Inquisitions; Including the Secret Transactions of those Horrific Tribunals* (London 1810), "a virtual repertoire of the pictorial history of *The Inquisition*" (Peters 228), and the records from the Barcelona tribunal, translated and published in 1828 by Samuel Goodrich under the title *Records of the Spanish Inquisition* in Boston (cf. Peters 284).

Poe certainly was cognizant of Prescott's account of the "Establishment of the Modern Inquisition" and his reference to the use of torture:

> This, which was administered in the deepest vaults of the Inquisition is admitted by the secretary of the Holy Office [i.e. Llorente] who has furnished the most authentic report of its transactions, not to have been exaggerated in any of the numerous narratives which have dragged these subterranean horrors into light. [...] The last scene in this dismal tragedy was the *act of faith* (auto da fe), [...] which [...] was intended [...] to represent the terrors of the Day of Judgment. [...] The unfortunate convicts were clad in coarse woolen garments, styled *san benitos* [...]. These were yellow, embroidered with a scarlet cross, and well garnished with figures of devils and flames of fire, which, typical of the heretic's destiny hereafter, served to make him more odious in the eyes of the superstitious multitude. (102-103)

This passage may well have inspired Poe's version of the torture chamber: "The figures of fiends in aspects of menace, with skeleton forms, and other more really fearful images, overspread and disfigured the walls." Shortly before the climax of the tale his narrator sees "spectral and fiendish portraitures" and continues: "Demon eyes, of a wild and ghastly vivacity, glared upon me in a thousand directions [...] and gleamed with the lurid lustre of a fire that I could not force my imagination to regard as unreal" (Mabbott 689, 695). Poe's tale seems to echo and illustrate Prescott's moral conclusion: "Many a bloody page of history attests the fact that fanaticism, armed with power, is the sorest evil which can befall a nation" (104). All this supports Alterton's thesis that "Poe intended the Inquisition to stand as the centerpoint in his story" (355). There is, however, much contextual evidence that makes Poe less an advocate of tolerance than a writer who chimed in with a pervasive anti-Catholic propaganda in order to cash in on the Nativist hysteria, which finally culminated in the Philadelphia riots in early May 1844 (cf. Billington 220-238) - only shortly after Poe had left that city for New York. It is interesting to note that Poe only added his motto of "tolerance" to the second version of "Pit" (*Broadway Journal* in May 1845) - although it had already appeared in Poe's "Pinakidia" in the *Southern Literary Messenger* in August 1836 (Mabbott 697). It seems that Poe and many of his contemporaries, who secretly shared anti-Catholic prejudices, were "sobered" by the Philadelphia riots and withdrew their support for the fanatical nativists in the American Republican party, which subsequently entered a "period of decline" (Billington 233-234). Any discussion of the merits of "Pit" will have to bear in mind the ambiguity that characterizes Poe's motives in writing and publishing this tale.

Poe and the Gothic Tradition

Lubbers discusses Poe's transformation of historical, philosophical, and fictional sources in "Pit" on the basis of his innovative, functionalist "blueprint" for writing fiction. Poe's increasing emphasis on symbolism and allegory (105, 117) denotes a tendency towards a constructivist and abstract approach to art, a practice of literary engineering (cf. Valéry, cited in Meyers 283), which helped to lay the groundwork for the modernist revolution in the early 20th century. At the same time Poe heavily relies on the trappings of Gothic fiction, which he transformed to his own ends (cf. Tate 468). Whereas the subterranean torture chambers and instruments of the Spanish Inquisition perfectly fit the Gothic pattern, the atrophied plot in "Pit" does not. According to Klein the typical Gothic narrative introduces an aristocratic villain and his covenant with the Devil. The victims, quite often innocent maidens, suffer a series of abductions, imprisonment, torture, rape, and narrow escapes until they are finally "saved."

The archetypal villain either is redeemed through repentance or has to face eternal punishment (269-270).

In "Pit" we do not meet an arch villain such as Poe's William Wilson or Schedoni in Radcliffe's *The Italian*. There is no covenant with the devil, nor does Poe make use of an "erotic inquisitor" like Lewis's Ambrosio or later Peter Arbuez in Victor de Féréal's [*i.e.* Mme. de Suberwick] bestseller *Les mystères de L'Inquisition et autres sociétés sécrètes d'Espagne* (1844), which was published only shortly after Poe's tale. In contrast to the covert illicit eroticism in "Ligeia" and "The Fall of the House of Usher" Poe in "Pit" presents an exclusively male world filled with Inquisitors, monks/torturers, the nameless victim/narrator, and Lasalle's soldiers. Both the Spanish monks and the French soldiers seem to function as cogs in a wheel, in a complicated machinery set up to test the narrator's fortitude (cf. Lüdeke's terminology: "a laboratory test in anxiety-psychosis," 125). The technology of physical and psychological torture is literally designed to first sever the victim's heart and seat of his soul ("[...] the crescent was designed to cross the region of the heart." [Mabbott 691]) and then to destroy his sanity by forcing him to face the horrors of the pit. The confrontation between the machinery of torture and the victim's innermost being, totally laid bare to the probing eyes of the Inquisitors, between blind technology and the despair of the narrator's soul, marks the "Ultima Thule" of the evolution of mankind and the search for "absolute knowledge."

Poe was able to encode "Pit" and focus on the mechanisms of torture and psychological terror because his readers were familiar with the Gothic genre. One could easily read "Pit" as a vignette or a central chapter from a long Gothic novel in the making, in which the torture scene in the Inquisitorial vaults is just one of the many trials of the innocent victim-protagonist before his redemption. There are a number of elements that link *The Italian* and *The Monk* to Poe's tale. Once Vivaldi in *The Italian* enters the dungeons of the Inquisition in Rome he reads the motto over the entrance: "Hope, that comes to all, comes not here!" (200) - an echo of Dante's inscription over the gate of Hell. Vivaldi is confronted by Inquisitors who are presented as "demons" (197), their faces "sculptured by passions of dark malignity, or fierce cruelty" (356). Radcliffe's description of torture, however, pales in comparison with the lurid scenes in Lewis's *The Monk* in which Ambrosio kidnaps and drugs the helpless Antonia, whom he finally rapes and kills in a sepulchral cave (327-328, 334-335). In a parallel plot Agnes, pregnant with child, realizes that she is tormented according to the "idea that to afflict my body was the only way to preserve my soul" (352). First buried among "mouldering bodies" (344), she is then left with the putrefying corpse of her stillborn child, and later insects, toads, lizards and worms crawl over her body (354). This may well have inspired Poe's use of the rats in his tale, although he refuses to emulate Lewis's "graveyard" horrors.

Despite a number of borrowings and parallels Poe transforms the Gothic model. The traditional convolutions of the Gothic plot are radically telescoped into the torture scene. The villain-victim relationship is de-individualized, the function of the villain pluralized in the anonymous apparatus of the Inquisition. The helpless maiden is replaced by a male prisoner, the moral concern of individual guilt and innocence disappears before the immediacy of torture. The victim no longer has a name or a face, his identity is reduced to a diaphanous state of suffering, a total transparancy of what is left of his self. Evil cannot longer be located in an individual character such as Ambrosio or Schedoni, in Poe's story it is transformed into an institutional mechanism, which - although created by human beings - has blotted out any vestiges of humanity in its operators. Despite the desperate efforts of Poe's anonymous victim/narrator it is the *deus ex machina* which finally saves his life. It is not the perseverance of the individual but another institutional force, the French army, which manages to destroy the machinery of the Spanish Inquisition. One powerful institution, representing a feudal order and guided by a medieval concept of religious fanaticism, is now replaced by another powerful force, the modern army, representing the Republican ideal and motivated by the spirit of Enlightenment.

The individual, Poe's victim/narrator, although saved in the end, is caught between these two contending forces. He does not have an impact on the outcome of that struggle. One might read this confrontation as Poe's version of a morality play in which the ideals of republicanism and rationalist thinking triumph over the dark powers of feudal tyranny and religious fanaticism. But the "vision" of the pit thwarts this perspective. One wonders whether the whole theatrical machinery of trial, torture and liberation served a "design" and only was set up to confront the narrator with the "revelation" of the pit. In that case the narrator, Poe and the readers are left with the problem of the origins of that "design" - and the seasoned theological/ philosophical "argument by design" which tries to prove the existence of God. Poe, "a religious man whose Christianity, for reasons that nobody knows anything about, had got short-circuited," strived to create his own theodicee and to invent a trans-Christian, pantheistic model of the world in his "astrophilosophical discourse" *Eureka* (Tate 433, 456). But at the end he may well have been confronted with the same old conundrum from which he set out in the beginning.

Lasalle, Joseph Napoleon, and the Peninsular War

In a text with almost no reference to traditional markers of individuality one wonders about the use of a very real place name (Toledo) since Poe quite often tends to be vague about his settings. One also wonders why the nameless narrator is rescued from his fall into the abyss by the "outstretched arm" of General Lasalle (Mabbott 697). Poe anchors his tale in a verifiable historical moment as well as a precise geographical place. This strangely contrasts with his symbolic use of the pendulum as "scythe of Time" and the bottomless pit, with the implication of a transcendence of time and space. Poe may have intended this for an aesthetics of contrast in a combination of the finite detail and the idea of infinity, but the names give additional clues to background and meaning of the story.

Mabbott has traced Poe's source for General Lasalle's visit to the "palace of the Inquisition" in Toledo in Thomas Dick's *Philosophy of Religion* (1825) and in a filler in the *Portsmouth Journal* [New Hampshire] of June 2, 1832:

> On the entry of the French into Toledo during the late Peninsular War, General Lasalle visited the palace of the Inquisition. The great number of instruments of torture, especially the instruments to stretch the limbs, and the drop-baths, which cause a lingering death, excited horror, even in the minds of soldiers hardened in the field of battle. (679-680)

Immediately after the surrender of Madrid Napoleon Bonaparte on December 4, 1808 issued his famous Chamartin decree ordering the suppression of the Spanish Inquisition. On December 9, 1808 the French, who under General Pierre Antoine Dupont already had occupied Toledo in the spring, set fire to San Juan de los Reyes and soon after to other churches and religious buildings in the city (cf. Muñoz Herrera 145-147). General Antoine Charles Louis Lasalle (1775-1809) distinguished himself during Napoleon's campaigns in Prussia and Poland in 1806-1807. In 1808/1809 as a commander of a division of light cavalry he valiantly served under General Jean Baptiste Bessières, who operated in the Basque region and had to keep open the lines of communication between Burgos and Bayonne after the Madrid Revolt on May 1, 1808. Lasalle's "madcap" attack then won the day for the French at Medina de Rio Seco on Bastille Day (July 14) 1808. This decisive victory paved the way for Joseph Bonaparte - proclaimed King of Spain by his brother on June 6 - who now was able to enter Madrid a week later (cf. Connelly 105; cf. Chandler 278). Because of his prowess Lasalle was probably chosen to accompany Napoleon to Madrid and then may have been sent on to the headquarters of General Horace François Sebastiani in Toledo to organize the suppression of the Inquisition there. On March 29, 1809, near the Portuguese border, Lasalle at the head of the 26th Dragoons led the decisive attack which won the important Battle of Medellín for Marshall Claude Victor, after which Lasalle was awarded the title "Count of the Empire." He was killed in the battle of Wagram/Austria in July 1809 (cf. Chandler 239-240, 278).

Poe may have read about Napoleon's Spanish adventure in Robert Southey's *History of the Peninsular War* (1823-1832), but he knew William Frances Napier's *History of the War in the Peninsula* (1828-1840), which he reviewed in *Graham's* in November 1841 (Mabbott 700). Poe probably was inspired to write his "Spanish tale" by the presence of Joseph Bonaparte, who after his flight from Spain had arrived in New York late in August 1815. In 1816 he settled at Point Breeze on the Delaware river near Bordentown, NJ. His mansion soon became a center of hospitality for members of the Bonaparte clan and for visitors from all walks of life. It also was transformed into a focus of transatlantic social and political activities. Joseph Bonaparte became "a man of consequence in the United States" (Ross 260; cf. Connelly 250-255, 269).

In the spring of 1824 and again in July 1825 the Marquis de Lafayette visited Joseph in what seems to have been an attempt to enlist him in a conspiracy to replace Charles X with Napoleon's son, the Duke of Reichstadt (cf. Ross 260; cf. Connelly 272). If Poe ever met Joseph Bonaparte it must have been through Lafayette, who during his stay in Baltimore had paid homage to Poe's grandfather, who as Assistant Deputy Quartermaster had spent $ 40,000 of his own money for the Patriot cause. In October 1824 Poe had served as a hand-picked member of Lafayette's honorary bodyguard during his visit in Richmond (cf. Meyers 1-2, 17). After his dishonorable discharge from West Point in March 1831 Poe shortly toyed with the idea of joining the French army with the help of Lafayette, when Joseph Napoleon was preparing his return to France (cf. Meyers 50; cf. Ostrom 44-45).

So far Poe scholars have not unearthed an official French report about Lasalle's activities against the Inquisition in Toledo. Muñoz Herrera has discovered a manuscript written by Lorenzo Frías "Sumario de lo occurido en Toledo durante la invasión francesa, en relación con el movimiento general de la guerra de la independencia, por un religioso," which castigates the brutality and rapacity of the French and Polish soldiers during their destruction of many religious buildings in Toledo (145-157). There is also a report written by the Polish officer Lumanusk (commander of the 9th Regiment of the Polish Lancers), who upon the order of Marshal Soult had to organize the suppression of the Inquisition in Madrid. Poe may have read this report, which was later reprinted as an appendix to Féréal's *Les mystères de l'Inquisition* in 1844.

Lumanusk writes that only after a fierce battle with the Spanish guards, which leaves several of his soldiers dead, he finally manages to enter the palace of the Inquisition, where he is welcomed by the Grand Inquisitor and his staff as though nothing had happened, and then is readily shown through all the chambers in the building. Lumanusk, almost willing to believe that all the stories about the terrors of the Inquisition were mere tattle, is ready to end his inspection when the French officer de Lille asks him to pour water onto the luxurious marble floor. When the water swiftly disappears in one of the crevices the French to the dismay of the monks discover a secret stairway to the subterranean torture chamber of the Inquisition, adjacent to which they find a number of prison cells with rotting corpses and skeletons of the victims. They finally happen upon about a hundred men and women of all ages, all naked and in chains, and free them from this "antechamber of Hell." After discovering "all kinds of the instruments of torture that human genius or demons could invent" Lumanusk's soldiers become so enraged that they start to apply them to the monks. Lumanusk without interfering turns away from this "terrible drama" which now unfolds before his eyes and only ends after all the monks have been tortured and probably been killed. Then he has his troops blow up the building and its vaults: "The palace of the Inquisition in Madrid no longer existed!" (Féréal 535-540; Helbing 133-136)

The "Lumanusk report" can be read as a supplement to Poe's tale, with the focus of the "camera eye" on the actions of the French liberators. There is another striking affinity between Poe's rendering of the descent and Féréal's description of the torture chamber of Sevilla (chapter 23) - allegedly based on Llorente:

> In the midst of a great rotunda in a deep vault below the Palace of the Inquisition, which was only dimly lighted by two torches, four men in shrouds surrounded a weak and sad man [...]. An oppressive, humid air like an unhealthy fog filled these subterranean chambers with graveyard vapors. The craggy walls of this cavern-like place, oozing with a film of moisture, were covered with instruments of torture, satanic inventions of the ascetic and ferocious imagination of the monks. [...] You descended to this place of hell on numerous narrow and winding stairs, which were covered with damp moss that made you slip at every step. The servants of the Inquisition, however, have a *pied marin* [the firm step of seasoned mariners] and know every nook and cranny of this terrible labyrinth." (Féréal 207; Helbing 125; translation from the German edition)

Féréal then proceeds to describe the torture of Manuel Argoso, the former governor of Sevilla, arrested by the Grand Inquisitor Peter Arbuez in order to get hold of his beautiful daughter Dolores. This and chapter 29 illustrate the three or four major forms of torture that have been recorded in Montanus and Llorente: *garrucha* (pulley), *potro* (rack), *toca* (water torture), fire torture (Montanus, 53-66; cf. O'Brien 38-55; cf. Kamen 173-177). Poe does not make use of these models of torture that have been verified by historians. He prefers the imaginary variants of the pendulum and the contracting red-hot iron walls, which he gleaned from spurious historical or fictional sources (cf. Mabbott 699-700).

Toledo

In contrast to Féréal's "realistic" rendering of Spanish local color Poe is much more vague and ambiguous. This is probably due to the fact that Mme. de Suberwick [i.e. the writer behind the pseudonym of M.V. de Féréal] had a first-hand knowledge of Spain, since she also is on record as the author of the illustrated *L'Espagne pittoresque* (1848), whereas Poe unlike Washington Irving only had access to second-hand information about Spain. Poe remained vague about his topic in order to heighten the effect of "the gossamer web of *some* dream" (Mabbott 682) and his digression on the borderline between the conscious and unconscious states of mind. Poe's narrator tells us that "there came thronging upon my recollection a thousand vague rumors of the horrors of Toledo" (Mabbott 685). Poe conjured up the familiar romantic theme of the ruins of Toledo that his contemporary readers knew from numerous accounts of English travellers, which flooded the British and American book markets in the 1830s. The new interest in Spain had started with the British intervention in the Peninsular War and was then kindled by Sir Walter Scott's poem "Vision of Don Roderick." Walter Savage Landor with his tragedy *Count Julian* (1812) and Robert Southey with his narrative poem "Roderick, the Last of the Goths" (1814) followed suit. After the Peninsular War the romantic interest in the Moorish past of Spain was revived by French participants in the war, who now returned as travellers, and English "pioneer tourists" such as Edward H. Locker and Henry David Inglis, as well as the Americans Washington Irving and Alexander Slidell Mackenzie. By 1830 Spain had become the "Mecca of the Romantic movement," and an avalanche of travellers converged upon a Toledo in ruins, which as "Dama Melancolía" and with its "saturnine" and "disquieting landscape" became its emblematic focus (Muñoz Herrera 25, 51, 56, 85; cf. Caro Baroja 217-223).

Tate's reference to Poe's "power [...] of the melancholy, heroic life" (432) may help to explain his affinity with the Toledo setting. Poe's vision of that city was probably influenced by Mackenzie's "prolix codification of the human iconosphere" in his *A Year in Spain* (1829) and by the popular image of Toledo as a "mummified city of the Middle Ages, where the banner of the romantic rebellion is weaved by the descendants of those who had to live through centuries of despotism." In view of the dream-like state of Poe's narrator it is interesting to note that a "dream scenography" suffuses many of the contemporary descriptions of the city (Muñoz Herrera 95, 83, 63-64). In the context of the emerging romantic perspective Poe must have come to see Toledo as a mirror of Spanish history, a concept later given expression by Perez Galdós: "Toledo es una historia de España completa" (Nieto 106). In this perspective Toledo had once been a model place of tolerance and coexistence between Moors, Jews and Christians well into the 15th century, known as the "Jerusalem of the West." After the introduction of the Inquisition under Ferdinand and Isabella in 1478 and the subsequent persecution and expulsion of the Jews in 1492 a long period of oppression and religious fanaticism followed. These centuries of intolerance finally were ended by the Napoleonic invasion, in the wake of which Spain now languished in a period of internal unrest and civil war which pitted liberals against traditionalists. To sympathetic contemporary observers this strife could only be ended by a return of tolerance, to be furthered by an evocation of the healing heritage of legends and lore of Toledo.

The oldest and most famous legend was about the cave of Hercules, the place of Roderick's "vision," which later became the secret center of black magic. Other magic places were the haunted palace of the alchemist Don Enrique de Villena, and the "Casa del duende" (the goblin's house) that burnt the night when God punished the witches of Toledo. The "Bitter Well" commemorates the legend of Rachel, who drowned herself, when she saw the face of her royal lover Alfonso at the bottom of this well. But Toledo also was a major birthplace of anti-Jewish black legends such as ritual murder of innocent children and poisoning of guileless Christians (cf. Caro Baroja 158-171, 100-101, 104-108). All these legends were closely interwoven with the most persistent theme of Toledo as the center of black magic in Europe. During the centuries of Moorish hegemony in Spain:

[...] Saragossa, Toledo, and the University of Salamanca (founded in the 12th century) gained throughout all Europe an evil notoriety as hotbeds of necromancy, nurseries and thriving-grounds of sorcerers. Toledo, in particular, was so ill-famed that we find it incidentally spoken of in popular poem and story as a seminary of magic. It is said that at one period a Chair of Black Magic was openly established there, and certainly Guazzo [i.e. Francesco Mario Guazzo. *Compendium maleficarum.* 1608; Engl. TL 1929] speaks of a seven years' course of the Black Arts and Magic at Toledo. [...] These horrible and ill-famed schools were gradually driven underground and finally rooted out by Queen Isabella the Catholic (1451-1504), who thoroughly purged Toledo and Salamanca of these abominations. (Summers 102-103; cf. Bächtold-Stäubli "Hochschulen der Zauberei", vol. IV, 140-148; cf. Caro Baroja 160-162)

The Narrator and Occult Traditions; Heresy and Guilt

Poe may have first learnt about Spain's heritage of black magic and occultism in Scott's *Letters on Demonology and Witchcraft* (1830 [Letter VII, 129]) and William Godwin's *Lives of the Necromancers* (1834). He also may have known that Scott had been condemned as a "satanic" writer by the Spanish Inquisition (Muñoz Herrera 75). All the tidbits of Toledo folklore have left an echo in Poe's tale. The theme of witchcraft and sorcery is closely connected with the identity of the narrator. Poe's "reductionist" approach to the genre allowed him to rely on his readers' familiarity with the mechanisms of the Gothic tale and with the romantic landscape of Toledo presented in the travelogues. He also could refer his readers to the popular genre of the "Spanish captivities," narratives of sailors and travellers who survived the dungeons and tortures of the Spanish Inquisition, the most popular of which was William Lithgow's account, published in 1632 (cf. Peters 190-199; cf. van der Vekene 157-175; cf. Max 103-323). However, Poe's choice of Toledo clearly implies a background of black magic and sorcery for the trial of his narrator.[1]

---

[1] Although Dédieu speaks of an "omnipresence of magic" in Toledo, he largely exonerates the Inquisition there: "Jamais cependant, ni à Tolède, ni dans aucune des Inquisitions espagnoles, la répression de la magie n'occupa la place prépondérante qui lui était dévolue par l'Inquisition italienne." There were cycles of action against *hechiceras* (magic practices), but since the Spanish Inquisition hardly believed in witches it proceeded very cautiously in cases involving *brujería* (sorcery) in order to prevent any execution by fire (309-328; 309, 320, 324).

Poe's readers also would remember three famous prisoners of the Inquisition: Benvenuto Cellini, Casanova, and Cagliostro. Cellini's *Autobiography* gives an account of his sufferings when imprisoned by Pope Paul III in Castel Sant' Angelo in 1538-1539. Two passages in Cellini's book bear a close resemblance to Poe's story:

> I was carried down below the garden into a very dark, dank room full of tarantulas and noxious worms. They threw a miserable hemp mattress on the ground, and that evening I was left without food, locked in behind four doors. [...] Little by little I felt strength ebbing, till my strong constitution had become used to the *purgatory* I was suffering. [...] they bore me away by the light of a great burning torch. I thought they intended to throw me into what is called the *Sammalò pit, a fearful place which has swallowed up a great many living men who have been hurtled down into a well in the foundations of the castle"* (214-215, 219; italics WK).

Whereas Cellini, who is rescued by the intervention of the Cardinal of Ferrara, attributes his redemption to God's grace, Casanova finally manages to escape from the "lead dungeons" of the Inquisition in Venice solely by his own acumen and strength: "I have always believed that when a man takes it into his head to accomplish some project and pursues it to the exclusion of anything else, he must succeed in it despite all difficulties; [...]" (IV, 221-222). Poe does not agree with Cellini's view, but he also argues against Casanova's voluntaristic credo. He nevertheless gleans items from their narratives for his tale, such as Casanova's description of the prisons of the Inquisition in Venice:

> These nineteen underground prisons have every resemblance to tombs but they are called "wells" because they are always flooded by two feet of sea water, which comes in through the same grated hole by which they receive a little light; [...] The prisoner, unless he enjoys being in a salt bath up to his knees all day, has to sit on a platform where he also has his pallet and on which at dawn a jailer puts his water, his soup, and his ration biscuit, which he has to eat at once, for if he delays *enormous sea rats would tear it from his hands.* (IV, 258-259; italics WK)

The most interesting element, however, is the scene of Casanova's arrest after having been denounced by the jeweler Manuzzi for possession of heretic books:

"[...] they were the *Key of Solomon*, the *Zecor-ben*, a *Picatrix*, a complete treatise on the planetary hours favorable to making the necessary perfumes and conjurations for conversing with demons of all classes. Those who knew that I had these books thought I was a magician, and it rather pleased me" (200). Casanova realizes that he is arrested for the possession of these books, but he feels "not guilty of anything" (197). In a very Poe-like manner, he suddenly seizes a cold hand in the dark and suspects that a corpse has been placed near him. Although he then realizes that he has grasped his own left hand, which is numbed by the cold, this experience destroys his former self-confidence: "I realized that I was in a place where if the false seemed true, *realities must seem dreams*; where the understanding must lose half of its privileges; where a *distorted imagination* must make *reason the victim either of chimerical hopes or terrible despair*" (205-207; italics WK). Poe's disquisition in "Pit" on the nature of dreams and the borderland between consciousness and states of unconsciousness is a variation of the theme introduced by Casanova. Casanova is confronted with one major "guilt" of his own making. He tells us that he was pleased with the idea that people believed him to be a great magician. Although he never will accept the accusation of being a heretic, he seems to realize that he suffers because of his own vanity and his occult leanings, which clearly contaminate his enlightened ideas.[2]

This strange combination of enlightenment posturings and a propensity for occult practices is mirrored in Casanova's "brother in spirit" Cagliostro, aka Joseph Balsamo, who died a prisoner of the Italian Inquisition on August 26, 1795. If Cellini and Casanova are ambiguous personalities and show streaks of roguish behavior Cagliostro is the unchallenged master charlatan of the 18th century who managed to amalgamate a broad spectrum of current ideologies and to profit from the occult leanings and the credulity of his followers, many of them members of the European nobility. Giovanni Barberi in his *Compendio*

---

[2] Almost all the books he mentions are *grimoires*, compendia of black magic and necromantic arts. The *Key of Solomon* or *Clavicula Salomonis* and the treatise on planatary hours contained magic formulas to conjure demons, whereas the *Picatrix* is a collection of recipes based on astrological "secrets", designed to prepare charms and talismans. The *Zecor-ben* is the *Zohar*, the central book of the Spanish Cabala, with elements of magic and mysticism that fascinated Casanova (cf. Bächtold-Stäubli III, 1170-1171; cf. Biedermann 193, 467, 381-383, 347, 399-400).

della vita e delle geste di Giuseppe Balsamo denominato il conte Cagliostro (1791) gives a full account of Cagliostro's trial by the Roman Inquisition, at the end of which he was sentenced to death for the "restitution and propagation of the [cult of] Egyptian Masonry" on March 21, 1791. Two weeks later this verdict was commuted to life imprisonment by Pope Pius VI (cf. Kiefer 595). Like Casanova Cagliostro showed a strong streak of vanity. Before the Roman tribunal he claimed to have acted upon a divine inspiration in order to further the interests of the Catholic church. He proclaimed himself to be both an atheist and a follower of the Roman Catholic creed, but then confessed to have been in the service of the Devil (cf. Kiefer 576-577, 584-586). Cagliostro's breakdown and confession served as a vindication of the Inquisition, which reduced the "super-simulacrum" to a cheap fraud, but above all it came as a blow to the proponents of Enlightenment, who had prided themselves as beacons of rational thought and now were confronted with the dark undercurrent of occultism and superstition, the pervasive "Cagliostro-syndrom of the epoch" (Kiefer 634, 617). There is a strange affinity between these prisoners of the Inquisition and Poe, who "was defined by the unbearable tensions in his paradoxical character" (Meyers 57). There also are ingredient of a juggler and a charlatan in Poe, "some of his erudition was clearly bogus." At the same time he shares a "tendency toward megalomania" (Meyers 74, 184) with those famous prisoners of the Inquisition. Tate argues that Poe in *Eureka* "tried to put himself not in the presence of God, but in the seat of God" (453). Meyers mentions Poe's "satanic pride" when he shocked his friend Lambert Wilmer by declaring: "My whole nature utterly *revolts* at the idea that there is any Being in the Universe superior to *myself*!" (Meyers 58) The narrator's sufferings and hallucinations in "Pit" may well be a projection of Poe's hidden fears about the consequences of his own version of a "satanic" philosophy. They certainly reflect the haunting efficiency of the Puritan psychology illustrated in Milton's presentation of Satan in Hell (*Paradise Lost* I, 34-49; I, 209-210) and Jonathan Edwards's vision in "Sinners in the Hands of an Angry God" (cf. Oliver 74-75) – even in an apostate like Poe.

In this perspective the narrator's silence about his "guilt" as well as Poe's reversal of trial and torture[3] indicate that in the context of Christian theology the problem of "guilt" for Poe is a foregone conclusion. The trial simply is a ritual, both the judges and the "culprit" just go through the motions. The "conditio humana" is defined by a series of punishments in form of physical and psychological torture as an inescapable consequence of existential "sinfulness" of man.

The Network of Four Central Symbols

This view may account for Poe's pervasive use of apocalyptic language and imagery (cf. Hirsch 649) and his allusions to purgatory. Malloy argues that the "apocalyptic framework" of the tale "suggests that Poe is rewriting the biblical story of the Fall as a Neoplatonic estrangement from the divine [...]" (89). The "reductionist" if not "abstract" plot is complemented with multi-facetted layers of Biblical and mythological allusions. Structure is simplified, imagery multiplied. One can see this as a major contribution in the development of a slowly emerging modernist and formalist "technology of art." The "framework" of the tale is defined by the four major symbols of the "menorah," the "pendulum," the contracting red-hot iron walls, and the pit. The seven candles have been traced back to Revelation 1:12-14 (Hirsch 646) as a kind of "apocalyptic marker," but they also represent the Menorah, which in medieval art became the symbol of the Jewish religion. In the context of Poe's tale it points to the Jewish heritage of Toledo as well as to the end of religious and cultural tolerance, which started with the coming of the Inquisition, originally introduced as an instrument against the Jewish religion (cf. Peters 77-86). It may also refer to the possible nature of the narrator's heresy. The Menorah as an evolution from the old Babylonian "tree of light" has been interpreted as a symbol of the divine light that suffuses the world and a representation of *logos* and *sophia* (Philo of Alexandria), of divine wisdom, spiritual light and salvation (Lurker 358-359). It symbolically controls the introductory scene of the judgment and introduces the ambiguity of the tale: intolerance, persecution and

---

[3] This does not square with the historical fact that torture was only applied during the trial as a means to "elicit a confession", but not after the verdict (cf. Kamen 174-176; cf. Monter 74-75; cf. Dédieu "Procédure inquisitoriale" 152-153).

perversion of the original ideals of Christianity on the one hand, promise of revelation and salvation on the other hand. The final revelation is of such a terrible nature that Poe's narrator in the end would rather have sidestepped it. The logical consequence of the tale is an endless continuation of the terrors that have flooded his soul.

After the transfer to the torture vault and the narrator's (retrospective) disquisition on the levels of awareness on the threshold of dream and reality the "pendulum" becomes the focus of attention. Critics have already referred to Poe's use of the "scythe of time" in "The Psyche Zenobia" (cf. Mabbott 353-354). The implicit reference to the representation of death as the "grim reaper," who relentlessly cuts down life, enhances the Gothic atmosphere of the tale. The mathematical precision in the movement of the "pendulum/scythe" helps the narrator to calculate his escape. It shows that this danger can be "sized up" and overcome by rational calculation. This "measuring" of a danger becomes impossible with the "bottomless pit" because "graspable" reality is transformed into immaterial "transcendence" or simply "the void."

The "scythe" also evokes Saturn, who as Chronos was often shown with this symbol of Time. He was also seen as a representation of Melancholy, an embodiment of the "saturnine" qualities attributed to that temperament. This allusion to Saturn tallies with the romantic perception of Toledo as an emblem of melancholy. The cult of melancholy with all its ramifications was familiar and even seemed to guarantee a certain degree of pleasure. In contrast, the terrors of eternal punishment in the fiery pit contained a more or less imminent threat that had to be taken seriously. However, those terrors had been the stock-in-trade of popular theology for centuries, and the success of the Gothic tales attested to its cathartic function. Once, however, God was eliminated from the picture, all "verities" anchored in the traditional Christian concept of the world disappeared or at least lost their familiar contours. "Nothingness" and "meaninglessness" (or absurdity as its modern term) began to take over the world as new horrors. Although most of his contemporaries did not seem to realize this paradigmatic change, Poe was very much disturbed by it and tried to confront and fathom its consequences in his fiction, especially in his "pivotal" Spanish tale.

Before the narrator is confronted with the ultimate horrors of the bottomless pit he is offered an "alternative" choice of death: "I could have clasped the red walls to my bosom as a garment of eternal peace. [...] At length for my seared and writhing body there was no longer an inch of foothold on the firm floor of the prison. I struggled no more, but the agony of my soul found vent in one loud, long, and final scream of despair. [...]" In that moment he comes to realize "that *into the pit* it was the burning iron to urge me" (Mabbott 696-697). It seems as though all his tortures, even his hairbreadth escape from the pendulum, have been carefully designed and orchestrated to make him fall into the bottomless pit. Torture and execution by ecclesiastical and wordly powers – thus runs Poe's argument - are terrible but familiar punishments. The metaphysical terrors, however, which await the inquisitive philosopher upon the final discovery of the secrets of the world are forever unbearable for the human mind.

Poe critics discovered possible sources for the contracting red-hot iron walls in some tales published in *Blackwood's* (cf. Mabbott 700; cf. Bonaparte's "birth-anxiety" thesis, 586). There was, however, a source much closer to the actual history of Toledo. Mackenzie in *A Year in Spain* (1829) tells his readers about his visit to the ruins of the *Quemadero,* the furnace of the Inquisition of Toledo, which had been destroyed upon orders of the liberal city government on June 16, 1820. With a reference to Llorente Mackenzie describes the *Quemadero* as a "paradigm of the intolerance" responsible for the ruin of Toledo: "It consisted of a huge hollow statue of plaster, erected upon a stone oven. The fire was kindled beneath, and the victims being let down from above perished slowly, rending the air with horrid yells" (Mackenzie 45; cited in Muñoz Herrera 80; cf. Max 88-89). The French Sébastian Blaze in his *Mémoires d'un apothicaire* (1828) describes the furnace as he had seen it during his visit in 1812/1813:

> se ve un macizo de cantería de alrededor de tres metros quadrados y de dos metros de altura. Era allí arriba donde se elevaban las piras de la Inquisición; era allí, sobre esa "hoguera" donde se hacían los "auto da fé." Las autoridades religiosas y civiles de Toledo, los habitantes de esta ciudad y sus alrededores, venían a congregarse en esta vasta llanura en torno al horno, y podían gozar del espectáculo divertido de la quema de un judío o de un brujo. [...] Subí a esta permanente caldera y encontré huesos humanos calcinados, observé que la tierra que le cubre en ciertos lugares era untuosa y grasienta. La hierba crece ahora en

abundancia, testimonio de que hace tiempo que no se quema allí a nadie. (Blaze 329; cited in Muñoz Herrera 79)

There is a picture of the *Quemadero* of Sevilla in Féréal (417) which was drawn on the basis of Llorente's description of the auto-da-fés in Sevilla:

> The great number of persons condemned to be burnt, obliged the prefect of Seville to construct a scaffold of stone near the town, name Tablada; it was called Quemadero, and still exists. Four statues, of plaster, were erected on it, and bore the name of the *Four Prophets*; the condemned persons were enclosed alive in these figures, and perished by a slow and horrible death. (Llorente, *Critical History* 37)

The "quemadero" refers to another Biblical allusion, the "baptism by fire" suffered by Shadrach, Meshach, and Abednego who were thrown into the fiery furnace because they refused to worship the golden statue of Nebuchadnezar, but survived the ordeal with the help of God (Daniel 3:19-30). This fictional illustration of Biblical parables and symbols again emphasizes the pervasive ambiguity of the tale. Poe could not have forseen the terrible prophecy in the trial of Shadrach, Meshach and Abednego - and concomitantly in his own tale - for the European Jews in the 20th century. In this perspective the survival of the narrator despite his "vision" still contains a tiny grain of hope, which, however, is forever burdened with the "awareness" of horrors Poe only imagined, but which less than a century later were to become a terrible reality.

Purgatory

The parable of the fiery furnace and its link with the symbol of the pit finally evokes the concept of the purgatory, which by definition is a place of terrible suffering, but also a state of transience promising final redemption. The "bottomless pit" has its original source in Revelation, where Satan "was cast into the lake of fire and brimstone, where the beast and the false prophet *are*, and shall be tormented day and night for ever and ever" (20:2,3,10). Through Milton its echo sent ripples through much of English literature. This heritage of "fire and brimstone" is contaminated with the classical one that Poe found in the 33rd Canto of Dante's Hell, set in the Ptolomaea, the third circle of the traitors' hell:

> as soon as any soul becomes a traitor,
> as I was, then a demon takes its body
> away - and keeps that body in his power
> until its years have run their course completely.
> The soul falls headlong, down into this *cistern*;
> and up above, perhaps, there still appears
> the body of the shade that winters here
> behind me; [...] (307)

Since wells were often regarded as points of entrance to the underworld in European folklore throughout the centuries (Bächtold-Stäubli I, 1679), this allusion in conjunction with the reference to Dante evokes the question of the nature of a possible "betrayal," for which Poe's narrator is about to be punished by his impending "fall" into the pit. It could be the heretic's repetition of Satan's rebellion, but it could also be an emulation of the traitorous act committed by Prometheus in divulging one of the best-kept secrets of the Gods to humankind. Poe may well intend to illustrate the fate of the romantic artist, who rebels against what he sees as the fundamental injustice in God's creation, and the sacrilege inherent in his emulation of God's original creative act, which also betrays the secrets of creation to the world.[4]

In the 1840s Poe's readers probably remembered a more recent model of the "pit", described by Maria Monk in her "convent tale" *Awful Disclosures* (1836). Soon after she has entered the Hotel Dieu Nunnery in Montreal she learns that it is a secret brothel for the priests. Nuns refusing the service expected from them are killed, their babies are immediately baptized and then strangled:

---

[4] An interesting emblem shows a smoking well full of snakes, telling the reader that his condemnation is the result of his own sins (*Emblemata* 1247). Another emblem illustrates the theme of the Well of Democritus: *Veritas* hides in a well, but Democritus reveals her whereabouts to Chronos (*Emblemata* 1816). Here again a network of allusions links "betrayal" with the emblems of Truth, Time, and the Pit as the entrance to a chthonic realm.

> As I proceeded [...] I observed before me, a hole dug so deep into the earth that I could perceive *no bottom.* [italics, WK] I stopped to observe it - it was circular, twelve or perhaps fifteen feet across, in the middle of the cellar, and unprotected by any kind of curb, so that one might have easily have walked into it in the dark.
>
> The white substance which I have observed, was spread all over the surface around it; [...] It immediately occured to me that the white substance was lime, and that was the place where the infants were buried, after being murdered, as the superior had informed me. [...] Here then I was in a place which I had considered as the nearest imitation of heaven to be found on earth, amongst a society where deeds were constantly perpetrated, which I had believed to be most criminal, and now found the place in which harmless infants were unfeelingly thrown out of sight, after being murdered. (48-50)

This is another example of Poe's astute amalgamation of Biblical, classical and learned references with those of the most lurid popular stories and legends of his time. The allusion to Maria Monk's "lime pit" reinforces the echoes from the Gothic novels and invokes the "Black Legend" and the Nativist propaganda "unveiling" Catholic atrocities on American soil.

Jacques LeGoff has traced the evolution of the idea of the purgatory in the context of the "process of spacialization of thought," dating its emergence at the turn of the 12th and 13th centuries (13, 267). The apocalyptic "infernalization of the Purgatory" at the end of the 13th century and the predominance of the "baptism by fire"-model incorporate ancient Indo-European mythologies of fire (403; 21-22).

This new idea was popularized in two major Irish texts about an imaginary journey to the Purgatory: *Vision of Tundale* and *Saint Patrick's Purgatory*, the influence of which is clearly reflected in "Pit". Tundale travels through a symbolic landscape, witnessing numerous tortures meted out to the sinners according to the nature and severity of their transgressions. When he finally arrives at the entrance to Hell he sees a "rectangular pit, shaped like a cistern, out of which emerges an effulgent and fetid flame filled with demons and souls, which fly up in the air like sparks to be extinguished and then to fall back into the depths" (LeGoff 256-257). *Saint Patrick's Purgatory*, probably written by the Cisterciensien monk H. de Saltrey between 1190 and 1210, was one of the bestsellers of the Middle Ages (LeGoff 266). According to the legend Jesus showed St. Patrick a round and deep pit in a desert-like place which the missionary enclosed with a wall. Later, the key to the entrance was kept by the prior of the church near "St. Patrick's Purgatory." H. de Saltrey describes the imaginary journey of the knight Owein, who is burdened with many sins. Sometimes between the years 1135 and 1154 Owein fearlessly starts his adventurous descent into St. Patrick's pit, where he is attacked by devils who try to burn him at the stake. He survives this and other tribulations by invoking the name of Jesus. Like his predecessor Tundale he witnesses a whole range of tortures applied to sinners who are clamped down by red-hot nails. Some are boiled or roasted in an infernal kitchen, others fastened to a rotating wheel of fire or plunged into tubs filled with boiling metal. After crossing a river of fire Owein comes to a fiery pit with dark and stinking flames full of sparks of rising and falling souls. He is told by his demonic companions that this is the Gate of Hell (LeGoff 263). The popularity of "St. Patrick's Pit," which - despite a condemnation by Pope Alexander VI in 1497 - became a favourite destination for pilgrims since the end of the 12th century, helped to change the symbolic meaning of wells: The former gateways to hell now became the entrance to the Purgatory - the new "ante-chamber promising the entry to Paradise" (LeGoff 268, 273, 484). Besides this "infernal inspiration" (Clifton) by the legend of St. Patrick Poe is illustrating the process of measuring the boundaries of (eschatological) time and space (cf. Lawes; cf. LeGoff 311), only to discover new dimensions of metaphysical terror. The importance of the legend of St. Patrick for Irish Catholicism and immigrant culture in the United States links Poe's use of this legend with the anti-Catholic and anti-Irish riots in Boston in 1834 and Philadelphia in 1844. In this perspective legend, metaphysical speculation and contemporary politics are inextricably interwoven in his tale.

Crime, Punishment, and Torture: The Ambiguous Role of the Audience

Poe's tale also echoes the contemporary debate about the reform of the penal system. Already in 1764 Cesare Beccaria in his *Essay on Crimes and Punishments*, which was to become the Bible of liberal legal reform, had attacked the use of torture:

> This custom seems to be the offspring of religion, by which mankind, in all nations, and in all ages, are so generally influenced. We are taught by our infallibly church, that those stains of sin, [...] are to be purged away, in another life, by an incomprehensible fire. Now infamy is a stain, and if the punishments and fire of purgatory can take away all spiritual stains, why should not the pain of torture take away those of a civil nature. I imagine, that the confession of a criminal, which in some tribunals is required, as being essential to his condemnation, has a similar origin, and has been taken from the mysterious tribunal of penitence, where the confession of sins is a necessary part of the sacrament. (43-44)

Beccaria traces the theological fundaments behind the traditional defense of torture as a "crucible" of truth and "Pit" can be read as a fictional illustration of Beccaria's arguments.

Moreover, Poe's tale is a contribution to the "genealogy of the modern 'soul'" (Foucault 29). Foucault analyzes the paradigmatic change in the system of trial and punishment between 1760 and 1840, when the public display of the "body as the major target of penal repression" in torture or execution was replaced by the soul. Even the "great theatrical ritual" of the guillotine was in the end "placed behind prison walls and made inaccessible to the public." The traditional process of grounding the verdict on the triad of law, offence and offender was now supplemented by a "whole set of assessing, diagnostic, prognostic, normative judgements concerning the criminal" and the "offender's soul", which "turned the assertion of guilt into a strange scientifico-juridical complex" (Foucault 8-9, 15, 18-19). Poe's tale in all its stages from judgment through physical and psychological torture closely mirrors this process of transformation toward a modern concept of man: The traditional idea of the body as a prison of the soul is now reversed so that "the soul is the prison of the body" (Foucault 30). This fundamental change, however, entails yet another damage to the integrity of the individual. Epictetus in the introductory chapter of his widely read *Enchiridion* had stressed the inviolability of the human soul in contrast to the vulnerability and ephemeral condition of the human body (11). The modern process of inversion now also allowed the dissection and destruction of the soul, the last sacrosanct region on the anthropological map - with disastrous consequences for the 20th century, which saw a renaissance of torture and an elaborate culture of "creative cruelty", taught in "colleges of atrocity" (Sofsky 86, 233). The torture chambers are transmuted into "laboratories of destructive fantasy," in which the victim is slowly dissected and totally depersonalized in a process systematically destroying will, language, and the soul of a human being. Space is transformed into a dramatic "stage of torture" upon which the "absolute, permanent presence of pain" destroys any notion of time (Sofsky 92-98). Sofsky reminds us that the many narrative and pictorial visions of torture in Hell are not just phantasmagorias but representations of social and historical reality (84).

From the vantage point of the end of the 20th century we cannot content ourselves with a traditional structural, metaphysical, or psychological reading that culminates in an evaluation of the "aesthetic" merits of Poe's tale. The persistent popularity of Poe's story referred to by Mabbott raises disturbing questions about the fascination with the "total situation" of torture (Sofsky 98) presented in "Pit."

One may argue that Poe's contemporaries and his readers in the 20th century of necessity cannot share the same perspective and that their respective "fascination" with the tale has to be evaluated in a different context, and moreover, that the readers of fiction cannot be compared with audiences infatuated with popular rituals of violence. However, after the nightmares of the 20th century, Poe's readers can no longer flinch from an assessment of their own emotional involvement and cathartic distancing from the historical, social, and metaphysical implications inherent in Poe's "Spanish" tale.

Works Cited

Alighieri, Dante. *The Divine Comedy: Inferno.* A Verse Translation by Allan Mandelbaum. New York: Bantam, 1982.

Alterton, Margaret. "An Additional Source for Poe's 'The Pit and the Pendulum'." *Modern Language Notes* 48:6 (June 1933): 349-356.

Bächtold-Stäubli, Hanns, ed. *Handwörterbuch des deutschen Aberglaubens.* [1927] 10 vols. Berlin: de Gruyter, 1987.

Beccaria, Cesare. *An Essay on Crimes and Punishment.* Boston, MA: Branden, 1983.
Biedermann, Hans. *Lexikon der magischen Künste.* München: Heyne, 1991.
Billington, Ray Allen. *The Protestant Crusade 1800-1860: A Study of the Origins of American Nativism.* [1938] Gloucester, MA: Peter Smith, 1963.
Bonaparte, Marie. *The Life and Works of Edgar Allan Poe: A Psycho-Analytic Interpretation.* London: Imago, 1949.
Caro Baroja, Julio. *Toledo.* Barcelona: Ediciones Destino, 1988.
Casanova, Giacomo. *History of My Life.* [1967] 12 vols. Vols. III & IV. Baltimore: Johns Hopkins UP, 1997.
Cellini, Benvenuto. *Autobiography.* London: Penguin, 1998.
Chandler, David G. *Dictionary of the Napoleonic Wars.* London: Arms and Armour Press, 1979.
Clark, David Lee. "The Sources of Poe's 'The Pit and the Pendulum'." *Modern Language Notes* 44:6 (June 1929): 349-356.
Clifton, Michael. "Down Hecate's Chain: Infernal Inspiration in Three of Poe's Tales." *Nineteenth-Century Literature* 41:2 (Sept. 1986): 217-227.
Connelly, Owen. *The Gentle Bonaparte: A Biography of Joseph, Napoleon's Elder Brother.* New York: Macmillan, 1968.
Dedieu, Jean-Pierre. "La procédure inquisitoriale. Les droits de la défense. Le cas espagnol." *Ketzerverfolgung im 16. und frühen 17. Jahrhundert.* Ed. Silvana Seidel Menchi, Hans Rudolf Guggisberg, Bernd Moeller. Wiesbaden: Otto Harrassowitz, 1992. 147-158.
Dedieu, Jean-Pierre. *L'administration de la foi: L'inquisition de Tolède, XVIe-XVIIIe siècle.* Madrid: Casa de Velázquez, 1989.
Epictetus. *Enchiridion.* Amherst, NY: Prometheus Books, 1991.
Esdaile, Charles J. *Spain in the Liberal Age: From Constitution to Civil War, 1808-1939.* Oxford: Blackwell, 2000.
Féréal, Victor de [i.e. Mme. de Suberwick]. *Die Geheimnisse der Inquisition und anderer geheimer Gesellschaften Spaniens.* [Brünn: Fr. Karafiat, 1864] Holzminden: Reprint-Verlag, n.d. [originally published as *Les mystères de l'inquisition et autres sociétés secrètes d'Espagne.* Paris: P. Boizard, 1844.]
Foucault, Michel. *Discipline and Punish: The Birth of the Prison.* [1975] New York: Vintage, 1979.
Helbing, Franz. *Die Tortur: Geschichte der Folter im Kriminalverfahren aller Völker und Zeiten.* 2 vols. [1910] Augsburg: Bechtermünz, 1999.
Henkel, Arthur, and Albrecht Schöne, eds. *Emblemata: Handbuch zur Sinnbildkunst des XVI. und XVII. Jahrhunderts.* Stuttgart: Metzler, 1996.
Hirsch, David H. "The Pit and the Apocalypse." *Sewanee Review* 76 (1968): 632-652.
Kamen, Henry. *Inquisition and Society in Spain in the 16th and 17th Centuries.* London: Weidenfels & Nicolson, 1985.
Kiefer, Klaus H., ed. *Cagliostro: Dokumente zu Aufklärung und Okkultismus.* Leipzig: Kiepenheuer, 1991.

Klein, Jürgen. *Der Gotische Roman und die Ästhetik des Bösen.* Darmstadt: Wissenschaftliche Buchgesellschaft, 1975.
Lawes, Rochie. "The Dimensions of Terror: Mathematical Inquiry in 'The Pit and the Pendulum'." *Poe Studies* 16:1 (June 1983): 5-7.
LeGoff, Jacques. *La naissance du purgatoire.* Paris: Gallimard, 1981.
Lewis, Matthew G. *The Monk – A Romance.* London: Penguin, 1998.
Link, Franz. *Edgar Allan Poe.* Frankfurt/Main: Athenäum, 1968.
Llorente, Juan Antonio. *A Critical History of the Inquisition of Spain.* [1823] Williamstown, MA: John Lilburne Co., 1967.
Llorente, Juan Antonio. *Historia Critica de la Inquisición en España.* 4 vols. Madrid: Hiperión, 1980.
Lubbers, Klaus. *Die Todesszene und ihre Funktion im Kurzgeschichtenwerk Edgar Allan Poes.* München: Hueber, 1961.
Lüdeke, Henry. *Geschichte der amerikanischen Literatur.* Bern: A. Francke, 1952.
Lurker, Manfred. *Wörterbuch der Symbolik.* Stuttgart: Kröner, 1991.
Mabbott, Thomas Ollive, ed. *Edgar Allan Poe: Tales and Sketches, Volume I: 1831-1842.* [1978] Urbana, IL: U of Illinois P, 2000.
Malloy, Jeanne M. "Apocalyptic Imagery and the Fragmentation of the Psyche: 'The Pit and the Pendulum'." *Nineteenth-Century Literature* 46:1 (June 1991): 82-95.
Maltby, William S. *The Black Legend in England: The Development of Anti-Spanish Sentiment, 1558-1660.* Durham, NC: Duke UP, 1971.
Max, Frédéric. *Prisonniers de l'Inquisition.* Paris: Seuil, 1989.
Meyers, Jeffrey. *Edgar Allan Poe: His Life and Legacy.* New York: Cooper Square Press, 1992.
Milton, John. *The Poetical Works of John Milton.* London: Macmillan & Co., 1882.
Monk, Maria. *Awful Disclosures of the Hotel Dieu Nunnery.* [1836] Nancy Lusignan Schultz, ed. *Veil of Fear: Nineteenth-Century Convent Tales by Rebecca Reed and Maria Monk.* West Lafayette, IN: NotaBell Books/Purdue UP, 1999.
Montanus, Reginaldus Gonsalvius. *Die Praktiken der spanischen Inquisition.* [1568] Translation and annotations by Franz Goldscheider. Berlin: Alf Sänger, 1925.
Monter, William. *Frontiers of Heresy.* Cambridge: CUP, 1990.
Muñoz Herrera, José Pedro. *Imagenes de la melancolía: Toledo (1772-1858).* Toledo: Graficas Toledo, 1993.
Nieto, Luis Moreno. *Toledo en la literatura.* Toledo: Imprenta de la diputación provincial, 1975.
O'Brien, John A. *The Inquisition.* New York: Macmillan, 1973.
Oliver, Lawrence J., Jr. "Kinesthetic Imagery and Helplessness in Three Poe Tales." *Studies in Short Fiction* 20:2-3 (Spring-Summer 1983): 73-77.
Ostrom, John Ward, ed. *The Letters of Edgar Allan Poe.* 2 vols. Cambridge, MA: Harvard UP, 1948.
Peters, Edward. *Inquisition.* Berkeley, CA: U California P, 1989.

Prescott, William H. *History of the Reign of Ferdinand and Isabella the Catholic.* [1838, 1843] Ed. C. Harvey Gardiner. London: Allen & Unwin, 1962.

Quinn, Arthur Hobson. *Edgar Allan Poe: A Critical Biography.* [1941] Baltimore: Johns Hopkins UP, 1998.

Radcliffe, Ann. *The Italian; or, The Confessional of the Black Penitents: A Romance.* Ed. Frederick Garber. London: OUP, 1968.

Reynolds, David S. *Beneath the American Renaissance: The Subversive Imagination in the Age of Emerson and Melville.* Cambridge, MA: Harvard UP, 1988.

Reynolds, David S. "Poe's Art of Transformation: 'The Cask of Amontillado' in Its Cultural Context." Kenneth Silverman, ed. *New Essays on Poe's Major Tales.* Cambridge: CUP, 1993. 93-112.

Ringe, Donald A. "Poe's Debt to Scott in 'The Pit and the Pendulum'." *English Language Notes* 18:4 (June 1981): 281-283.

Ross, Michael. *The Reluctant King: Joseph Bonaparte, King of the Two Sicilies and Spain.* London: Sidgwick & Jackson, 1976.

Scott, Walter. *Letters on Demonology and Witchcraft.* [1830] Ware, Hertfordshire/UK: Wordsworth Editions, 2001.

Sofsky, Wolfgang. *Traktat über die Gewalt.* Frankfurt/Main: Fischer, 1996.

Summers, Montague. *Witchcraft and Black Magic.* [1946] London: Arrow, 1964.

Tate, Allen. *Collected Essays.* Denver, CO: Alan Swallow, 1959.

Vekene, Emil van der. "Ehemalige Inquisitionsgefangene berichten: Memoirenwerke und Erlebnisberichte des 16. bis 19. Jahrhunderts." *Glaubensprozesse – Prozesse des Glaubens? Religiöse Minderheiten zwischen Toleranz und Inquisition.* Ed. Titus Heydenreich, and Peter Blumenthal. Tübingen: Stauffenburg, 1989. 157-175.

Wülfing, Wulf. "Napoleon-Bibeln: Anthologien als Medien der Mythisierung von Figuren der Geschichte." *Wege der Literaturwissenschaft.* Ed. Jutta Kolkenbrock-Netz, Gerhard Plumpe, and Hans Joachim Schrimpf. Bonn: Bouvier, 1985. 184-204.

Regional Aspects in T. S. Eliot's Poetry

Angela M. Senst

"I am afraid no scenery except the Mississippi, the prairie and the North East Coast has ever made much impression on me," writes T. S. Eliot in 1930 ("To E. McKnight Kauffer" 211). This declaration for distinct rural American regions comes as a surprise in a poet who is generally praised for his urban imagery and its adequacy to express the plight of the uprooted modern man. Critical attention usually focuses on Eliot's universality, while regional aspects of his poetry are neglected. Even the rural imagery Eliot employs in poems like "The Dry Salvages" is used to prove him an American rather than a regional poet because writers and critics alike have created and sustained the myth of America as *nature's nation*. Consequently, literature which makes use of imagery taken from nature is automatically classified as 'American' – despite the fact that it is impossible to determine whether famous regional poems such as Robert Frost's "The Tuft of Flowers," "Mending Wall," or "Mowing" are indeed set in New rather than in Old England. Moreover, the regionalist movements which arose throughout the country in the 1920s understood themselves as bulwarks against cosmopolitanism (Jordan, Introduction xii), which for them symbolized the "congested, proletarianized, centralized, and standardized future toward which the country seemed irreversibly to be declining" (Dorman xii). By creating exemplary "mythic communities" they hoped to recover what modern America lacked but needed: a sense of community, roots in the land, and the values of tradition (Wilson, Introduction x). Seen against this background it is not surprising that the cosmopolitan poet Eliot was not considered "one of them," since his poetry laid bare the cultural malaise the regionalist movements tried to oppose. Michael Kowalewski, however, argues for a less restrictive definition of *regionalism*, which takes into account "the full spectrum of places within a given area" and includes both rural and urban landscapes (180). And indeed, as long as we do not narrow our understanding of *region* to rural areas only but realize that different cities possess specific cultural patterns and distinctive local identities (cf. Ludwig 28), not only T. S. Eliot's rural, but also his urban imagery does indeed qualify as *regional*.

In order to examine the regional aspects of T. S. Eliot's poetry it is necessary to determine what exactly is meant by the term *regionalism* – a task more easily set than solved, since literary criticism seethes with vague attempts at defining why some poetry qualifies as *regional*. What started out as the *local color movement* of the late 19th century was soon rejected because it was thought to be primarily interested in the picturesque and "suggested distortion, exploitation, and exaggeration of regional material" (Nordström 15). *Regionalists* of the 1920s and '30s, however, prided themselves on the fact that their literature presented a "serious investigation or reflection of place," whereas nowadays contemporary writers like to talk about the *sense of place* inherent in their work and reject the term *regionalism* for its suggestions of provinciality and narrow perspective (Nordström 15). A closer look at the literary texts themselves, however, reveals that it is literature transcending the mere descriptive which continues to be read and discussed – indifferent of the fact when it was written and which of the labels are given to it. In his analysis of the American regional movement Robert L. Dorman is convinced that some of the greatest artists "used the provincial and familiar as raw material which they shaped according to presumably 'universal' philosophical, psychological, and moral themes" (xiii). To give only two examples: Sarah Orne Jewett's "A White Heron" is more than just a sentimental description of life in rural Maine and Robert Frost's poems continue to be read not only for their accurate depictions of New England, but because they touch upon questions still essential to our life.

These difficulties notwithstanding, there are several elements that recur in the various definitions of *regionalism*. All of them acknowledge the shaping power a particular environment has on its inhabitants and define the *region* itself in terms of a shared geographical and cultural history, but it is especially the new regionalism emerging in the 1970s that made cultural identity its key issue, and explains regionalism "in terms of the experience of a social group more than in terms of place" (Wilson, Introduction xiii). Within regional literature the *region* is not merely setting, but rather a combination of values, beliefs, and customs, which the regional writer is well aware of and strives to convey to the reader in order to enable him to sense a particular environment. Since the regional writer is both participant and reporter of the region (Holman 11), he is as much writing for the insider as for the outsider. While the insider is able to recognize setting and atmosphere and may experience a sense of belonging, the outsider is given the possibility to acquire information about another place and to become familiar with a way of living so far unknown to him. In order to evoke an actual sense of the region, *regional literature* therefore uses specific cultural, historical and geographical detail (Jessup 9). This does not necessarily mean, though, that the regional writer is giving a historically correct picture of time and place. Often, he rather records "not what is factual, but what is believed in spite of any facts" (Holman 7). As James R. Shortridge points out, a place's image serves as a cultural symbol, which explains why the image is more important than the reality of life in a particular place (60). This thesis is confirmed by Stephen Nissenbaum, who speaks of the "invention" of New England and reminds us "that by 1860, when small-town New England was first being sentimentalized as a seat of pastoral Yankee stability, the region as a whole had become the single most urban part of the nation – the most industrial, the most Catholic, the most heavily immigrant in population" – facts that New England regionalists either ignored or marginalized (106) in order to create the myth of rural New England. The necessity to create unifying cultural symbols also explains the extensive use of stereotypes in regional literature: If both writer and reader alike are more concerned about the cultural projection than the depiction of 'reality,' the regionalist author has to resort to preconceived images in order to fulfill his audience's expectations by confirming and strengthening what he and his readers regard as typical of a particular region.

At first sight Eliot's literary criticism reveals a surprising closeness to regionalist thought: Whether he singles out authors whom he considers "landmarks of a national literature" (*American Literature* 17) or calls Dante the "most *European*" poet ("What Dante" 134), Eliot praises literature for containing "strong local flavour combined with unconscious universality" (*American Literature* 17). In doing so he echoes the regionalists' credo that "regionalist art is not limited to the provincial in the narrow sense but seeks to express in the regional the universal" (Hönnighausen 358). Like many contemporaries Eliot rejects "provincialism" for its "distortion of values," by which he means "applying standards acquired within a limited area, to the whole of human experience; which confounds the contingent with the essential, the ephemeral with the permanent" ("Classic" 69). He expresses sympathy for the Southern regionalist manifesto *I'll Take My Stand*, praises Virginia for possessing a distinct characteristic culture ("[...] to cross into Virginia is as definite an experience as to cross from England to Wales, almost as definite as to cross the English channel"), and deplores the "monotony exerted by the industrial expansion" (*After Strange Gods* 16). He stresses the importance of "local loyalties" (*Notes* 52) and points out the "crippling effect upon men of letters, of not having been born and brought up in an environment of a living and central tradition" (*After Strange Gods* 53). Being convinced that clinging to an old tradition, or attempting to re-establish it, always contains the danger of sentimentality (*After Strange Gods* 19), Eliot rejects the regionalist work of his contemporaries for exactly the same reasons they put forward against the work of the earlier *local color school*. According to Eliot, the "true" regionalist should rather try "to grow a contemporary culture from the old roots" (*Notes* 53). While the emphasis on "culture" foreshadows concepts of region that are presently discussed by the *new regionalists*, the emphasis on "contemporary" challenges sentimental nostalgia. The image Eliot creates of a particular region is not designed as a positive counter-image against urban America, but strives to convey an awareness of the poet's subjective reality. Since Eliot conceives of himself as a person who was never given the possibility to develop strong local loyalties (Read 15), the reality he presents in his poetry is an analysis and depiction of the uprootedness of modern man and thus differs widely from the idealizing myths created by more conventional regionalist writers.

In his introduction to the *Adventures of Huckleberry Finn* Eliot explains that it is only intimate knowledge of a particular region that enables a writer to use *place* in a significant way:

> There are, perhaps, only two ways in which a writer can acquire the understanding of environment which he can later turn to account: by having spent his childhood in that environment – that is, living in it at a period of life in which one experiences much more than one is aware of; and by having had to struggle for a livelihood in that environment – a livelihood bearing no direct relation to any intention of writing about it, of *using* it as literary material. (334)

Consequently, the places Eliot employs in his own poetry are taken from these two spheres of experience. His poetry gives a true account of the environment of his childhood years, namely St. Louis with the Mississippi river, and the New England coast, where the Eliot family spent their summer holidays, and where Eliot attended Harvard University. And it makes use of English places, mostly London, where Eliot worked as schoolmaster, Extension Lecturer, in the foreign department of Lloyd's Bank, and finally as publisher.

Since Eliot is convinced that "universality can never come except through writing about what one knows thoroughly" (*American Literature* 18), his urban imagery is that of St. Louis with descriptions of Paris and London superimposed (Moody 79). The thorough knowledge of the locale thus ensures an immediacy of perception that establishes Eliot's reputation as the cosmopolitan poet in poems like "The Love Song of J. Alfred Prufrock" or "The Waste Land." The fact, though, that Eliot mixes images from different cities in order to create a unified image of urban life, conceals Eliot's heightened awareness of a specific locale: "[...] cosmopolitanism can be the enemy of universality – it may dissipate attention in superficial familiarity with the streets, the cafés and some of the local dialect of a number of foreign capitals" (*American Literature* 17-18). To the regionalists of the 1920s all cities looked the same, anyway: "New York knows more of Paris and London than it does of the Middle West." (Carey McWilliams, qtd. in Dorman 117). Responses to Eliot's poetry seem to confirm this apprehension: Because of "the yellow smoke that slides along the street / Rubbing its back upon the window panes" (24-25) it was long assumed that the setting in "Prufrock" is London with its characteristic yellow smog. However, A. David Moody points out that Eliot's home town St. Louis had its own fogs which were yellowed by its own factories (78). Moreover, the women, who "come and go / Talking of Michelangelo," (13-14; 35-36) convey the atmosphere of educated Boston at the beginning of this century, which Eliot got to know while he was a student at Harvard University (cf. Sigg 18-20). They are easily recognizable as stereotypes – not the Yankee farmer stereotype Robert Frost creates, but stereotypes nonetheless. The ending of "Prufrock" confronts the reader with an equally ambiguous setting, since it is impossible to decide whether Prufrock's encounter with the mermaids takes place at the Boston seashore or at Dover Beach. Another example of the superimposition of landscapes can be found in the first part of "The Waste Land," despite the fact that place names make it quite easy to identify the city described as London and enable the reader to become part of the crowd flowing over London Bridge: "up the hill and down King Williams Street, / To where Saint Mary Woolnooth kept the hours" (66-67). In part III, 'The Fire Sermon,' the reader accompanies the "Thames-daughters" on their journey downstream, passing Greenwich, the Isle of Dogs, Highbury, Richmond, Kew, Moorgate and Margate Sands in order to encounter at the mouth of the river – Carthage. With the invocation of this name London is linked with the fate of ancient cities of culture, in particular Jerusalem, Athens, Alexandria, and Vienna, to which it is likened in part V.

But there are also instances in "The Waste Land" which refer to specific places: While alluding to Spenser's *Prothalamion*, the description at the beginning of part III gives a detailed account of how the Thames river banks must have looked during summer nights and on this specific winter evening:

> The river's tent is broken; the last fingers of leaf
> Clutch and sink into the wet bank. The wind
> Crosses the brown land, unheard. [...]
> The river bears no empty bottles, sandwich papers,
> Silk handkerchiefs, cardboard boxes, cigarette ends
> Or other testimony of summer nights. The nymphs are departed.
> And their friends, the loitering heirs of City directors;
> Departed, have left no addresses. [...]
>
> A rat crept softly through the vegetation
> Dragging its slimy belly on the bank
> While I was fishing in the dull canal
> On a winter evening round behind the gashouse [...] (173-190)

Although the beginning could be a description of any river, the fact that 'City' is spelled with a capital 'C' leaves no doubt that this is the "City of London," the center of the British Empire. The scene rendered is depressing: The reader does not know whether he should not be glad that a rat is the only other living creature the speaker encounters on the river banks because the testimonies of summer nights suggest dirt, desperate loneliness and cheap sex. It is a comment on society's moral values and it manages to convey the feeling of what it must have been like to live in this environment, and thus creates a heightened awareness of the locale.

Another instance of "a literature as no other locality could produce, a literature that could not have been written in any other time, or among other surroundings" (Garland 26) is the pub scene in part II, 'A Game of Chess,' in which Eliot tries to imitate the particular diction of the speakers:

> When Lil's husband got demobbed, I said –
> I didn't mince my words, I said to her myself,
> HURRY UP PLEASE ITS TIME
> Now Albert's coming back, make yourself a bit smart.
> He'll want to know what you done with that money he gave you
> To get yourself some teeth. He did, I was there.
> You have them all out, Lil, and get a nice set,
> He said, I swear, I can't bear to look at you.
> [...]
> You ought to be ashamed, I said, to look so antique.
> (And her only thirty-one.)
> I can't help it, she said, pulling a long face,
> It's them pills I took, to bring it off, she said.
> (She's had five already, and nearly died of young George.)
> [...]
> HURRY UP PLEASE ITS TIME
> HURRY UP PLEASE ITS TIME
> Goonight Bill. Goonight Lou. Goonight May. Goonight.
> Ta ta. Goonight. Goonight. (139-171)

In this dialogue between two women in a pub shortly before closing time the repeated calls "HURRY UP PLEASE ITS TIME" enable the reader to recognize the place as an English pub and not an American bar. The word "demobbed", which is a British slang abbreviation of 'demobilized' and was first recorded in 1920 ("Demobbed"), makes it possible to date the scene shortly after WWI. The people referred to are poor, they have rotten teeth due to malnutrition, and it is poverty that forces Lil to abort her child. Apart from the historical information Eliot's own reading of "The Waste Land" conveys a true auditory picture by imitating the women's accent. Being convinced that "the structure, the rhythm, the sound, the idiom of a language, express the personality of the people which speaks it" ("Social Function" 19), Eliot stresses that "the music of poetry [...] must be a music latent in the common speech of its time. And that means also that it must be latent in the common speech of the poet's *place*" ("Music" 31) – it is a distinctly regional idiom. In the poem "Preludes" accurate description and, as Moody points out, American language and speech rhythms make it possible to identify the scene as an American town: "lot" and "block" are American usages, the English expression of "shades" as it is used in this poem is "blinds", whereas "blinds" in Eliot's usage is a Southern expression of what people from other American regions would call "shutters" (79-80).

These examples show that Eliot's urban imagery is rich in details of time and place and demonstrate how thorough knowledge of the locale enables him to express in the regional the universal. By describing what he believes to be the reality that surrounds him, Eliot evokes an awareness for the uprooted modern man in an anonymous city who "can connect / Nothing with nothing" ("The Waste Land" 301-302). Avoiding the danger of sentimentality inherent in the regionalists' refusal to acknowledge the change from a rural to an urban society and their clinging to an old tradition in a vain attempt to re-establish it, Eliot's poetry captures the mood of disillusionment that prevailed in the Western world after WWI. Eliot's depictions of urban environments, however, do contribute to the birth of yet another myth: the cultural symbol of the modern city signifying loneliness, anonymity, and moral corruption.

Especially Eliot's late poems, in which rural landscapes prevail, drew critical attention to Eliot as an American poet. True to his own remark that "[a] writer's art must be based on the accumulated sensations of the first twenty-one years" (Review 167), many of his rural landscapes point to his American childhood and youth. Among the poems that make use of this scenery the first movement of "The Dry Salvages" readily comes to mind because it employs both imagery from the Mississippi river and the North East Coast. At the beginning of "The Dry Salvages" an epigraph refers the title to an actual place, "a small group of rocks, with a beacon, off the N.E. coast of Cape Ann, Massachusetts." Thus supplying the outsider with inside-knowledge Eliot robs the insider of the exclusive sense of belonging which the latter must have felt when he – unlike the outsider – already in the title recognized the actual place. Moreover, Eliot adds information the insider, too, has probably never heard of and thus defamiliarizes the latter from the familiar scene: Eliot's insertions "presumably *les trois sauvages*," i.e. "the three savages," and his comment on the pronunciation of *Salvages*, which is supposed to rime on *assuages*, forces both readers – the insider as well as the outsider – to ponder on the dialectic nature of these rocks. They might – especially in a storm – be as dangerous as the stereotypical savage, with whom not only readers of early American fiction readily associate wild untamed natural power. At the same time the reference to the verb 'to assuage' gives a positive meaning to the rocks which could serve as a safe haven for shipwrecked persons. By forcing the insider to get a new perspective on familiar scenery, Eliot effectively plays on regional conventions, and continues to do so at the beginning of the poem proper. Having read title and epigraph, the reader expects a poem about the East Coast, but instead he is confronted with a river personified as a

> [...] strong brown god – sullen, untamed and intractable,
> Patient to some degree, at first recognized as a frontier;
> Useful, untrustworthy, as a conveyor of commerce;
> Then only a problem confronting the builder of bridges.
>   [...] ever, however, implacable,
> Keeping his seasons and rages [...]. (2-8)

The geographical and historical information in this passage, in particular the allusion to the frontier, make it easy to identify the river as the Mississippi, which Eliot remembers from his childhood, and which he describes in his introduction to *Adventures of Huckleberry Finn*: "[...] the [Mississippi] river with its strong, swift current is the dictator to the raft or the steamboat. It is a treacherous and capricious dictator. At one season, it may move sluggishly [...] at another season, [...] it runs with the speed such that no man or beast can survive in it" (332). With the pulsating rhythm of the river (11-14), the scenery changes. In the following lyric passage Eliot manages to evoke an awareness of the seashore that is as intense as Mark Twain's presentation of the Mississippi, which Eliot held in high esteem (Introduction 333). In lines 16-37 the reader is not only given a visual image of the sea, but all his senses are engaged, and thus he becomes able to experience the sea:

> The sea is the land's edge also, the granite
> Into which it reaches, the beaches where it tosses
> Its hints of earlier and other creation:
> The starfish, the horseshoe crab, the whale's backbone;
> The pools where it offers to our curiosity
> The more delicate algae and the sea anemone.
> It tossed up our losses, the torn seine,
> The shattered lobsterpot, the broken oar
> And the gear of foreign dead men. The sea has many voices,
> Many gods and many voices.
>   The salt is on the briar rose,
> The fog is in the fir trees.
>   The sea howl

> And the sea yelp, are different voices
> Often together heard: the whine in the rigging,
> The menace and caress of wave that breaks on water,
> The distant rote in the granite teeth,
> And the wailing warning from the approaching headland
> Are all sea voices, and the heaving groaner
> Rounded homewards, and the seagull:
> And under the oppression of the silent fog
> The tolling bell (16-37)

In this passage the sea behaves like an unruly living creature. It reaches into the granite and tosses flotsam and jetsam onto the beaches. After an enumeration of these "hints of earlier and other creation" the imagery changes from the visual to the auditory, when rhythm, alliteration and onomatopoeia convey an awareness of a region that is dangerous and beautiful at the same time. Like many regionalist writers Eliot thus uses the particular place to lure the reader into the revelation of a universal truth. But it is, in fact, irrelevant to the interpretation of "The Dry Salvages" whether the reader is able to identify the actual place, since sea and river are used as universal symbols. Intimate knowledge of a particular environment is, however, essential for the writer who strives to express in the regional the universal.

Eliot's later poems often contain similar passages (e.g. in the other quartets, "Landscapes" or "Marina"), but his poetry always avoids the danger of sentimentality. It is not used to create an image of a positive tradition that serves as a model of our modern times, but instead presents life as it is: fragmented, a "heap of broken images" ("The Waste Land" 22), which his collage technique adequately mirrors. By arranging seemingly unconnected detailed accounts of every-day-life next to imagery taken from mythology or literature Eliot makes it impossible for the reader to surrender to the scenery, but forces him to reflect on it. Unlike more conventional regional literature Eliot's fragments do not allow the reader to enjoy the completeness of the illusion. This play on regional conventions explains why the regional aspects of Eliot's poetry are so easily overlooked. Despite the fact that Eliot's poems do indeed manage to express in the regional the universal, his bleak depictions of reality are seldom labeled *regionalist* because his poetry does not employ "realistic local details to develop a generally positive image of the region it describes" (Jessup 5). According to

Winks "one best understands how people conceive of themselves regionally by observing what they take collective pride in. And this, over time, is best measured by what they consciously choose to preserve from the culture (mythical or real) that they have historically defined for themselves through operable truths and vital lies" (31). Eliot's poetry, however, exposes these placid regionalist illusions as sentimental, and his negative depiction of life in the cities is nothing to take pride in. By combining realistic local details with classical and mythological allusions Eliot creates a mirror-image of the fragmented modern world which contemporaries recognized as their daily environment. They were able to identify with Eliot's personae and felt that he gave a true account of what it was like to be a modern man in an anonymous city.

Works Cited

"Demobbed." A Supplement to the Oxford English Dictionary. 1972.
Dorman, Robert L. *Revolt of the Provinces: The Regionalist Movement in America, 1920-1945*. Chapel Hill: U of North Carolina P, 1993.
Eliot, T. S. *After Strange Gods: A Primer of Modern Heresy*. New York: Harcourt, Brace and Company, 1934.
- - -. *American Literature and the American Language: An Address delivered at Washington University on June 9, 1953*. St. Louis, MO: Washington U, 1953.
- - -. *The Complete Poems and Plays*. London: Faber & Faber, 1969.
- - -. An Introduction to *Huckleberry Finn*. 1950. *Adventures of Huckleberry Finn*. By Samuel Langhorne Clemens. Ed. Sculley Bradley et al. 2nd ed. New York: Norton Critical Edition, 1977. 328-335.
- - -. "The Music of Poetry." 1942. Eliot, *On Poetry* 26-38.
- - -. *Notes Towards the Definition of Culture*. London: Faber & Faber, 1948.
- - -. *On Poetry and Poets*. London: Faber & Faber, 1957.
- - -. "The Social Function of Poetry." 1945. Eliot, *On Poetry* 15-25.
- - -. "To E. McKnight Kauffer, a letter from T. S. Eliot." *T. S. Eliot: Essays from the* Southern Review. Ed. James Olney. Oxford: Clarendon Press, 1988. 211.
- - -. "What is a Classic?" 1944. Eliot, *On Poetry* 53-71.
- - -. "What Dante Means to Me." 1950. *To Criticize the Critic and Other Writings*. London: Faber & Faber, 1965. 125-135.
- - -. Rev. of *Turgenev*, by Edward Garnett. *Egoist* 4 (1917): 167.
- - -. "The Waste Land." Rec. 1947. *T. S. Eliot Reads*. Audiocassette. New York: HarperCollins, 1971.

Garland, Hamlin. "New Fields." *Crumbling Idols: Twelve Essays on Art Dealing Chiefly With Literature Painting and the Drama*. 1894. Ed. Jane Johnson. Cambridge, MA: Belknap, 1960. 21-26.
Holman, David Marion. *A House Divided: Regionalism and the Form of Midwestern and Southern Fiction, 1832-1925*. Diss. U of Michigan, 1983. Ann Arbor: UMI, 1983.
Hönnighausen, Lothar. "Region, Nation and the Definition of American Identity in the Early Twentieth Century." *Negotiations of America's National Identity*. Ed. Roland Hagenbüchle, and Josef Raab, in cooperation with Marietta Messmer. Atlantic Perspectives 9. Vol. 2. Tübingen: Stauffenburg, 2000. 348-361.
Jessup, Emily Decker Lardner. *Embattled Landscapes: Regionalism and Gender in Midwestern Literature, 1915-1941*. Diss. U of Michigan, 1985. Ann Arbor: UMI, 1985.
Jordan, David. Introduction. *Regionalism Reconsidered: New Approaches to the Field*. Ed. David Jordan. New York: Garland, 1994. ix-xxi.
Kowalewski, Michael. "Bioregional Perspectives in American Literature." *Regionalism Reconsidered: New Approaches to the Field*. Ed. David Jordan. New York: Garland, 1994. 29-46.
Ludwig, Hans-Werner. "Province and Metropolis; Centre and Periphery: Some Critical Terms Re-examined." *Regionalität, Nationalität und Internationalität in der zeitgenössischen Lyrik*. Ed. Lothar Fietz, Paul Hoffmann, and Hans-Werner Ludwig. Tübingen: Attempto, 1992. 28-48.
McWilliams, Carey. "Young Man, Stay West." *Southwest Review* 15 (Spring 1930): 301-9.
Moody, A. D[avid]. "T. S. Eliot: The American Strain." *The Placing of T. S. Eliot*. Ed. Jewel Spears Brooker. Columbia: U of Missouri P, 1991. 77-89.
Nissenbaum, Stephen. "Inventing New England." Wilson, *New Regionalism* 105-134.
Nordström, Lars. *Theodore Roethke, William Stafford, and Gary Snyder: The Ecological Metaphor as Transformed Regionalism*. Uppsala: Almqvist & Wiksell, 1989.
Read, Herbert. "T. S. E. – A Memoir." *T. S. Eliot: The Man and His Work*. Ed. Allen Tate. London: Chatto & Windus, 1967. 11-37.
Shortridge, James R. "The Persistence of Regional Labels in the United States: Reflections from a Midwestern Perspective." Wilson, *New Regionalism* 45-70.
Sigg, Eric. "Eliot as a Product of America." *The Cambridge Companion to T. S. Eliot*. Ed. A. David Moody. Cambridge: Cambridge UP, 1994. 14-30.
Wilson, Charles Reagan, ed. *The New Regionalism*. Jackson: UP of Mississippi, 1998.
Wilson, Charles Reagan. Introduction. Wilson, *New Regionalism* ix-xxiii.
Winks, Robin W. "Regionalism in Comparative Perspective." *Regionalism and the Pacific Northwest*. Ed. William G. Robbins, Robert J. Frank, and Richard E. Ross. Corrallis, OR: Oregon State UP, 1983. 13-36.

Interrogating Whiteness: Perspectives on 'Race' in Texts by James McBride, Shirlee Taylor Haizlip, and Edward Ball

Eva Boesenberg

If the twentieth century was, as W.E.B. Du Bois suggested, the century of the color line, its figurations towards the end of this period contrasted markedly with those at the time of his writing. Family memoirs such as Edward Ball's *Slaves in the Family* (1998), James McBride's *The Color of Water* (1996), and Shirlee Taylor Haizlip's *The Sweeter the Juice* (1994) draw intricate chiaroscuro landscapes that foreground black/white interrelatedness even as they attend to the specificity of lived racial experience. Analyzing their representations of 'race,' I argue that these texts contest the purity and exclusivity of whiteness as well as the essential quality and homogeneity of blackness. Focusing on families that are black as well as white, they emphasize the social and cultural construction of racial identity and the internal heterogeneity of racial groupings. In the process, they assess the value of whiteness as a form of social capital while also calculating the costs incurred by its realization. Conversely, McBride's narrative of his mother's life details her rationale for living among black people and represents her Jewish heritage as "whiteness of a different color," to borrow Matthew Frye Jacobson's apt formulation (1-12, 161-199).

The narratives' focus on racial variability and the hybridity of personal experience corresponds to multigeneric discourses that incorporate a variety of authenticating documents and photographs corroborating their claims to historical factuality. Speaking from the intersections of cultural entitlement and previously silenced or marginalized orality, they construct dialogic portrayals of racial individuality from a multiplicity of competing as well as collaborating voices. In this endeavor, the central metaphor and structural paradigm organizing the texts, the image of family and kinship, proves to be particularly effective yet also restricting, an issue I will discuss in greater detail towards the end of this article. Although they are exceptional in their sustained attention to interracial family ties, collectively the texts suggest that crucial but explosive issues such as black/white heterosexual relations may be discussed less defensively and more candidly in the future.

Interrogating Whiteness

Outlining factual relations of kin between blacks and whites, both Edward Ball and Shirlee Taylor Haizlip reveal notions about the purity of the white 'race' as fantasies of racial superiority and innocence. Owing to the different racial positions from which they begin to narrate their families' histories, however, their stories proceed along differential lines of inquiry. Predictably, Ball's investigation of slave life on the plantations of his ancestors and his visits to some of the slaves' descendants meet with hostility especially from some of his older kin, who view his enterprise as a desecration of their cherished genealogy. For a clan that convenes periodically to enjoy a common sense of value grounded in the family's past fame and fortune, a closer look at the 'darker side' of their legacy promises nothing but unsavoriness and controversy. Yet Ball's text clearly honors his paternal ancestors, representing their lives empathetically and in great detail while adducing additional historical information for a more densely circumstantial portrayal of contemporary realities.

What alters "the look of the past" (62) more irrevocably than any disdain on the side of the author is the close attention the text pays to information about *all* of the plantations' former inhabitants. There is a subtle irony in the fact that the Balls' own records contradict many of the white lies circulating within the extended family, such as the Balls' supposed aversion to the disruption of slave families or their reluctance to inflict physical punishment (56). If whiteness is understood not only as "a location of structural advantage and race privilege" but also as "a 'standpoint' from which people look at themselves, at others, and at society; and a set of cultural practices that are usually unmarked and unnamed," as Martha R. Mahoney summarizes Ruth Frankenberg's findings in *White Women, Race Matters*

(330-331), it is the last two aspects of white identity that are questioned most consistently in Ball's family memoir.

The most serious challenge to the family's habitual ways of seeing themselves and their routine marginalization of African Americans in their image of the past, however, arises not so much from a recognition of their predecessors' callousness or brutality but from the evidence of interracial heterosexual unions. Where family members like Dorothy, whom the text depicts as "marinated in Ball family lore" (50), assert that, in contradistinction to occurrences in Thomas Jefferson's household, there was very little – if any – "cohabitation" in the Ball homes (58), and represent mulatto or quadroon mistresses as a "French invention" shunned by the English (57), Edward Ball discovers circumstantial evidence that strongly suggests the contemporaneity of miscegenation with the history of the Balls in America.

The original patriarch of the clan, Elias 'Red Cap' Ball who almost certainly sustained a long-term sexual relationship with his (mixed-race) slave Dolly after the death of his second wife (in a form closely resembling Thomas Jefferson's cohabitation with Sally Hemings, down to the children's manumission in the father's will while their mother remained enslaved [Wood 23]) was not the only one among the Ball men to father sons and daughters with partners of African descent. The text cites numerous instances of interracial sex or even long-standing unions involving male members of the Ball lineage. As the book's title implies, slaves thus turn out to be biological rather than merely symbolic family members, a fact that fundamentally revises the boundaries and texture, as well as the meaning of consanguinity. No longer an unproblematic source and signifier of personal worth and entitlement, bloodlines reveal a genealogy that comprises transgression and possibly coercion as well as honor and romance.

One consequence of this reconfiguration is Edward Ball's discovery of relatives among the descendants of slaves he seeks out. The chapters that represent such meetings with their forthright discussions of slavery, racism, and the personal ties between those present complement the more conventionally historiographic sections in terms of narrative form as well as content. The black families' oral traditions not only substantiate and add to Ball's own findings; the dialogic structure of the chapters in which the author becomes visible as a sometimes hesitant or bewildered *participant* in a revision of the past also characterizes a more democratic form of historical narration that corresponds to his thematic approach.

Where Ball's text deconstructs one family's supposedly consistent and homogenous tale of historical whiteness by acknowledging the presence and impact of those formerly rendered invisible on account of their 'race' and subordination, Shirlee Taylor Haizlip's memoir recounts her efforts to complete her mother's and thus her own black genealogy by tracking down its missing white members. Yet these are not symmetrical projects, for the absence of Haizlip's white relatives is conscious and intentional: These 'lost' uncles, aunts and cousins relinquish their family ties in return for the social capital of whiteness with its attendant benefits such as social status and freedom from racial discrimination. Their often unexpected disapperance and the subsequent denial of any connection to their darker-skinned relatives are experienced as traumatic betrayals by those left behind.

Haizlip's mother is an extreme case in point, for her "brothers and her one sister, her father, her father's mother and all her aunts and uncles except one chose to live another life" (75). Orphaned perhaps even more radically than in the customary meaning of the term, she grows up in a series of foster homes, a socialization that produces a deep-seated melancholy her daughter endeavors to alleviate with her project of familial reconstitution (33). Again the picture that emerges from her minute mapping of the family history defies a binary logic of 'race', emphasizing gradations of skin tones and hair textures instead. The color line appears less as a natural bar than an intersection, a site of frequent crossing and re-crossing, the certainties of 'race' that it promises thoroughly undermined by family members' decisions to "pass" (34).

Despite its lack of ontological reality or biological grounding, however, the *effects* of the black/white dichotomy are substantial. Like Ball's text, Haizlip's corroborates an understanding of whiteness as property cogently theorized by Cheryl Harris, a form of entitlement one might, elaborating on Pierre Bourdieu, describe as a form of social capital. Where Ball speaks of "an intangible sense of worth" and a sense of historical rootedness conveyed by his ancestry (13), detailing his inheritance as "a great fund of cultural capital, including prestige, a chance at education, self-esteem, a sense of place, mobility, even (in some cases) a flair for giving orders"(14) although his progenitors were unanble to pass on their estates or financial resources, Haizlip notes that many of her relatives "left the race" in order to obtain better employment and higher wages (63-64, 69). More so than Ball, however, Haizlip also notes that the mobilization of whiteness also entails a price, a policing of identity that amounts to a denial of self (71-72). For the idea of racial purity on which whiteness (unlike blackness) is based demands a rigorous disavowal of all things black, including one's kin and the 'tainted' aspects of one's past. Whereas whiteness is premised, like property, on the right to exclude, blackness allows for heterogeneity and internal difference. Thus black family members may freely acknowledge all of their relatives while those living as white risk losing caste by association.

De-Essentializing 'Race'

The family memoirs of Haizlip, Ball, and McBride deconstruct what Kendall Thomas calls "the metaphorical illusion of an authentic racial identity" (127) not only with regard to monolithic whiteness, however. Through their detailed attention to the historical specificity of black and white lived experience, their "material interest in actual, embodied black existence" (Thomas 127), they also question any unitary ideology of blackness. McBride and Haizlip specifically address the situation of mixed-race African Americans, whose position is at once precarious and privileged. While Haizlip recounts some incidents in which her "lack of color" became an occasion for scorn, she cites many more instances in which racial privilege and social status accrued to light skin or Caucasian features (13, 34, 56, 78-79, 94).

Her description of Washington's "colored aristocracy" (78/79) as well as her own childhood reveals the confluence and mutual reinforcement of financial, educational and social capital (such as relative whiteness) even within a context of blackness. Thus admission requirements for an elite African American club in the early twentieth century included "fair skin, light eyes, thin lips, a high-bridged nose and an automobile" (79).

But Margaret Morris, the narrator's mother who grew up in this rigidly stratified social environment, sustains at best an ambivalent relation to the white privilege she inherits, for to her whiteness signifies above all the abandonment by her kin. In choosing a spouse whose skin color is significantly darker than hers (a pattern subsequently reiterated by her daughter), she opts for the 'safety' of black identification and "a stable, older figure from a large, close family" (98) rather than the entitlements pertaining to a light complexion. The effects of forgoing racial privilege are mitigated by the family's eventual attainment of an upper class lifestyle, though. Her husband effectively parlays his educational and overall cultural capital as well as his spiritual and social authority as a clergyman in the black community into real estate and a more than comfortable existence that encompasses stylish cars, elegant clothes, vacations in fashionable holiday resorts, and ivy league educations for most of his children.

This combination of economic wealth and – at least in his own case – the absence of privilege based on skin color, the apparent disjunction or at least attenuation of the presumed link between 'race' and property occasionally overtaxes the imagination of white contemporaries who are incapable of reconciling such a foreign sight with their expectatons of racial hierarchy within the United States. The narrator's father delights in confounding such stereotypical notions of 'race,' countering inquiries after the family's country of origin with a polite: "The country of Connecticut" (178).

The circumstance that the narrator's own racial positioning similarly defies the notion of any neccessary connection between skin color, 'race,' and social status is not merely due to the rise of a black middle class in the post-World War II era. Haizlip notes at the outset that many readers might not recognize her as black if they saw her, since the tone of her skin falls within the customary parameters of whiteness. It is nurture rather than nature that determines her self-identification as black, she avers: "...we have lived as, worked as and mostly married black people. Our psyches, souls and sensibilities are black" (13). Paradoxically, this recognition also generates her later empathy with the white family members, whom she comes to regard as "black people who had become white" (266). But the contingency and constructedness of 'race' does not negate its visceral power, with both aspects resonating in the language of the text's concluding chapter (267). Even though 'race' may be biologically insignificant for the human species, as the last paragraph suggests, it signifies an enduring legacy of individual as well as national self-division.

The painful aspects of such internal fragmentation emerge with greater force in James McBride's *The Color of Water*. His family memoir, like Haizlip's, revolves around the reconstruction of his mother's life, but with a significant difference: where Margaret Morris's relatives disappear into whiteness, Ruth McBride "came over to the African-American side," as her son phrases it (274). By marrying a black man, she went beyond the pale of the living for her Jewish family who said kaddish and sat shiva for her, performing the traditional funerary rites to mark her symbolic death (2). With a mixed-race family, McBride's mother points out, living among whites was not a viable option in the 1940s: "*I stayed on the black side because that was the only place I could stay. The few problems I had with black folks were nothing compared to the grief white folks dished out*" (232). There are more positive moments of identification with her African American milieu as well: the love for her husband, the generosity of his family, and blacks' general lack of a judgmental attitude towards her (240, 247, 109).

Unlike Haizlip's white kin, however, Ruth McBride never completely 'fits' in her black environment, a fact of which young James is sorely aware at an early age. While his mother appears content with a life centered on her large family and the church, ignoring unpleasant or jarring aspects of her surroundings, the son perceives the discrepancy between his mother's color and that of their neighbors as a threat not only to her safety but also to his own. Again and again, he expresses his anxiety about the circumstance that his family is not "just one color" (103). His insecurity is intensified by his mother's evasiveness concerning matters of 'race.' When confronted with the question: "Am I black or white?", she retorts: "You're a human being... Educate yourself or you'll be a nobody!" (92). Queries concerning her own racial identity are met with "I'm light-skinned" – and the immediate introduction of a different topic (xvii).

As a result, James – like all of his brothers and sisters – suffers from what he describes as "color confusion" (52). While his brother Richie attempts to solve this dilemma by imagining himself as green – a third term that elides the black/white-polarity (52) -, James seeks refuge in the image of "a boy who lived in the mirror" (90). This imaginary double, his "true self," is at liberty, well-off, and unencumbered by his mother's ethnicity (91). The narrator's perplexity concerning his identity that is reflected in a figure both self and other – or rather, the self as other – continues well into adulthood. It is only by engaging his mother's journey to the black side of the color line that he finally manages to unravel, and reconcile himself to, his complex heritage and individuality.

Consequently, *The Color of Water* is a dialogic text whose narrative alternates between the stories of mother and son in a form of call-and-response loosely organized around the correspondence between their interwoven tales. The mother's account, set in italics, appears in the chapters with uneven, her son's in those with even numbers, while the title, as Ada Savin observed, typographically combines both voices. The son's tale frames and contextualizes the mother's, echoing it at times (as in the chapters "Lost in Harlem" and "Lost in Delaware"); more generally, it reflects the ways in which the narrative he elicits illuminates and transforms his self-perception. Whereas Ball's conversations with the descendants of people enslaved on his progenitors' plantations open up a unitary tale of family pride and supposed social superiority to a diversity of 'other' voices that undermine its presumptions, McBride's dialogues with his mother produce a form of synthesis and closure, if not of her story, then at least of his.

Whiteness of a Different Color

What enables the narrator to eventually accept his family's and his own mixed-race heritage is the discovery, not of his mother's whiteness, but of her Jewish descent. As she dredges up memories of her first-generation immigrant family and a youth circumscribed by her materialistic and racist father's domestic tyranny, sexual abuse, and days spent in a store rather than a home, her decision to flee to the North and to share her life with a beloved black man and his family, in which "kindness was a way of life" (236), becomes eminently understandable, even though it entails leaving her mother and sister behind.

Rachel Shilsky's metamorphosis into Ruth McBride (2) involves a dual cross-over, a transition not merely from whiteness to living among and with black people, but perhaps even more importantly from the Jewish faith to Christianity. Her life centers not so much on cordial relations with her neighbors as on her large nuclear family and the New Brown Memorial Baptist Church she founds with her first husband (249-258). As her son describes her at a time of emotional hardship: "Ma was utterly confused about all but one thing: Jesus" (165).

Despite the centrality of Christianity in Ruth McBride's life, she does not disparage her parents' faith or blame it for the deprivations of her childhood. She carefully distinguishes between Jews and white people, "occasionally talk[ing] about 'the white man' in the third person, as if she had nothing to do with him, and in fact she didn't," as her son observes (32, cf. 87). Whiteness thus emerges as internally stratified in McBride's text, a category in which the history of different immigrant groups registers in distinct ways. Reflecting on the complex reconfiguration of Jewish Americans as white delineated by historians such as Karen Brodkin Sacks or Matthew Frye Jacobson, *The Color of Water* points to the distance still separating Americans of Jewish descent and 'lily-white' Anglo-Saxons.

This discrepancy facilitates James McBride's coming to terms with his mixed-race identity. Once he has retraced his mother's sojourn not only to Suffolk, Virginia, where she grew up – in a manner that tropes the slave narratives' paradigmatic journey, as Savin observes -, but to the Jewish faith and culture that characterized her formative years, the narrator can (re)define himself as "a black man with something of a Jewish soul" (103).

His encounters with members of Suffolk's Jewish community are marked by unusual frankness and a reception "as if I were one of them...as if there were no barriers between us" (224). In light of the fact that religious community appears to transcend 'race' in their eyes, the narrator concludes that Jewish identity may indeed constitute a divergent version of whiteness, a notion subsequently reinforced by a close friendship with a Jewish colleague. In the course of this development, McBride also endeavors to reconcile his mother to her Jewish past, a project that is only partly successful. Although she recovers some of her early history in the process of narrating her story to her son, who effects a reunion with her childhood friend Frances, for example, she remains aloof from Jewish life and religious ceremony even though she is no longer averse to acknowledging her previous connections to it (284).

The transformation of personal identity thus turns out to be more comprehensive and more beneficial for the son than for the mother. In the end, his tale is one of achievement: his own, but even more so Ruth McBride's. Her children's professional success validates her emphasis on education, upward mobility, and religion, a version of the American Dream that, as the narrator points out, derives much of its energy from the traditional Jewish passion and veneration for knowledge but eschews its crudely economic application figured in the maternal grandfather's callous materialism and disregard for others.

Yet James McBride's story illustrates, more insistently than Haizlip's, the difficulties of mixed-race people to find their place in a society that continues to view 'race' predominantly as a matter of two mutually exclusive categories. This may be due to the lack of economic privilege which shielded Haizlip from some 'race-related' pain and perplexity. While Haizlip, too, dwells on what Gordon S. Wood has termed "the ambiguities and absurdities of racial definitions" (28), her sense of personal identity appears less massively affected by their vicissitudes.

Reconfiguring the American Family

All three texts project journeys of self-discovery in which the narrator's sense of self is fundamentally revised and expanded. The image of psychoanalysis Ball employs to describe his own project (13) is pertinent for all of them, for it is the return (and recognition) of the repressed that allows them to attain a more comprehensive understanding of themselves as well as their families and the past. Physically as well as imaginatively retracing their relatives' steps – with Ball traveling to the places in West Africa from which some of his black kin were forced to undergo the dreaded "middle passage," McBride journeying to his mother's former abode and into Jewishness, and Haizlip following her mother's siblings into white residential areas in Anaheim and elsewhere – the narrators, in true *Bildungsroman* fashion, return from their expeditions more knowledgeable and mature, but also somewhat staggered by their findings.

The reconfiguration not only of their individual self-understanding but of their families has important ramifications for an understanding of U.S.-

American national identity. Where some kin figured as property in the Balls' 'unreconstructed' vision, and "family" initially served as a metaphor not only of community but at times also of exclusion and racial hierarchy in Haizlip's and McBride's narratives, the kinship structures that materialize towards the end of the texts are more inclusive, egalitarian, and diverse.

A crucial component in the formation of these new families is the rehabilitation of interracial sexual unions or 'miscegenation.' Although it is well-nigh impossible to determine to which degree coercion entered into those relationships conducted during and under slavery (generally between white men and enslaved women), long-term, apparently monogamous alliances like those between William Harleston, one of Ball's ancestors, and Kate Wilson (271-277) suggest that genuine affection was involved. Although the paucity of records generates the danger of "conceding too much" to the men's viewpoints when describing these liaisons, as Lewis and Onuf caution in their discussion of the parallel case involving Thomas Jefferson and Sally Hemings (11), the descendants of Kate Wilson also draw a rather benign picture of her association with Harleston, preserving it as a common-law marriage in the family's oral tradition (Ball 272). Shirlee Taylor Haizlip remembers her forebear judge James D. Halyburton – through whom she is distantly related to Martha Washington – with similar fondness (44).

Obviously, the situation is qualitatively different for twentieth-century interracial marriages such as Ruth McBride's. Her son describes her alliances with both his father and his stepfather as thoroughly affectionate and characterized by mutual respect, if somewhat idiosyncratic. In light of the fact that Ruth raised twelve children, virtually all of whom became professionals, even her former neighbors concede: "She led a good life" (227).

This acceptance and endorsement of interracial marriage is by no means uncontroversial even in the contemporary U.S.A. Clarence Walker cites a 1997 opinion poll in which fully 30 % of those interviewed opposed black-white marital unions (187), and many scholars have noted the extreme discomfort with 'miscegenation' evident in academic discussions of Jefferson's relation with Sally Hemings (Gordon-Reed 247). In all three texts here discussed, the detailed representation of mixed-race existence further involves the recognition that the idea of 'untainted' whiteness – just as the concept of an authentic blackness – is a fantasy grounded in a willful ignorance of historical facts as well as a misperception of contemporary reality. In view of "History's" crucial role for many Americans' self-understanding, the reconstructed past they present poses quite a challenge to the conventional saga of racial hierarchy and white distinction. If stalwarts such as Thomas Jefferson and Martha Washington can be shown to have black or mixed-race descendants, the nation's pedigree begins to look variegated indeed.

History's new look corresponds to a different sound, for it is the result of written records being reinterpreted in a dialogic dialectics with previously marginalized oral traditions. The texts' thematic explorations are continued and complemented on a level of form by narrative techniques that foreground the interactive quality of their formative discourses, implying that any truth about the shared history will necessarily be multivocal.

In order to promote the recognition that, as Walker puts it, "America is not a white country," all three narratives effectively deploy the metaphor of the family and of consanguinity. While this is a powerful rhetorical strategy for countering ideas of natural racial separateness and inequality, it generates problematic effects in other regards. At best, it can be employed to construct what Scott L. Malcomson in *One Drop of Blood* terms "imagined families of race" (507) which would no longer require the painful separation of children, "friend from friend, into races" (7) he remembers from his own youth. The *American* family, he contends, is necessarily (at least) white, black, and Native American *at the same time*; therefore, "[w]hen white Americans are among themselves and do not see that there are people missing from the family,...then they are failing fully to understand what it means to be an American" (506).

On the other hand, the concept of "the family" has been, and continues to be mobilized in the service of extremely conservative, sexist and racist social politics by the 'Moral Majority,' segments of the Republican Party, and other organizations of the political Right. A number of cultural critics have also commented on the politically counterproductive figurations of 'healthy' family structures in black nationalist discourse (Gilroy 305-313, Williams 144-145). Issues of political representation, of class or unequal economic opportunity are difficult to address within a paradigm of family relations. Generally, the familial constellations in Ball's, McBride's, and to a lesser extent Haizlip's text, always unquestioningly heterosexual and more often than not hierarchical in character, tend to reinscribe patriarchal and heterosexual privilege even as they attempt to dismantle inequalities of 'race.' Rarely does a queer uncle make a furtive appearance (Haizlip 240-241). And certainly, the aura of chaos and 'aberration' that surrounds the households headed by females is everything but innocuous in the context of 'race.'

Further, the narratives of economic success and upward social mobility presented by Haizlip and McBride may camouflage the persistence of racial discrimination. However, such a narrative strategy also avoids articulating African Americans as victims, a representational routine whose pitfalls many black critics have deplored. If the texts – Ball's included – err on the side of sanguineness, they nevertheless communicate the continuing importance of 'race' in the twenty-first century. Their optimism may be inspired by a perception of generational discontinuity in the attitudes concerning interracial relations as well as the thorny and knotty aspects of the past. Ball's younger relatives support him in his endeavor while the older ones are hostile or indifferent at best; in Haizlip's family, it is a young white man, Jeff, who eagerly claims the narrator's mother as his "Aunt Margaret" while even her sister Grace remains somewhat hesitant (258-259, 265). Younger Americans, the texts thus suggest, may be less inclined to reify notions of 'race' or to police the color line.

It may still be too early to speak of a "blurring" of the color line, a phrase recently employed by Anette Jacobsen in a similar context, but the family memoirs of Shirlee Taylor Haizlip, James McBride, and Edward Ball fruitfully complicate its character and shift its terrain. Most significantly, they challenge the uniformity, transparency, and ontological status of whiteness, imagining in its stead a particularized, historically specific, and above all dialogic web of racial relations. If "membership in a race, like membership in a national community, is 'imagined,'" as Kendall Thomas suggests (131), these texts open up novel ways of imagining both.

Works Cited

Ball, Edward. *Slaves in the Family*. [1998] New York: Ballantine Books, 1999.
Bourdieu, Pierre. *La distinction. Critique sociale de jugement*. Paris: Les éditions de minuit, 1979.
Frankenberg, Ruth. *White Women, Race Matters: The Social Construction of Whiteness*. Minneapolis: U of Minnesota P, 1993.
Gilroy, Paul. "It's a Family Affair." *Black Popular Culture*. Ed. Gina Dent. Seattle: Bay Press, 1992. 303-316.
Gordon-Reed, Annette. "'The Memories of a Few Negroes': Rescuing America's Future at Monticello." *Sally Hemings & Thomas Jefferson*. Ed. Jan Ellen Lewis and Peter S. Onuf. 236-252.
Haizlip, Shirlee Taylor. *The Sweeter the Juice: A Family Memoir in Black and White*. New York: Simon & Schuster, 1994.
Harris, Cheryl I. "Whiteness as Property." *Harvard Law Review* 106 (June 1993): 1709-1791.
Jacobsen, Anette. "Blurring the Color Line." Paper presented at the CAAR-Conference on "Colorlines – The Meanings of 'Race' for the Twenty-First Century," Cagliari, March 23, 2001.
Jacobson, Matthew Frye. *Whiteness of a Different Color: European Immigrants and the Alchemy of Race*. Cambridge, MA: Harvard UP, 1998.
Lewis, Jan Ellen, and Peter S. Onuf. "Introduction." *Sally Hemings & Thomas Jefferson: History, Memory, and Civic Culture*. Ed. Lewis and Onuf. Charlottesville: UP of Virginia, 1999. 1-16.
Mahoney, Martha R. "The Social Construction of Whiteness." *Critical White Studies: Looking Behind the Mirror*. Ed. Richard Delgado and Jean Stefancic. Philadelphia: Temple UP, 1997. 330-333.
Malcomson, Scott L. *One Drop of Blood: The American Misadventure of Race*. New York: Farrar Straus Giroux, 2000.
McBride, James. *The Color of Water: A Black Man's Tribute to His White Mother*. New York: Riverhead Books, 1996.
Sacks, Karen Brodkin. "How Did Jews Become White Folks?" *Race*. Ed. Steven Gregory and Roger Sanjek. New Brunswick, NJ: Rutgers UP, 1994. 79-85.
Savin, Ada. "'It's Not the Color of Your Skin': Intertwining Black and Jewish Diasporas in James McBride's *The Color of Water*." Paper presented at the CAAR-Conference on "Colorlines – The Meanings of 'Race' for the Twenty-First Century," Cagliari, March 23, 2001.
Thomas, Kendall. "'Ain't Nothin' Like the Real Thing': Black Masculinity, Gay Sexuality, and the Jargon of Authenticity." *The House that Race Built*. Ed. Wahneema Lubiano. New York: Random House, 1998. 116-135.
Walker, Clarence. "Denial Is Not a River in Egypt." *Sally Hemings & Thomas Jefferson*. Ed. Jan Ellen Lewis and Peter S. Onuf. 187-198.
Williams, Rhonda M. "Living at the Crossroads: Explorations in Race, Nationality, Sexuality, and Gender." *The House that Race Built*. Ed. Wahneema Lubiano. New York: Random House, 1998. 136-156.
Wood, Gordon S. "The Ghosts of Monticello." *Sally Hemings & Thomas Jefferson*. Ed. Jan Ellen Lewis and Peter S. Onuf. 19-34.

Romance, Madness, and Woman's History

Charlotte Lennox's *The Female Quixote* Revisited

Sabine Volk-Birke

> Mrs. Clayton and I had a furious argument about reading books of a bad tendency; I stood up for preserving a purity of mind, and discouraging works of *that kind* – *she* for trusting to her *own strength* and *reason*, and bidding defiance to any injury such books could do her, but as I *cannot presume* to depend on my own strength of mind, I think it safest and best to *avoid* whatever may prejudice it.
> (Howes 61)[1]

The controversy about the contribution of romance to the tradition of narrative in general and to the 18th century novel in particular is still very much alive today. In this context, Charlotte Lennox's *The Female Quixote*, which appeared in 1752, plays an important role, as is testified by its critical reception in the eighteenth century as well as by the various interpretations it received from contemporary critics affiliated to different schools and persuasions. To some extent, Lennox follows the pattern of the courtship novel; the plot concentrates on the life of the heroine Arabella, well-born, beautiful, and rich, from the time her father chooses a husband for her until this marriage takes place – a development that takes little more than a year and implies that her history, in other words what is worth telling, ends when she is about eighteen years old. This conventional pattern is modified and subverted by the power of literature. Arabella, who is brought up in total seclusion by a father who had withdrawn from public life, finds English translations of French romances, mainly by Mlle de Scudéry and La Calprenède, in his library, and reads them as true and reliable information about history, the relations between the sexes, conduct in public and in private, gender specific social customs, principles and ideals. When she applies these maxims to 'real' eighteenth century situations, her behaviour is

---

[1] The quotation is from a letter of 14 May 1760, written by Mary Granville Delany, the wife of Dr. Patrick Delany, Dean of Down, to her sister. Mrs Clayton is the widow of Dr. Robert Clayton, Bishop of Cork and Ross.

regarded as unintelligible, ridiculous, even mad. Before her marriage to Glanville can close the novel, she must be "cured", and her conversion to the use of reason indeed implies repentance, gratitude, and total acceptance of what is proper for a young lady at the time.

The novel has received two very different kinds of reading. Lennox's critique of romance as a genre and the pernicious influence of romance reading on a female audience was seen as the author's sole intention by its contemporary public. Although this reading is not denied by modern critics, they also draw attention to the subversive potential of romances and their empowering of women as Lennox's implicit critique of women's very real subjection to the rules made by men in a patriarchal society.[2]

Before I look at the use Lennox makes of romances, it will be useful to recall some of the landmarks in the debate about the nature and origin of the eighteenth century novel. I shall then briefly sketch some of the debts the novel owes to romance and finally concentrate on *The Female Quixote*, particularly concerning the issues of reading, story telling, authority, and women's right to their own history as opposed to their role in men's histories.

The genre of romance has had a tradition and critical reception which is not much less variegated than the complicated adventures of its protagonists. On the one hand, its ancient Greek, its medieval, its sixteenth and its seventeenth century representatives were immensely popular, on the other hand, they provoked satirical transformations and critical attacks. On the one hand, romances were widely read by courtly and aristocratic audiences, on the other hand they were regarded as primitive entertainment for the vulgar and the ignorant. On the one hand, their mythical and supernatural elements contributed materially to the fascination romances had for their audiences, on the other hand it was this element of the fantastic which discredited them with their opponents who looked for probability of plot. On the one hand, their heroes and heroines, who represented the virtues of courage, constancy, disinterestedness, chivalry, and gallantry, were admired by aristocratic readers who saw their own feudal value structure exemplified, on the other hand, the idealized heroes and heroines with their

---

[2] Cf. Doody's introduction to *The Female Quixote*; cf. also Roulston and Craft.

complicated rituals of courtship, love and battle appeared outmoded and laughable, if not dangerously misleading, to a sober middle-class public.

In the debate about the contribution of romance to the development of the novel there are basically two views, one for and one against. The former has recently been argued emphatically by Margaret Anne Doody in *The True Story of the Novel*, who begins by stating that "[r]omance and the Novel are one. The separation between them is part of a problem, not part of a solution" (15). The latter traces its ancestry down to Ian Watt, who maintains a clear distinction between literature before Defoe and after. In Watt's view, the eighteenth century novel has to be seen in contrast to a classical and medieval heritage: it rejects traditional plots. In the wake of Descartes and Locke, with their emphasis on method and sense perception, the primary literary criterion of the novel was, according to Watt, "truth to individual experience – individual experience which is always unique and therefore true" (Watt 13). The narrative method typical of this new genre of the novel is formal realism.

This creed is still recited in the 1980s, with unqualified assent, for example by Lennard J. Davis who states clearly that "romance is not usefully seen as a forebear of, a relative of, or an influence on the novel. The clear fact in the development of narrative during this period is that there was a profound rupture, a discursive chasm between these two forms" (25). Davis emphasizes that romances are set in an idealized past of a remote or legendary country, are based on the epic, designed for an upper class reader, value the preservation of virtue and chastity, are never written in the first person or letter form, mix fact and fiction, and claim to follow the rules of *bienséance* and *vraisemblance*. In contrast to these, the novel is set in more recent times and in the locale of the author, modelled on history and journalism, is more middle class in scope, shorter and more compact of plot, focuses on illegal doings and forbidden passions, tends to be written in first person and letter form, tends to deny that they are fictional and claims to be writing history or recording life as it is (cf. Davis 40).

One of the most significant recent contribution to this theory of the eighteenth century novel is J. Paul Hunter's book *Before Novels. The Cultural Contexts of Eighteenth Century English Fiction*. Hunter views himself in the Watt tradition, which he wants to modify, but which he basically accepts. He explains the eighteenth century novel within a framework of cultural historicism, drawing on the history of mentalities and anthropology as methodological approaches. In many respects, this is fascinating. Clearly, a theory of the eighteenth century novel needs to include, as Hunter demands, interaction between so-called high and low culture, oral culture, the power of readers to create texts, the significance of non-verbal texts, and, above all, an inclusive sense of novels that comprehends titles that are untypical, unsuccessful, non-canonical as well as the best known work by the best writers.

All this sounds very open-minded and unprejudiced. However, there is one premise Hunter makes, like Watt, from the beginning. He wants to "demonstrate the independence of the novel from previous narrative models because of its popular, non-'literary' status at its beginning, and detach its fortunes especially from the history of romance" (Hunter xix). In his view, the novel must be seen as an alternative to romance, as a genre which has replaced romance in a functional sense, without owing anything to romance, certainly without having descended from romance.

Hunter has powerful eighteenth century allies, whom I will mention later, but he also had twentieth century opponents before the publication of Doody's book. It seems that the question of the significance of romance has become a battle ground for literary critics of different persuasions. There are a number of voices which argue convincingly for the relevance of romance within a concept of the 18th century novel. Karl Heinz Göller's valuable study on the beginnings of the English novel under the title *Romance und Novel* (1972) is not generally known among Anglo-American scholars.[3] Göller's argument is that the eighteenth century novel did not spring complete, like Athena, from Zeus' head, but is the result of a complicated process of transformation, and he shows in his book how many features of the novel were already present in medieval romance. He outlines how the tradition of medieval chivalric romance, which continues in prose until the sixteenth century, and the picaresque tradition, merge in the eighteenth century, as one can see in Fielding's, Smollett's and Sterne's use of

---

[3] Margaret Schlauch's book *Antecedents of the English Novel. 1400-1600* (Warszawa 1965) which deals with a similar period is quoted more frequently. This book is also, in a sense, in the Watt tradition, as it aims at tracing the antecedents of realistic and circumstantial story-telling in the 18th century manner.

traditional forms and motifs. The episodic plot structure of the picaresque novel gives way to an overall pattern in which individual events contribute to the aim of the journey and are therefore not interchangeable. Göller points out that these are not original creations of the 18th century novel, but can be traced back to the Middle Ages.

We cannot speak about the relationship between old romance and new novel, however, without taking into account the influence of the Greek romances, which were introduced to England in the Renaissance by Lyly, Sidney, and Shakespeare, and the French romances of the seventeenth century, written in the tradition of the Greek romances, which constituted a second wave of romance literature in England in the second half of the seventeenth and the beginning of the eighteenth century. They existed side by side with the romance parodies that were written in the tradition of Cervantes' *Don Quixote* and Scarron's *Roman Comique*.[4]

The Greek romances follow typical patterns and contain a number of stock characters and situations. Usually the setting is pastoral, the hero falls in love with the heroine at first sight, but then they are separated and each has to undergo a series of adventures alone. The hero excels in various actions which demonstrate his courage, the heroine defends her chastity which is continually threatened by a succession of men. The action is not propelled by character development or connected through cause and effect, but consists of a series of episodic events. Shipwrecks and other disasters play an important part, together with Fortune, the Gods, or Providence. Often the parentage of hero or heroine is established satisfactorily in the final denouement. Although there are realistic elements in romances, the overall plot line is not realistic. When the lovers are finally united, the romance ends, and romance convention allows for the reformation of the rake who makes a good husband after all.

The French romances were first read in the original by the English court circle. Royalist families regarded romances as a genre which reflected aristocratic values, they were impervious to the anti-fiction propaganda of the Puritans. After 1652 French romances were translated into English, then English imitations of the genre followed. The English romances fall roughly

---

[4] Cf. Doody, *The True Story*: "Romance and the Novel are one. The separation between them is part of a problem, not part of a solution" (15).

into two categories: passionate romance, which is a modification of French heroic romance, and religious romance, which is Greek heroic romance shortened and christianised.

In passionate romance, the heroine is faced with a conflict between duty and love. She falls in love with a rake, who is, of course, unacceptable to her parents. It would be her duty to give him up, and indeed in French heroic romance the heroine never marries the hero as long as her parents object to him. In English passionate romance, this pattern changes. Love is shown as an uncontrollable power which cannot be counterbalanced by duty. The heroine corresponds with the rake and elopes. The rake, predictably, seduces or even rapes the heroine, and of course she becomes pregnant. The rake then abandons the girl, who suffers a number of misfortunes – so here the adventure section comes after the union with the lover. The heroine repents eventually and blames her folly in long self-accusations. In some versions of this type of romance, however, the rake is reformed and marries the girl.

Religious romance, which dominates the works of Jane Barker and Penelope Aubin, has no conflict between love and duty, the lovers are chosen correctly. They suffer a series of misfortunes, but there is no excitement through attempted rapes. The virtue of the heroine is never at issue. Aubin stresses in her prefaces that she shows characters which ought to be imitated. A divine providence rewards virtues and punishes vices in the end.

Congreve's *Incognita* or Behn's *Oroonoko* can certainly be read within a tradition of romance, and many works of Delariviere Manley and Eliza Haywood which were very popular with contemporary readers clearly also classify as romances. Northrop Frye goes so far as to say that "[w]hen the novel was established in the 18th century, it came to a reading public familiar with the formulas of prose romance. It is clear that the novel was a realistic displacement of romance, and had few structural features peculiar to itself" (38).

Hubert McDermott shows convincingly in his book *Novel and Romance* that both, Richardson and Fielding, drew extensively on the romance tradition, despite their protestations to the contrary. Clearly, the foundling theme which is exploited in *Joseph Andrews* and in *Tom Jones*, the latent excellent qualities of the hero, his white skin and birthmark, the last minute discovery of noble parentage and consequent grouping of couples, the seduction and rape theme in all its variations, complete with the threat of incest, the numerous coincidences at Upton and in London, all these are romance plot patterns and motifs, as are the journey, the heroic and mock-heroic battles, Tom's gallantry to women, his adoration of Sophia, his despair when she is offended with him, and his wish to marry her as the focal point of all his actions.

The same holds true for Richardson, who also used romance patterns in *Pamela* and *Clarissa*. Mr B., a version of the traditional libertine of passionate romance, expects Pamela to follow the example of the heroine of passionate romance, who forgets all about duty and falls for the hero before marriage. He never doubts his success – and certainly a number of romances teach him patterns of female behaviour which justify his view. However, Pamela stars in a different production, which works according to different rules. Her role models are the heroines of religious romances, so that Mr B., who sees himself as the hero of passionate romance, is annoyed that she does not play her part properly. Her head may be turned by romances indeed, as he suspects angrily, but if it is, then she follows Mrs Aubin's role models. When Mr B. complains that Pamela assumes airs, as if she was a mirror of perfection, he characterizes her as a heroine of religious romance. But the basic plot situation corresponds rather to Mr B.'s tableau of passionate romance: When Pamela is left without protection after Lady B.'s death and falls in love with Mr B., contemporary readers would have expected the same ending as Mr B., namely the rape and ruin of Pamela, to which she half-consents.

Clarissa is clearly closely akin to the romance of passion, too. Lovelace sees himself as the seducer par excellence, and he believes that every woman is at heart a rake, in other words, all women act like heroines in passionate romance, they can all be overcome and in the end they will consent, "once subdued [...] always subdued" (430). Secret correspondence and elopement are there, in a sense, Clarissa even loves him, so he assumes that the rest will follow naturally. The famous fire scene in which Lovelace gains entrance to Clarissa's room at night when she is undressed has precedents in romances. Lovelace's belief that it is always in his power to repair all damage by marriage is also a romance convention. Even the

Harlowe family see Clarissa as the heroine of passionate romance, who refuses an honourable suitor because she wants to elope with the rake. When she has left her parents' house with Lovelace, they immediately assume, again in complete accordance with the romance pattern, that she is ruined and that marriage only can make an honest woman of her.

Burney's *Evelina* draws the story of her parents, that is, the basis of all the action, from the same source, mixing passionate and heroic elements. Caroline Evelyn, to escape from a forced marriage, consents to an elopement with Sir John Belmont, who marries her, but later on denies the marriage, so that Evelina's mother, pregnant and deserted, looks like a heroine from passionate romance, but is, in reality, a figure from heroic romance. Sir John Belmont answers to the pattern of the rake, whose reformation is delayed and comes in two parts, the first being the amends made to his supposed daughter, the second being his contrition at the end of the book when he is reconciled with Evelina and has accepted not only her mother as his legal wife, but also Evelina as his legitimate daughter. The fact that Evelina looks so much like her mother emphasizes the connection between the violence of his repentance and his desire to make up for the wrong he inflicted on his wife, so in a sense this scene is a variation on the reformation of the rake which leads to marriage in some versions of passionate romance. Sir Clement Willoughby is a younger embodiment of the rake who would like to see Evelina acting according to passionate romance, whereas Evelina herself is always the heroine of heroic romance. The parallels between daughter and mother are striking, but Evelina, although she is in love with Lord Orville, remains obedient to her guardian and willing to subordinate her passion to her duty.

It seems to me that far from being reduced in stature, the novel gains a new dimension when we take these influences into account. Richardson clearly wrote in opposition to the image of women which was propagated in passionate romance. He wanted to show a heroine whose virtue was not a thin coat of varnish, a heroine whose concept of her own integrity was not restricted to virginity in a narrowly technical sense. Neither is Clarissa's conflict simply one between love and duty, although she regards obedience to her father as paramount, and although she must come to see that she has fallen in love with Lovelace. The issue for her lies much deeper – she is fighting for her right to determine her life according to her own concept of right and wrong. The epistolary form gave Richardson a narrative technique which could bring out the dramatic as well as the psychological implications of the plot much more clearly than either an omniscient narrator or an autobiography could have done. Moreover, he shows a woman who expresses herself by writing – Clarissa's style is an integral feature of her self-portrait.

However, although Fielding and Richardson relied on their readers' knowledge of romance plots and situations, they followed the fashion of the time in rejecting the genre explicitly. This has often been ascribed to a large extent to the fact that women constituted a significant part of the reading public, who had to be kept away from dangerous fantasies. Authors and critics were supposed to have taken this fact on board – it had consequences for the type of plot and the portrayal of character considered appropriate. Brewer observes that by the end of the 18th century

> the female novel reader had become the epitome of the misguided reading public. She was depicted as filled with delusive ideas, swayed by false ideas of love and romance, unable to concentrate on serious matters – all of which would lead to frivolity, impulsiveness and possibly sexual indiscretion. Such a woman embodied what critics saw as the literary marketplace rather than the literary public; as pure pleasure and the pursuit of private ends rather than as pleasure combined with moral virtue.

He continues, however, to claim that "this figure was, of course, a fiction. To judge from all we know about 18th century readers – diaries, membership lists from circulating libraries and so on – the flighty novel reader was just as likely to be male as female" (Brewer 193).

Nevertheless, romances provoked particular criticism.[5] Their reading clashed with the training necessary to make a good wife. Romances encouraged extravagant ideas, because they softened the mind by love, and because readers fooled away so many days, even years, which they could use for a better purpose. As Hunter points out, cultural anxiety about idleness is pervasive from the middle of the seventeenth to the end of the

---

[5] How one should reconcile the popularity of so many works written in the romance tradition during the second half of the 17th and the first half of the 18th century remains an unsolved problem.

eighteenth century (cf. Hunter 275ff.). Arabella is also blamed for these faults, partly by the narrator at the beginning of the novel, partly by the Doctor who manages to 'cure' her of her delusions.

Nearly all mid-century novelists denounced the influence of romances on young girls as pernicious and took care to make their readers understand to which extent their own stories were conceived within different traditions and informed by different aims. Richardson fears that romances "inflame and corrupt" (McDermott 149), his aim in *Pamela* was to "turn young people into a course of reading different from the pomp and parade of romance writing" (206). Fielding's narrator talks slightingly about idle romances which are filled with monsters in *Tom Jones* and points out that the universal contempt with which romances are generally regarded makes him cautiously avoid the term in relation to his own work. Lennox, who, as a female author, had to be even more careful, since her writing was not only seen as an influence on readers but also as an expression of her own morality, may have used her satire on romance in *The Female Quixote* on the one hand to show that she wrote in accordance with literary fashion, and on the other hand to clear her name and refute implicit charges of sexual availability. As she depended on the income provided by her writing, she needed to be a financially successful and therefore morally impeccable author (cf. Levin).

When we look at contemporary reality we can clearly see how decisive the right choice of a husband is for a woman. Although Lord Hardwick's *Marriage Act* of 1753, insisting on a number of official formalities, successfully terminated clandestine marriages in England, and thus prevented fortune hunters from eloping with adolescent heiresses and making themselves not only their domestic but also their financial masters, the women were still subject to paternal or conjugal control. As their marriage made them legally one with their husband (*femme couverte*), they lost all their rights over their property (except for settlements which could be negotiated between father and husband, generally to provide for widowhood) and their children. Divorce was impossible, no matter what the husband's behaviour. Romances, if they empower women, albeit only before marriage, are indeed a most misleading educational experience. But the attacks on this genre still beg several questions. If the romance was really a defunct genre, why flog a dead horse? If nobody took romances seriously any more, why did authors like Richardson and Fielding so much as mention them when discussing their own productions? How can Mr B. complain that Pamela's head is turned by romances, how can Lovelace call Clarissa's fear of rape the romantic notions of a girl? And how were readers able to enjoy the finer points of irony in *The Female Quixote* if they did not know every major character and plot complication from Scudéry and La Calprenède?

Lennox's complex and at times even contradictory use of romances is illuminating in this context. Far from simply being pretexts that are revealed as dangerous and misleading, romances function on several planes and are refracted in the readings of different characters, the most important of which are Arabella's mother, Arabella, Sir George, and the Countess. I shall discuss Sir George and the Countess at a later point. The first reader was Arabella's mother, who had bought them to "soften a Solitude which she found very disagreeable" (*FQ* 7). After her marriage, she had been transferred from civilisation (we do not learn where exactly she lived) to her husband's remote and secluded Castle, surrounded by grounds which had been laid out to "appear like the beautiful product of wild, uncultivated Nature. But if this Epitome of *Arcadia* could boast of only artless and simple Beauties, the Inside of the Castle was adorned with a Magnificence suitable to the Dignity and the Immense Riches of the Owner." (*FQ* 5) Romance, it seems, is exactly the genre which corresponds to this setting: a perfect rural Arcadia (Sidney's romance is not implied gratuitously), a husband rich and cultivated (as well as idiosyncratic), the beautiful and intelligent woman carried away – but the sequence is missing, there are no further adventures, there is not even social contact. Instead, Arabella's mother reads romances, a genre still fashionable at her time. Her experience takes place in her imagination and seems to have no consequences for her reality.

Arabella, brought up in total seclusion, with no other diversion than running about "like a Nymph" in the park and talking to her father and her attendants, is the second reader: she claims her maternal heritage when she begins to read the romances. On the one hand, she is presented as artless, unspoilt, and simple, on the other hand, she is introduced into the cultural symbolic order through romances by her mother, albeit posthumously. On the whole, what is mentioned explicitly about her reading gives rise to the suspicion that she has taken in only certain aspects of the texts. Arabella concentrates on the finer points of etiquette as regards the choreography of courtship and women's power over men. Allusions to Scudéry's society, the element of social criticism, apparently escape her. She has fully understood the poetics of romances, however, and she has also absorbed the idealism of their heroes and heroines. In contrast to most of the people who surround her, Arabella is generous and loyal, not least in her relation to other women, whom she does not view as potential rivals in the competition of the marriage market. So although Arabella does take the romances very much at face value, in other words, is not capable of a contextualized or allegorical reading, she has absorbed the 'spirit' of romances. It is important to stress that they did not inflame her passions, as they were supposed to do, neither did they corrupt what the eighteenth century called her virtue. When the heroine embarks on this reading, she has little reason to suspect these books, as her father had moved them from her mother's closet to his library, thus giving them official status. The library as a collection and as a room may have been newly established by the Marquis. Brewer states that although in 1650 few country houses had libraries, during the eighteenth century they became almost universal (cf. Brewer 184).

But Arabella commands a paternal heritage, too. Her father becomes her teacher when she is four years old, and instructs her not only in reading and writing, but also in French and Italian. He admires her intelligence and intends to "render her Mind as beautiful as her person was lovely" (*FQ* 6). Thus Arabella receives two different and apparently independent educations, which cultivate her reason and her imagination. Since her mother's and her father's influence never come into contact with each other, Arabella becomes something like a split personality. At least this is the way Lennox presents her. At the age of seventeen, she is totally bewitching not only on the basis of her beauty, but also on the basis of her rational discourse. She can talk so well that her uncle, Sir Charles, "express'd much Admiration of her Wit, telling her, if she had been a Man, she would have made a great Figure in Parliament, and that her Speeches might have come perhaps to be printed in time" (*FQ* 311). On another occasion he claims that she "sometimes talked as learnedly as a Divine" (*FQ* 314). This is high praise indeed; it shows that women could talk about serious subjects with perfect rhetoric, and were in no way inferior to men in this respect. Their gender does not exclude them from capacity, although it excludes them from practice in public.

But the reverse of this admiration which Arabella draws invariably from the men is the horror with which they react to her speeches and behaviour in connection with love and courtship. This culminates in Sir Charles wondering if Arabella "was not really disorder'd in her Senses" and eventually concluding that she is mad. He asks himself whether "he ought not to bring a Commission of Lunacy against her" (*FQ* 339). In other words: the paternal heritage, a rational education, is not only safe, it alone guarantees social integration culminating in marriage. Her father, her uncle, and Glanville, like most other men, have never read romances; Glanville even refuses to do so when Arabella asks him to. They avoid this mental landscape altogether, keeping on the safe side. In contrast, the maternal heritage, romance reading, threatens Arabella's position to the extent of making her an outcast, who is likely to end up in Bedlam.[6] What is seen as her wilful disregard of social custom puts her almost beyond the pale and brings her, despite her undoubted chastity, close to a fate that Hogarth had depicted in 1735 for the abandoned rake. The danger of romances could not be demonstrated more dramatically.

Moreover, her reading of romances exposes Arabella to danger from a different quarter. Sir George, the only man in the novel who is "perfectly well acquainted with the chief Characters in most of the *French* Romances; could tell every thing that was borrowed from them, in all the new Novels that came out" (*FQ* 130), needs to be seen as a contrast to the virtue and generosity of the heroine. As a man, he reads romances as fiction and is thus not affected by them, but his moral principles are shown as deficient from the start. He is interested in Arabella's money and social position, deceives Glanville and his sister about his intentions, and attempts to manipulate the heroine on the basis of her romances. His first attempt collapses because he is only able to imitate some plot conventions, but has not understood the ethical code of romance, so that Arabella, far from falling for him,

---

[6] It is Glanville's true love that keeps her out of real trouble. In a sense, she tests his devotion in an eighteenth century context as severely as the romance heroines test their lovers between the covers of books. Glanville goes with unwavering loyalty through ordeals in public which no self-respecting suitor could have reason to expect; by way of comparison Solmes, who reacts with scarcely veiled sadism to Clarissa's recalcitrance, can be read as a contrast to Glanville's virtues.

reproaches him severely. His second attempt is more successful. He manages to slander Glanville and to make Arabella believe that he cannot honourably marry her. However, it is this trick that makes Arabella aware of her love for Glanville, a feeling she had not properly identified before. Here, as in other passages of the novel, the satire on romance is ambiguous. Although Arabella imagines threats and attacks by a number of men who have no intention of hurting her, she comes into contact with real dangers she does not suspect: abduction, rape, whores disguised as respectable women and employed in the service of deceit, fortune hunters, these are all possibilities within the 'real' eighteenth century scenario. Incest, a typical feature of romance, is also something contemporary readers would not dismiss as impossible, even though Arabella only imagines this danger. When the men try to convince Arabella that reality does not include any of the dangers she reads about in romances, they either ignore the facts or lie.

It comes as no surprise that Arabella can only be integrated into society, that is, marry the man who loves her, after she is cured of her folly. The dialogue which leads to Arabella's conversion to reality is conducted by a Divine, who is introduced as "the Pious and Learned Doctor ---" – some critics suspect that this chapter of the novel was written by Dr Johnson. The learned Doctor, who is responsible for Arabella's conversion, is not familiar with Romances himself. When Arabella mentions a number of heroines, he admits he has not heard of most of them, "[t]he rest I faintly remember some Mention of in those contemptible Volumes with which Children are sometimes injudiciously suffer'd to amuse their Imagination; but which I scarcely expected to hear quoted by your Ladyship in a serious Discourse" (*FQ* 374). Here romance is less than a feminized genre, it is not even fit for the entertainment of children. In the French salons and even in English polite society, romances had been a very respectable genre read and discussed across the gender divide by educated ladies and gentlemen. Scudéry's poetological considerations in the preface to *Ibrahim* show her to be conscious of a number of issues which the mid-eighteenth century reading presented by Lennox ignores completely. Not only was Scudéry aware of problems of plot construction, probability and historicity, not only did she refer to Greek models, she also incorporated (partly satirical) reflections on contemporary society, veiled by the geographical and temporal distance of her characters. Moreover, the portrayal of human emotions was one of her main aims. Far from creating unworldly flights of fancy, Scudéry responded acutely with her romances to a particular literary and social situation.[7] But in the reformation scene, the point of view propagated by the Doctor misrepresents Scudéry and gives her works a negative twist by pointing out to Arabella that romances, apart from being fictions and absurd, are criminal, because they "give new fire to the Passions of Revenge and Love; two Passions which, even without such powerful Auxiliaries, it is one of the severest Labours of Reason and Piety to suppress, and which yet must be suppressed it we hope to be approved in the Sight of the only Being where Approbation can make us Happy" (*FQ* 380). Both passion and love run counter to humility and compassion, two virtues that provide cornerstones of society, because they inspire acts of kindness. Ironically, Arabella has been shown in many situations as a model of kindness and compassion, so her reading has not had the effect described by the Doctor.

After this climax, conversion takes place immediately. The ending of *The Female Quixote* takes great care to annihilate all traces of a role model which demands public activity and public recognition of greatness. The future husband Glanville rejoices to find his bride "recovered to the free Use of all her noble Powers of Reason" [*FQ* 382] (listen to the allusion to Shakespeare's *Tempest* and Montaigne!), and he does not contradict her when she says

> To give you myself [...] is making you but a poor Present in return for the Obligations your generous Affection has laid me under to you; yet since I am so happy as to be desired for a Partner for Life by a Man of your Sense and Honour, I will endeavour to make myself as worthy as I am able of such a favourable Distinction. (*FQ* 383)

---

[7] Cf. Morlet-Chantalat, 19: "L'action principale, et un peu plus largement tout ce qui relève de la matière romaine, admet encore une analyse fondée sur les principes définis par les théoriciens de l'épopée. A l'autre pôle, bien des éléments de la conversation, portraits, descriptions de châteaux, nouvelles de la vie mondaine, relèvent de la gazette, et ne trouvent leur sens que par référence à une réalité extérieure à l'œuvre. Plus intéressantes, plus réussies, sont les parties de l'œuvre qui, dès la publication, semblent devoir leur succès à leur ambiguïté: certaines histoires intercalées, dont les données sont empruntées à l'actualité sentimentale du milieu des Samedis – et c'est ce qui intéresse des enjoués – mais auxquelles l'integration dans le roman va tendre à donner une significance exemplaire; [...] Cette rencontre entre une tradition culturelle et la recherche collective d'un milieu pour répondre aux nécessités de la vie sociale, c'est ce que montre d'abord la composition d'ensemble de la *Clélie*."

The taming of the shrew could not be more perfect. This is the correct attitude in all points: gratitude for being chosen by the man, under an obligation to him, therefore striving for ever to be worthy of him; all initiative must come from the man, he desires, she submits. We could come to the conclusion that given such a portrayal of female role acceptance, it is small wonder that Dr Johnson gave an all-night party in honour of Charlotte Lennox, complete with hot apple-pie and crown of laurel, that Richardson advised her and, together with Johnson, Fielding, and the Earl of Orrery helped her to get *The Female Quixote* published by Andrew Millar, one of the leading booksellers of the day, and that Fielding gave the book a favourable review in his new *Covent-Garden Journal*, as did Johnson in the *Gentleman's Magazine* (cf. Hanley 27-32).

Seen from this angle, the novel looks like the successful destruction of romance, once and for all. However, a number of critics have read Arabella's alternative world as a projection of wishes which could find no legitimate outlet in eighteenth century society. By insisting on customs of the romance world, particularly as regards the relation of the sexes, Arabella radically challenges the power structure in contemporary gender relations. Her wish to enjoy solitude when she is tired of company, her dismissal of men from her presence, or her command that they should be silent, far exceeds the limits of women's rights in polite society. One only has to read *Evelina* to see how vulnerable and powerless young women could be, and to which extent social rank gave men almost unlimited licence. But even if unmarried women were treated with a degree of respect, they could not fail to see that they were commodities on the marriage market. Even Arabella's loving father wants Glanville's courtship to be as brief as possible. In this respect, Arabella challenges received ideas. Indifferent to wealth herself, she cannot be bribed into marriage and she refuses to be hurried into it, particularly when she has not been able to find out how strong her lover's attachment is under pressure. These demands, however, obviously transgress the boundaries of women's rights.

But Arabella was not just unwilling to be married off as fast as possible. She disagrees with the whole system of education for women and with the concept of appropriate female occupations, asking the most unsettling question which has been provoked by her reading,

> What room, [...], does a Lady give for high and noble Adventures, who consumes her Days in Dressing, Dancing, listening to Songs, and ranging the Walks with People as thoughtless as herself? How mean and contemptible a Figure must a Life spent in such idle Amusements make in History? Or rather, Are not such Persons always buried in Oblivion, and can any Pen be found who would condescend to record such inconsiderable Action? (*FQ* 279)

She claims the right to remarkable actions for women, to actions which show women's courage and adherence to principles. One of the attractions of romance was that they gave a history not only to the heroes, but also to the heroines. The very fact that they were separated from their lovers or fiancés at the beginning of the action made it necessary for them to fend for themselves. Even if they suffered persecution and misery, danger of death, exile, shipwreck, and the threat of rape, they had a history, they were granted experience in the world. These actions ultimately lay claim to glory, and public fame. With these expectations, a woman has penetrated deeply into male territory. Such a concept of equality can only be brought forward within the limits of comedy, as this concept turns the world upside down, it is a carnival – or the route to Bedlam. If the claim is made seriously, *Clarissa* demonstrates what becomes of a woman who steps out of the boundaries of her father's house. In many ways, Richardson's novel figures prominently as pretext and commentary on *The Female Quixote* (cf. Bartolomeo 163-175). Respectable readers were supposed to turn away in dismay from Arabella's attitude towards women's biography. Women who insisted on the right to know best what was good for them were usually not admired for their intelligence or willpower, on the contrary, they were accused of displaying one of the worst of female vices, unreasonable stubbornness. Jane Austen is very much aware of this problem: when Fanny refuses to be married to Crawford, she falls into disgrace. Sir Thomas Bertram says to her, "you have now shewn me that you can be wilful and perverse, that you can and will decide for yourself" (Austen 241). Anne Eliot is persuaded to give up Wentworth. In both cases, the women were right and the authorities were wrong. The nineteenth century novel is still full of situations which vary the romance patterns and question the ability of women to decide for themselves: Dorothea Brooke, Little Emely, Ruth, and Tess, and up to a point Marie Melmotte. In comedy, Oscar Wilde was able to cash in satirically on the sentiment. When Lady Bracknell, conducting one of her gruelling interviews in *The Importance of Being Earnest*, is informed that the woman her nephew wants to marry has undergone the experience of "birth, baptism, whooping cough, registration, vaccination, confirmation, and the measles; both the German and the English variety" she comments critically: "Ah! A life crowded with incident, I see, though perhaps somewhat too exciting for a young girl. I am not myself in favour of premature experiences" (Wilde 304).

This Victorian attitude is closely related to that of the Countess in *The Female Quixote*. Presented as an admirable women in all respects (the proper role model for Arabella), the Countess attempts to reform Arabella, but is not able to do so, partly because Lennox removes her suddenly from the scene. Possibly conversion through a woman, and without a climactic accident, accompanied by a near fatal illness, would have been the wrong signal altogether. The Countess is an important figure since she has read romances and therefore understands Arabella much better than anybody else, Sir George included. Besides, her reading has not had any evil consequences on her social integration. Horrified by the idea of "adventures" for a woman (the sexual connotation is one aspect, the public attention focussed on the woman is certainly another), she is able to sum up her own life in one sentence, "And when I tell you, [...] that I was born and christen'd, had a useful and proper Education, receiv'd the Addresses of my Lord --- through the Recommendation of my Parents, and marry'd him with their Consents and my own Inclination, and that since we have liv'd in great Harmony together, I have told you all the material Passages of my Life" (*FQ* 327). This is an exemplary biography, which, as the Countess points out in the remainder of the sentence – differs "very little from those of other Women of the same Rank, who have a moderate Share of Sense, Prudence and Virtue." (*FQ* 327) Clearly, the message is that a respectable girl and future wife does not have a history[8] and indeed, under conduct book circumstances, she had very little opportunity of enjoying a life crowded with incident.

But the issue with romance concerns not only the main plot, it also influences narrative technique. The telling of histories (either by the protagonists themselves, or by their servants or confidants) as embedded

---

[8] Women like Moll Flanders, or Roxana, would find themselves beyond the pale in real life. In literature, their antecedents are found in the criminal biography, and Defoe as fictitious editor does his best to dissociate himself from his protagonists in the preface.

stories is an integral feature of the construction of romances. Lennox devotes a whole chapter to the theory and practice of this convention, making Arabella instruct her reluctant maid Lucy how to tell her mistress's history.

> [...] you should know as well as myself, and be able, not only to recount all my Words and Actions, even the smallest and most inconsiderable, but also all my Thoughts, however instantaneous; relate exactly every Change of my Countenance; number all my Smiles, Half-smiles, Blushes, Turnings pale, Glances, Pauses, Full-stops, Interruptions; the Rise and Falling of my Voice; every Motion of my Eyes; and every Gesture which I have used for these Ten Years past; nor omit the smallest Circumstance that relates to me. (*FQ* 122)

But this is not all. Apart from telling everything that happened from the heroine's birth, her appearance must be described minutely, and all her conversations "upon the Subjects of Love and Gallantry" must be repeated, so that the audience may be "so well acquainted with [her] Humour, as to know exactly, before they are told, how [she] shall behave" (*FQ* 123). Apart form her own mistress's thoughts, everybody else's thoughts must also be told. Not surprisingly, Lucy baulks at this demand – how should she know what other people think? The scene is partly funny, not least because the actual telling does not take place, since the prospective audience left while the poetics were discussed at length in a different room. On the other hand, Lennox uses the convention of the embedded story several times herself. Miss Groves's history, told by her maid, is scandalous in the context of eighteenth century propriety, although a modern reader might be more sympathetic to Miss Groves than a contemporary audience. The story serves several purposes. It has a number of features in common with passionate romance, exposing deviant female behaviour in the conflict between duty and love, and showing the rake acting without incurring any legal or social sanctions, thus the story re-inforces the warning to women. It shows lack of loyalty in the servant who tells the story, and it shows the complete innocence, generosity and magnanimity of the listener Arabella, who imposes *her* romance interpretation on the events and continues to give support to Miss Groves. The Countess's history, brief and uneventful, is told by herself, and functions as a contrast to Miss Groves's story, to the princess of Gaul's story, and to Arabella's history, setting the norm for female behaviour. Sir George tells his invented history, according to romance conventions, with the design to manipulate Arabella, but fails, and then finally instructs the supposed princess of Gaul, a prostitute hired for the purpose, to tell her invented history. This last story succeeds at first, but ultimately leads to the discovery of Sir George's plots and traps him in the marriage with Glanville's sister Charlotte. All these histories are revealing in many respects, concerning the tellers, the protagonists, and the audience. Lennox has been able to turn the romance conventions which she seems to debunk to excellent use in her own novel.

Moreover, the portrayal of 'humour', thoughts, and body language indicative of subtle shades of emotion, as well as conversations which reveal character dispositions rather than advance the plot, all key features of romance, are narrative techniques which Lennox imitates and puts to good use. The portrayal of thoughts and feelings in the eighteenth century novel has long been attributed to the tradition of the diary, the autobiography, spiritual as well as secular, the letter, and drama. Romance is largely missing from this list, despite the extensive depiction of inner life for example in Sidney's *Arcadia*. Lennox acknowledges the influence explicitly, referring to the custom of romance and novel writers of looking into the heart of the heroine, and even quoting an expression used by Scudéry (*FQ* 180). Arabella's emotional stress, the need to decide what to do, is mingled with memories of romance situations, and may lead to a monologue which expresses the result of the thought process. Clearly the pattern of set speeches, constructed with rhetorical mastery, as we find them still in the renaissance, leave their mark in *The Female Quixote*. But rhetorical forms of organization do not invalidate the portrayal of thoughts and emotions, unless one forgets that stream of consciousness is not a mirror of thought processes, but a different literary convention.

On the other hand, many conversations which serve, to some extent, to juxtapose romance conventions satirically to mimesis of eighteenth century customs and beliefs, reveal not only Arabella's wit, sincerity, and nobility of character as well as Glanville's suffering, torn as he is between admiration, love, and frustration, they also expose the unimaginative, manipulative, opportunistic, egocentric and even spiteful characters of the others. Austen's dialogues, although they revolve round different subjects, fulfill a similar purpose.

It seems to me that the relevance of romance for the history of the novel cannot not be confined to the satirical tradition established by a biased interpretation of Cervantes, and realism or verisimilitude defined in a narrow sense cannot be made the sole distinctive feature of a 'good' novel. Doody draws attention to the fact that the true great tradition of the novel,

> stretching back not only to Boccaccio but to Apuleius and Heliodorus, was still the literary heritage of European and English readers and writers born at the turn of the eighteenth century. This inheritance included Spanish novels of the sixteenth and French novels of the seventeenth century. The rise of Prescriptive Realism put an end to this culture of the Novel and made the Great Tradition largely invisible. (Doody 288)

Doody regards *The Female Quixote* as the literary document which crystalized this turning point. Contemporary fiction demonstrates clearly that the tradition of the novel, far from relying on verisimilitude only, presents alternative and fantastic worlds of such variety and invites readings on so many levels that it seems to be time for an unprejudiced look at the eighteenth century and before.

Works Cited

Lennox, Charlotte. *The Female Quixote*. Ed. by Margaret Dalziel, with an Introduction by Margaret Anne Doody. The World's Classics. Oxford: OUP, 1989. (*FQ*)

Austen, Jane *Mansfield Park*. London: Dent, 1963.

Bartolomeo, Joseph F. "Female Quixotism v. 'Feminine' Tragedy: Lennox's Comic Revision of *Clarissa*." *New Essays on Samuel Richardson*. Ed. Albert J. Rivero. London: Macmillan, 1996. 163-175.

Brewer, John. *The Pleasures of the Imagination. English Culture in the Eighteenth Century*, London: HarperCollins, 1997.

Craft, Catherine A. "Reworking Male Models: Aphra Behn's *Fair Vow-Breaker*, Eliza Haywood's *Fantomina*, and Charlotte Lennox's *Female Quixote*." *Modern Language Review* 86:4 (Oct. 1991): 821-838.

Davis, Lennard J. *Factual Fictions. The Origins of the English Novel*, New York: Columbia UP, 1983.

Doody, Margaret Anne. *The True Story of the Novel*. London: Fontana Press, 1998.

Frye, Northrop. *The Secular Scripture. A Study of the Structure of Romance.* Cambridge, MA.: Harvard UP, 1976.

Göller, Karl Heinz. *Romance und Novel. Die Anfänge des englischen Romans*, Regensburg: Hans Carl, 1972.

Hanley, Brian. "Henry Fielding, Samuel Johnson, Samuel Richardson, and the Reception of Charlotte Lennox's *The Female Quixote* in the Popular Press." *A Quarterly Journal of Short Articles, Notes, and Reviews* 13 (2000): 27-32.

Howes, Alan B., ed. *Lawrence Sterne: The Critical Heritage.* London: Routledge, 1974.

Hunter, J. Paul. *Before Novels. The Cultural Contexts of Eighteenth Century English Fiction.* New York: W.W.Norton, 1990.

Levin, Kate. "'The Cure of Arabella's Mind': Charlotte Lennox and the Disciplining of the Female Reader." *Women's Writing: The Elizabethan to Victorian Period* 2 (1994): 271-290.

McDermott, Hubert. *Novel and Romance. The Odyssee to Tom Jones.* London: Macmillan, 1989.

Morlet-Chantalat, Chantal. *La Clélie de Mademoiselle de Scudéry. De l'Epopée à la Gazette: Un Discours féminin de la Gloire.* Paris: Honoré Champion, 1994.

Richardson, Samuel. *Clarissa or The History of a Young Lady.* Ed. Angus Ross. Harmondsworth: Penguin, 1985.

Roulston, Christine. "Histories of Nothing and Femininity in Charlotte Lennox's *The Female Quixote*." *Women's Writing* 2 (1995): 25-42.

Schlauch, Margaret. *Antecedents of the English Novel. 1400-1600* Warszawa: PWN-Polish Scientific Publishers, 1965.

Watt, Ian. *The Rise of the Novel.* Harmondsworth: Penguin, 1970.

Wilde, Oscar. *Plays.* Harmondsworth: Penguin, 1971.

Games With/Out Frontiers: A Ludic Analysis of Salman Rushdie's *Grimus*

Jürgen Meyer

Setting the Scene

Salman Rushdie's assessments of his literary debut *Grimus* (1975) range from the resignation that it, "to put it mildly, bombed" (*IR* 1), to the apology for attempting "to take certain themes out of Sufi poetry, and use them in the context of a Western fantasy novel. So, it's a quest novel, it's a 'journey of the soul' kind of a novel" (Kumar 215). Bakhtinian approaches to *Grimus*, such as M Keith Booker's, have drawn attention to its subversive "transformations [...] quite central to the Menippean tradition to which Rushdie is such a clear heir" (Booker 980). Generally, in Rushdie's writings "the boundary between self and other is always problematic, his characters tend to be complex, multiple, and highly variable" (Booker 980). If "*Grimus* represents the beginning of a conception of literature as an orchestration of voices" (Cundy 24), this leads to its intertextuality and, from a post-colonial point of view, its politics. *Grimus* describes the cultural "clash between different systems of values and between the people of the *third world* and their *European* colonizers" (Johansen 33, author's italics). If critics insist generally on the fact that the novel was "a first novel" (Parameswaran 43), being merely a "test-run for the successful novels of the 1980s" (Cundy 12), they follow in Rushdie's own wake. But Uma Parameswaran concedes that "*Grimus* has been ingeniously thought out, and, though difficult to unravel, is precisely put together as a Rubik cube" (Parameswaran 42). The following analysis focuses on *Grimus* from such a ludic point of view. It may indeed open up a new dimension in the understanding of a leitmotif running through many of Rushdie's literary games.

Grimus is a tripartite novel and describes Flapping Eagle's quest for, and conflict with, the God-like Grimus, who wants to rule over life and death. The pre-history of the plot is that there was the 'trinity' of Grimus, Virgil Jones and Nicholas Deggle, who incidentally discovered a parallel universe, inhabited by the frog-like Gorfs. From their world they stole devices of the so-called "Conceptual Technology" which enabled them, by means of wishful thinking, to create the dimension of Kâf with its capital, the City of 'K'. They coaxed people under the promise of eternal life to this world, not mentioning to them that it was a world without everlasting youth. The first part of the novel ("Present") shows how Flapping Eagle is transferred from a mythic world where the siblings grew up, with its reservation for an Amerindian tribe, the Axonas, just off the 'civilised' town of "Phoenix",[1] into the artificial otherworld of Kâf. Here, he continues his search, guided by Virgil Jones who has turned into a Grimus' enemy. In part two ("Past"), Flapping Eagle passes the City of 'K' and witnesses all the victims of the eternal life temptation. These 'elect' spend a sad, impotent and actually undead life. Some of them have grown sick of their Struldbruggian existence and wait for an occasion to riot against Grimus who alone is able to rejuvenate. To keep this privilege for himself, he has retreated into an unnatural dimensional fold of Kâf world, a distortion of its gravitational field affecting both body and soul. As Flapping Eagle visits 'K', some of the inhabitants opt for death and commit suicide – a new development, as Flapping Eagle actually re-introduces Death into this world of immortals. Finally, he leaves 'K' and encounters Grimus (in part three, "Grimus"). They struggle for death or life. Although Grimus seems to win against the "Spirited Death" (*G* 236), he is finally overthrown by Flapping Eagle and, according to the instructions of the observing Gorfs, the winner restores the natural order, if at the expense of Kâf world and all the people existing there.

---

[1] One should hesitate to identify space and time with our known reality, as Johansen does when he locates the "Phoenix" in *Grimus* with Phoenix, Arizona (cf. *G* 29). Even if Flapping Eagle points out that he had grown up in the United States, the "Amerindian" tribe appears to span native American and Indian societies; likewise, whether "the time [is] consequently the near or remote future" (*G* 29) is a debatable point, since the 700 years which Flapping Eagle spent wandering across this world define it clearly as mythical. Likewise, the otherworldly dimension of Kâf can be associated both with the Caucasus and the Kashmir regions, but it may also be understood generally as "*al-Kahf*"/the cave (cf. Syed 138 f.).

Following Parameswaran's intuitive hint at the Rubik-cubic composition of the text, considering the frequency of both its linguistic quizzes and the density of its intertextuality, other ludic aspects of the novel appear to have gone unnoticed. Parameswaran pays attention to the often self-explaining punning techniques in *Grimus* (cf. Parameswaran 35-40), whereas Catherine Cundy and Ib Johansen focus on the profound intertextuality of the novel. They identify a wide range of literary references, such as Dante's *Divine Comedy*, Shakespeare's *Tempest*, Sterne's *Tristram Shandy,* Samuel Johnson's *Rasselas* and a number of native American trickster-myths, such as the *Walan Olum*. Mujeebuddin Syed analyses the influence of oriental (Muslim and Hindu) and occidental (Greek and Nordic) mythologies on the novel, especially of Attar's *Mantiq al-Tayr (The Conference of the Birds)*. This is an oriental classic equivalent to the Phoenix-myth, centring around the search of 30 birds (*"si morgh"*) for salvation in one god, Simorgh (cf. Syed 138f.). Grimus himself explains his own name, identifying it as an anagram of Simurg (cf. *G* 232f.). Finally, Syed sees "ample evidence of the book's subversion of religion, especially Islam" (Syed 145). Syed draws his conclusion from the final stages in the confrontation between Flapping Eagle and Grimus, not considering the Gorfs' function. As I hope to prove, putting a focus on their final instructions, the "iconoclastic intention" (Syed 146) seems not so much directed towards a particular religion but towards a generally totalitarian thought system, religious and political. Less attention has been drawn to the fact that the novel was a contribution to the Victor Gollancz Science-Fiction competition (cf. Cundy 12, and Reddy 5), but it contorts a number of notions and models developed in the "New Physics" (for a detailed discussion, cf. Meyer).

Such ludic backgrounds, both in their linguistic and literary dimensions, may indeed have been an original motivation and inspiration of the novel. After all, *Grimus* was written in the climate of general interest in game-theoretical descriptions of interactive processes (social, scientific, and literary).[2] In my discussion, I will focus primarily on the observation of

---

[2] In general, games have been an object of interest in various environments of social life (economics, cf. Davis), in the natural sciences (biology, cf. Müller) and the humanities (aesthetics or philosophy, cf. Heidemann, and cultural anthropology, cf. Huizinga, Turner and Köpping). Here they have been considered as 'representations' or 'simulations' of 'reality'. Still more recently, games have become a focus of interest in literary studies and literary theory (cf. Hutchinson and Iser). Thus, applications of game theory in a range of

game-theoretical phenomena in the individual performing strategies and their success or failure. The novel is clearly structured according to ideas and concepts of both puns and strategic games. And if "it is not so much the framing which delineates the ludic, but rather the potential to transgress frames, to subvert or merge or confound them" (Köpping 18), then *Grimus* is indeed the prototype of a ludic text. One may not identify any particular game – there are no 'real' chess moves; neither are there any obvious card-game tricks. But it is possible to recognise some rules in the game-context, the roles of players and stones, and the individual strategies. Some of these elements appear inconsistent, which raises several problems: In a board game, there is a clear liminal separation of interior and exterior levels, and of the systems 'game' and 'reality'. Here we are, however, dealing literally with games without frontiers: In *Grimus* any such clear-cut distinctions are ineffective, in fact non-existent. In Flapping Eagle's "quest" (*G* 225) there are elements of a paper chase played by his enemy Grimus, there are references to structurally incomplete jig-saw puzzles created by one of the central characters, Virgil Jones (cf. *G* 42f.), and there are various allusions to chess (once 'mis-played' as draughts, cf. *G* 116): Even if games do not remain within their known limits, they play a significant role as lexical markers of the ludic context. Following them, the reader will understand them as metaphorically as Flapping Eagle, when he echoes flattery by Grimus: "Played my hands well [...]. A revealing metaphor, don't you think? [...] This is a game, isn't it, a game you're enjoying?" (*G* 236) The reader may take such explicit hints as reading instructions and combine them in such a way that the ludic structure of the text itself becomes visible. Another such cross-liminal reading instruction is the *mise-en-abîme* story about the Angel of Death related at the centre of the plot (cf. *G* 141): The embedded narrative provides both an actual skeleton key to Flapping Eagle's quest and a programmatic self-description of the plot. To appreciate the textual game, readers have to play according to the rules in order to cope with an exuberantly playful text, which is more than just "exceed[ing] the cleverly allusive" (Cundy, 12).

Flapping Eagle's quest is motivated by the search for his sister, or by "the maze that led to Bird-Dog" (*G* 84), whom he assumes to have followed

---

disciplines have reached across the dividing lines between the sciences and the humanities.

Grimus who is masked as pedlar Sispy. Reflecting the beginning of his search, Flapping Eagle puts the focus on the initial conditions: Being orphans, young Flapping Eagle (then called Joe-Sue) and his adventurous sister Bird-Dog are only tolerated within their tribe. As a result, Bird-Dog is curious and fond of

> [...] the outside world. If it hadn't been for this fondness, she might never have met the pedlar Sispy; and then she might never have left [the Axona's tribe], and then I might never have left, and it would all have been different. (G 16f.)

This consideration refers to an important quality of a game, namely its repeatability (cf. Heidemann 48-52). Each new match sets the frame for the various 'realities' which may develop under different initial conditions. Thus, under different circumstances, such as a less adventurous sister, Flapping Eagle realises there would have been a host of other possible developments (and ultimately, stories); still, he cautiously adds a remark which turns out as an inference towards Grimus' final revelation at the end of the game: "Or perhaps there would inevitably have been a Sispy" (*G* 17). Very early on, Flapping Eagle is aware that he is involved in a game set on a level yet inaccessible to him. He is predetermined to participate passively until he is moved to take action in the game – which is to put an end to it, according to his function as the "eminently suitable angel of death" (*G* 234).

Playing the Game

Grimus can indeed be read as a "minutely planned" board, or strategy game (cf. *G* 232), in which Kâf world, being located in "that not-quite Mediterranean" (*G* 37), is a world within in a world – as any game is (cf. Heidemann 8). However, as this board is distorted by Grimus' magic, the "Grimus effect", one may realise that it consists of various levels in this hierarchy of nested worlds. The conflict is indicated in the rivalry between Grimus and Virgil Jones, but it is carried out between Grimus and Flapping Eagle. Long ago, Jones became Grimus' opponent because he denied the ethical legitimacy in the "*Great Experiment*" (*G* 214), a world without death. Jones' aim is the *withdrawal* from the Baconian ideals of absolute knowledge and the resulting option for everlasting life. The main conflict is therefore the (non-)acceptance of death in existence. There can only be complete victory or complete defeat, but no draw. Grimus plays an unruly game, acting out his 'master plan' against death. From his point of view, everything appears predetermined by him, and for some time it seems as though he were the winner, having placed a safe bet: "I have been constructing the Perfect Dimension, in which everything goes according to plan" (*G* 235), and he concludes his lecture with the words: "[...] here, it must be as I intended it" (*G* 235).

Grimus says that he has been playing a "perfect game of chess" (*G* 236) which seems completed as soon as he has achieved his ultimate aim: The transfer of his mind and personality to another individual's body, a virtually 'metempsychotic' move. Like any game, his works with various degrees of knowledge and information which the contesting teams need to keep in secret or to discover, and in doing so, they must use strategic devices within the limits of the rules. At the same time, participants depend on their competitors' tactics and, in case of a more complex interaction between various 'teams', chance. Thus, chaos and order, chance and free will, intuition and strategy intersect. In this 'game', Grimus' antagonist Jones has waited for an opportunity to put things right. Meeting Flapping Eagle, Jones realises the mental strength of his new friend and remarks at one point: "Interesting [...] that you should think of death as such a humanizing force" (*G* 55). Accordingly, he decides to use him as a 'stone' in the game. At various points in the development of his game, he reflects his moves (*"the irrevocable choice"*, *G* 60) knowing that each one will have a substantial effect on the course of the game. Likewise, Grimus says that, planning the game, he had set a number of "crossroad-points" in advance: Points of decision which in fact leave no room for a genuinely free choice to Flapping Eagle, but direct him to Grimus along what he calls "*line*[s] *of flux*" (*G* 235). "Do you deny that I have lured you here [...]?" (*G* 235), he asks in retrospection of the game, thus emphasising his own strategic supremacy, this being the equivalent to a prophesy told to Flapping Eagle even before the beginning of the actual quest: "It is your lot to be led by others; in the end you will accept this" (*G* 27).

Apart from the competition in the 'natural' world and in the Kâf-dimension, there is a third world: It is inhabited by the Gorfs who are all "Magisters Anagrammari". They live in the Gorfic "nirveesu" on the planet Thera under the rule of Dota. These frog-like stone creatures who think in imaginary "thought-forms" (cf. *G* 245) are capable of surfing the minds of others – they are, as it were, experts at metempsychosis. Usually, the main occupation of these creatures is an almost cabbalistic search for the linguistic "Divine Game of Order" (*G* 64), this being, obviously enough, an anagrammatic acronym of GOD. The tolerance for making up new acronyms and anagrams is limited by pure reason on the one hand, by chance on the other. Thus, their function is to act as a deity *ex machina* (see below). Only Koax, who is thrilled by action, leaves his dimension in obeisance to his fatal gambling bug and follows his "consuming passion" (*G* 67). He acts against the rules of his immaterial cosmos, interfering with the lower orders of existence by entering Flapping Eagle's mind and hoping for "a long, delectable time of endimions-shuffling, which was the next best thing he knew to the Divine Game" (*G* 73). Koax drives Flapping Eagle into abysses of linguistic puns which distract him from his quest. At first, Koax is rather disappointed at Flapping Eagle's inability to solve puns: "Even an idiot could have guessed that [...]. Even an idiot. That was the trouble with most people. They were so bad at games" (*G* 79 f.). But seeing that Virgil Jones, deeply worried about the success of his own strategic aim, helps his companion by logging in on Flapping Eagle himself, Koax is in much higher spirits: "This was better, he thought. This was something like it. If he had had hands, he would have rubbed them" (*G* 85). As Koax is discovered by Virgil Jones, they begin a 'combat of wits' about the legitimacy of partaking in the game against Grimus. If Jones has two objections against the gambling Gorf's presence, it is only the second of them which Koax finally accepts as "the correct move. [...] The first was a wasted move, which deprives you of perfection. Nevertheless, a score is a score is a score [...]" (*G* 93). After this concession, the witty Gorf strikes back by "intuition" (*G* 94): He points out that, for the solution of the main conflict, Virgil's presence is equally irrelevant. "It gives a little symmetry to the contest, wouldn't you say?" he snaps at his contestant (*G* 94). Koax's intuition causes a draw between these two combatants whose fight prefigures the final struggle between Eagle and Grimus.

After a first glance at the cross-liminal levels in the fictional game *Grimus* it is a small step to take a closer look at the narrative structure: At first, the plot appears to be an equivalent to a type of games which game-theorist Morton D. Davis describes as "zero-sum finite game with limited information" (cf. Davis 10). Such games are played by two teams and there is "only a finite number of alternatives at each turn, and the game is terminated in a finite number of moves" (Davis 10, footnote). In our case, the game is set by Grimus and it appears to be completed when he, against the resistance of others (esp. Virgil Jones), reaches his aim, namely his metempsychosis, i.e., his own self-transcendence (this being an important quality of any game, cf. Turner 37). For a long time, Flapping Eagle acts as a chess-piece moved both by Virgil Jones and Grimus in a game which he does not realise and later does not comprehend. However, as soon as Flapping Eagle becomes aware of his function as active player, he breaks the rules, liberating himself from the frames he has been put into. In an act of 'metalepsis', a leap across predefined limits, he obliterates the demarcations of the game-board on which he has been moved by Victor Jones and Grimus. But Eagle's liminal transition is only made possible by Grimus himself who first redefines and raises him in order to challenge him then as an active player, or contestant, an act which causes a new situation with unforeseen consequences.

Theoretically there are games which only allow linear and actually predictable developments, provided both players know the rules and limited strategies. Victory depends wholly on the player who has the first move and plays without making mistakes – the player who reacts is determined to lose, no matter what strategy he applies. It all depends on the first player's attention or carelessness; if he makes a mistake, then the second player may win. In such a so-called 'zero-sum game with limited information' (e.g., *Four in a Row*), the degree of victory is balanced by the degree of defeat. A draw is not possible. Davis points out that each player (or team) will apply a strategy according to the minimax-theorem: The equilibrium of chances is always at risk, and each player will attempt to take advantage, or to restore the balance if in a disadvantageous position (cf. Davis 39) – metalepsis, however, (such as assuming new roles, or changing positions arbitrarily) is no legitimate tactical means.

Even in a rather simple game it is hard to predict safely an opponent's actions following one's own move; there is always a margin of error in all prediction and action. Therefore, one may only work with statistical probabilities, displaying the mathematical chances of individual results after a move: It is shown in a so-called win-and-loss matrix. Some of Virgil Jones' reflections upon his own chances of success in the game against Grimus are a rather weak attempt at composing a functional equivalent of such a matrix: "Could he influence Flapping Eagle sufficiently to make the whole plan work?" But it leads him to, "[y]et again, uncertainty." On another occasion, Virgil Jones looks down at his distorted creation as "[a]n idea that didn't work", and wonders: "Did one abandon it, set oneself apart from it as he had done from the life of the island? Did one attempt to save it? Or did one agree to destroy it [...]?" (*G* 61). As he observes Flapping Eagle's dimension fever aggravated by the interference of Koax's 'abysmal' pun on the synonyms "Ethiopia" and "Abyssinia" (cf. *G* 77ff.), he worries about the key to his own success in the game against Grimus, and decides to take action – he has to use his ability of mind-travel in order to help Flapping Eagle out of the Gorf's distracting and paralysing puzzle (cf. *G* 79). These considerations show that Flapping Eagle is, at this point, still a passive stone. Following the minimax theorem, all the players try to figure out the most promising winning strategies. Accordingly, Grimus anticipates his contestant's win-and-loss matrix for the final moves:

> Since you do not know how to conceptualize the coordinates of your Dimensions [in order to return to the empirical world, J.M.], you cannot leave the island, said Grimus. You cannot stay among Kâf's inhabitants, bearing my face. Your only alternative is suicide, and once I have shown you my marvels you will not wish to do so. (*G* 233)

But Grimus assumes he's playing a 'zero-sum game with limited information', and he must realise that it works on a far more complex level. He has set the rules and strategic aims, but as he himself disregards or redefines them, he disturbs the game-cosmos. Moreover, it turns out that in the ludic construction of Rushdie's novel there are two pairs of players: Jones vs. Koax on one level, and Eagle vs. Grimus on another, which is more significant. Grimus who thinks himself to be in control of the whole game, is only aware of his own level; however, he is not aware of, and therefore cannot control, the subordinate fight between Jones and Koax. Neither does victory on one side necessarily imply defeat on the other: Even though the Stone Rose and the other instruments of *Conceptual Technology* (including the "Subsumer" which allows the final metempsychosis) serve the party who is in possession of these devices, they also imply serious disadvantages. As long as Grimus keeps the Stone Rose he is in possession of the key to absolute power, but at the same time he must seclude himself from the other inhabitants of his dimension and therefore cannot act freely: His 'absolute' power is in fact relative to the structural constellation of players and pieces. Likewise, as soon as three of his enemies (a "trinity of nemesis", *G* 247) 'win' the Stone Rose, they 'lose' on the existential level – because it means that they use the destructive force of this item in an inappropriate way. Moreover, the end of the game implies absolute extermination of all the participants involved: There are no winners, except Flapping Eagle whose victory it is to restore the natural order – even at the expense of his own life; his quest ends in a "voluntary *self-sacrifice*" (Johansen 28). Victory and loss are ambiguous and subject to interpretation, an advantage achieved on one level may turn out as a disadvantage on another.

In sum, there are three strategies at work in *Grimus*, with varying degrees of complexity. The strategy of the people of 'K' is the simplest: Without Grimus' permission they cannot attack him, and with it, they manage to destroy him and everything else, but not the object of their desire – the Stone Rose. Virgil Jones has more knowledge than they do, but less than Grimus. Therefore, he has a different, more sophisticated strategy than the inhabitants of 'K'. It reads "Wait your moment" (*G* 223), a premise which accounts for his behaviour even beyond the point where he decides that "there was little merit in staying put" (*G* 60), and which is the last in a whole series of admonitions for Flapping Eagle. Using first the defensive strategy of Virgil Jones, Flapping Eagle slips into a dramatic crisis near the final stages of the game. As soon as he has become a self-dependent player, his strategy is to withdraw from the match altogether: "But in the end it all depends on me, Grimus [...]. It all hangs on my choice and I tell you now I am not going to play" (*G* 236). Grimus, who appears to quit the game, explains his own strategy to his victim and coaxes Flapping Eagle to his secret place at the labyrinthine centre of the multi-dimensional game-board: "Seeing no reason not to" (*G* 237), Flapping Eagle follows passively everywhere Grimus leads him, and is inadvertently back into the game. Finally, he acts too carelessly:

Flapping Eagle touches the "*Subsumer*", as Grimus begs him to do, because he thinks that he "could not deny [this to] him. It was a small thing to concede." Grimus makes his winning move into Flapping Eagle's mind, and comments: "*My mother always told me, you've got to trick people into accepting new ideas*" (*G* 242). In his simple refusal to participate, Flapping Eagle thinks to have played his joker, and to have put an end to the game. But as Grimus' strategy works differently, he can redefine this refusal as an actual move: "[...] one of the greatest qualities of a well-formed concept is flexibility. One can turn disadvantages into advantages" (*G* 235). In the explanations of his own moves preceding his encounter with Flapping Eagle, Grimus declares himself winner in this unfair match. Indeed, this archetypal trickster, the "ancient infant", seems to win complete victory only *with* his opponent's refusal. It is too late when Flapping Eagle realises that there is actually no way to keep out of the game in Kâf dimension.

An actual psychomachia between the two characters takes place inside Flapping Eagle: Good "I-Eagle" finally defeats evil "I-Grimus" and resists the temptation of knowledge, power, and eternal life. For, rational thinker though he is, Grimus, who planned everything so well, has made a fatal mistake, too: Mixing the levels of chess-piece and player, he underrates Flapping Eagle's personal strength and continues to regard him as a passive object. Grimus analyses Flapping Eagle: "Your Ionic Pattern [...] is the strongest destructive pattern I have ever seen" (*G* 234). His 'psychoanalysis' also emphasises Flapping Eagles's power of intuition: "Chaos. The true weapon of the destroyer. Your unconscious mind knew exactly what it was doing" (*G* 236). But this alone is a one-sided conclusion. Forgetting to consider the factor 'strength', Grimus does not take into account that Flapping Eagle the player acts differently from Flapping Eagle the 'stone'. During the dimension fever, Flapping Eagle has learned to use both strategies of consciously playing on time *and* moving impulsively, i.e., unpredictably (cf. *G* 88f.). This volatile quality, signified in Flapping Eagle's name, is neither seen by Grimus nor by Virgil Jones, but it turns out to be the key to Flapping Eagle's victory. If Jones' passive strategy leads his friend into a severe crisis, Grimus' anarchy is itself flawed by his impatience. The king's road to success, one may say, is a combination of random and orderly tactics according to what is technically termed as 'mixed strategy principle'.

In the final combat between "I-Eagle" and "I-Grimus", Flapping Eagle acts similar to Grimus, continuing the game as his opponent thinks to have finished it. Grimus stops playing immediately after capturing Flapping Eagle's mind. His victim fights him down and then leaps, again, across the levels of the distorted game-board, this time for the consultation of Dota as an umpire. Dota declares that mind-surfing Koax had been no less harmful than Grimus; even if he has done little more than shuffle a few chess-pieces around (cf. *G* 250). But the Gorf's interference with Eagle's mind has created "a minor branch of the Divine Game to such a point that it threatened the Game itself" (*G* 66). Koax is banned from his "nirveesu" – this being a worse penalty than the former exclusion from the game by Virgil Jones, for it implies his death. Grimus, too, receives maximal reproof for mixing the cosmic levels of the game, or "endimions":

> *We are extremely perturbed about Grimus' misuse of the* [Stone] *Rose. It was never intended to be a tool for intraendimions travel. Nor a magic box for the production of food. It is a flagrant distortion of Conceptual Technology to use the Rose to Conceptualize a packet of* [...] *coffee.*
>
> *Most particularly we are worried about the subendimions* [i.e., sub-dimensions] *he has set up on the mountain-top. Subendimions are Conceptually unsound. A place is either part of an Endimions or it is not. To Conceptualize a place which is both a part of an Endimions and yet secret from it could stretch the Object to disintegration-point. We would like this ridiculous Concept to be dissolved forthwith.* (*G* 245f.)

Grimus has caused a lot more chaos: He confounds the hierarchical order in the distinction of supernatural beings ('Gods'), rational subjects and passive objects. Thus, in his game a player may turn into a piece, like Virgil Jones; a piece may become a player, like Flapping Eagle; finally Grimus himself acts as aleatory game-director (who sets the operative rules and defines the board), agonistic gamester (who strategically moves the pieces according to these rules) and mimicking trickster (who, using different masks, cheats the other contestants).[3]

---

[3] This typology refers to Wolfgang Iser's elaboration of his own reception theory. Iser puts Roger Caillois' main categories of games into a narratological context and applies them as types of narrative strategies; thus, *agôn* / 'confrontation' connotes the coherence in a plot, whereas *alea* / 'chance' emphasises its apparent contingency (often resolved by a superior 'power', such as fate etc.); finally, *mimicry* / 'masking' and *ilinx* / 'ecstasy' show its performative and subversive qualities (cf. Iser 453ff.). Moreover, Iser sees these

In the end, Flapping Eagle obeys Dota's orders and restores the original cosmos: Grimus' defeat becomes complete. But if Madhusudhana Rao concludes that "Flapping Eagle once again rearranges the a-temporal priorities in the marvellous World of Calf Mountain, into a more stable and secure order" (Rao 11), he ignores the implications of the ending: The extermination of the game-cosmos by Flapping Eagle symbolises a morally ambivalent act. For there is a disquieting tone in the kill-joy Dota's sentence: The Gorfs accept no place but their own cosmos, allowing mechanisms of imaginary puns and thought forms, but prohibiting practical ingenuity. Thus, the extinction of a whole universe, an artifice which was, in all its defects, no "utopia" (*G* 85), seems barely justifiable.[4] Leaving no space for games, nor indeed fictions, their vengeance on Grimus' robbery of Conceptual Technology appears "deprived of perfection" and, in its absoluteness, ethically corrupted: The resultant cosmic order is spoilt with totalitarian megalomania, just as Grimus' absolute individualism is. Ultimately, the Gorfs' collectivism, their thought-forms and rationality are blighted by the dialectics of enlightenment; both Grimus and the Gorfs use their knowledge as a power-instrument for their own ends, and not for the general welfare.

The ludic quality of Rushdie's first novel, particularly for the ethically ambivalent culmination in its ending, may be seen in the general context of Rushdie's manichaean world picture. M. Keith Booker has observed that a particular narrative technique pervades Rushdies novels: "We are given an account of events, then that account is retracted and we are given an alternative, contradictory account." Therefore "it is impossible to develop any satisfactorily stable understanding of the exact meaning and status of these problematic transformations" (Booker 985). One reason for this feature may indeed be that Rushdie inscribes all his fictional characters and actions a high degree of ambiguity and, after *Grimus*, he has continued to put his

---

dispositions as reading strategies and claims that it is in fact the reader's making sense of a text which leads to the inevitably playful conception and creation of new plots for never-ending stories: Iser alludes here to the interdependence of text and reader which leads to his assumption that the category "game" actually turns into an absolute ("Spiel [wird] gleichsam totalisiert", Iser 467); thus, in the reading act, the recipient enters the game and has to obey its rules, but actively contributes to its continuation.

[4] In fact, Rushdie's radically rational creatures, the Gorfs, may be seen in intertextual dependence of Swift's unreasonable rationalists who intend to leave no place for the alien Other, namely the Houyhnhnms in *Gulliver's Travels* IV (cf. Erzgräber).

novels in the context of games or, as in his most recent *The Ground Beneath Her Feet* (1999), sports. Thus, in the description of the ambiguities in life as Rushdie, behind the mask of his protagonist Saleem Sinai, explains them in *Midnight's Children* (1980), people and actions are subject to a complex interplay of chance, determination and strategy (or free will). There, in a chapter headlined "Snakes and Ladders" he dwells on the emblematic, or "metaphorical", quality in this board-game. Linking it to human existence, he generalises – in agreement with the ending of *Grimus* - that "[a]ll games have morals", and explains the crucial importance of a ludic mind capable of (re-)interpretation in order to cope with the contingency of life:

> [...] the game Snakes and Ladders captures, as no other activity can hope to do, the eternal truth that for every ladder you climb, a snake is waiting just around the corner; and for every snake, a ladder will compensate. But it's more than that; no mere carrot-and-stick affair; because implicit in the game is the unchanging twoness of things, [...]; in the opposition of staircase and cobra we can see, metaphorically, all conceivable oppositions [...], but I found, very early in my life, that the game lacked one very crucial dimension, that of ambiguity – because [...] it is also possible to slither down a ladder and to triumph on the venom of a snake... (*MC* 167)

Works Cited

Rushdie, Salman. *Imaginary Homelands*. London: Vintage, 1991. (Quoted as *IR*)
-----. *Grimus*. 1975. London: Vintage, 1996. (Quoted as *G*)
-----. *Midnight's Children*. 1980. New York: Bard/Avon, 1982. (Quoted as *MC*)
Booker, M. Keith. "Beauty and the Beast. Dualism as Despotism in the Fiction of Salman Rushdie." *English Literary History* 57:4 (1990): 977-997. Repr. in *Reading Rushdie: Perspectives on the Fiction of Salman Rushdie*. Ed. Mary D. Fletcher. Amsterdam, Atlanta, GA.: Rodopi, 1994. 237-254.
Cundy, Catherine. *Salman Rushdie*. Manchester/New York: Manchester UP, 1996.
Davis, Morton D. *Game Theory. A Nontechnical Introduction*. With a Foreword by O. Morgenstern. New York: Basic Books, 1970.
Erzgräber, Willi. "'Reason' und 'Nature' in Swift's *Gulliver's Travels*, Buch IV." *Papers on Language and Medieval Studies Presented to Alfred Schopf*. Ed. Richard Matthews and Joachim Schmole-Rostosky. Frankfurt/M.: Lang 1988. 69-88.

Fletcher, Mary D., ed. *Reading Rushdie: Perspectives on the Fiction of Salman Rushdie*. Amsterdam, Atlanta, GA: Rodopi,, 1994.

Heidemann, Ingeborg. *Der Begriff des Spieles und das ästhetische Weltbild in der Philosophie der Gegenwart*. Berlin: de Gruyter, 1968.

Huizinga, Johan. *Homo ludens: Vom Ursprung der Kultur im Spiel*. [1938] Reinbek: Rowohlt, 1991.

Hutchinson, Peter. *Games Authors Play*. London: Methuen, 1983.

Johansen, Ib. "The Flight from the Enchanter: Reflections on Salman Rushdie's *Grimus*." *Reading Rushdie*. Ed. Mary D. Fletcher. 23-34.

Iser, Wolfgang. *Das Fiktive und das Imaginäre: Perspektiven literarischer Anthropologie*. [1991] Frankfurt/M.: Suhrkamp, 1993.

Köpping, Klaus-Peter. "The Ludic as Creative Disorder: Framing, De-Framing and Boundary Crossing." *The Games of Gods and Man: Essays in Play and Performance*. Ed. Klaus-Peter Köpping. Münster: LIT, 1997. 1-39.

Kumar, T.Vijay. "'Doing the Dangerous Thing': An Interview with Salman Rushdie." *Rushdie's Midnight's Children: A Book of Reading*. Ed. Menakshee Mukherjee. Delhi: Pencraft International, 1994. 212-227.

Meyer, Jürgen. "GUT and QED, and Other 'P2C2E': 'Processes Too Complicated to Explain' and Rushdie's New Physics." *Lost Worlds & Mad Elephants: Literature, Science and Technology 1700-1990*. Eds. Elmar Schenkel and Stefan Welz. Glienicke/Cambridge, MA: Galda + Wilch, 1999. 331-349.

Mueller, Ulrich, ed. *Evolution und Spieltheorie*. Munich: Oldenbourg, 1990.

Parameswaran, Uma. "New Dimensions Courtesy of the Whirling Demon: Word-Play in Grimus." *Reading Rushdie*. Ed. Mary D. Fletcher. 35-44.

Rao, Madhusudhano M. *Salman Rushdie's Fiction. A Study – The Satanic Verses Excluded*. New Delhi: Sterling Publishers, 1992.

Reddy, P.B. "*Grimus*: An Analysis." *The Novels of Salman Rushdie*. Ed. G.R. Taneja und R. K. Dhawan. New Delhi: Indian Society for Commonwealth Studies, 1992. 5-9.

Syed, Mujeebuddin. "Warped Mythologies: Salman Rushdie's *Grimus*." *ARIEL* 25:4 (1994): 135-151.

Turner, Victor. *From Ritual to Theatre: The Human Seriousness of Play*. New York: PAJ Publications, 1982.

Social Competence and Linguistic Performance in Elizabethan Parliaments

Hans-Dieter Metzger and Dietmar Schneider

1. Principal Preconditions: Authority and Order

Amongst the received truths of Tudor history, the existence of a holistic Elizabethan world picture occupies an apparently secure place. Ever since in 1943 E. M. W. Tillyard reconstructed this vision of a fixed, static, and unchanging world as the prominent mode of perception and recognition, numerous scholars have underscored that the idea of an ordered universe was the key concept of the age. Most of them agree that until the end of the 16th century the idea of order functioned as a dynamic modus capable of explaining various changing social attitudes and facts without necessitating a conscious value reassessment (Tillyard, Suerbaum 475-529, Gelfert 14-20, Ronan, Lovejoy). The basic assumption of this theory says that God created an immutable ordered cosmos, defined by hierarchy and interrelation. God himself is divine essence, John Aylmer wrote in 1559, "spread throughout the world and ingrafted in every part of it" (Aylmer, sign. C 3). According to this theory, God's will assigned to every single entity its specific position or stage within a divinely ordained chain of existence. This underlying premise - the universal structuring power of the cosmos - reaches far back in intellectual history and can be found in numerous Western writers, commencing with Homer, Plato, Ovid, and the apocalyptic authors of Holy Scripture, and continued by medieval theoreticians such as Thomas Aquinas. Under the Tudors this traditional concept acquired new prominence, though in a modified version. Instead of the overcrowded medieval versions, its 16th century counterpart displayed a much more clarified hierarchy and presented the monarch as the unrivalled focus in closest proximity to God. The reason for the clarification is all too obvious: the 'king-tailored' variant was much more effective in supporting the post-reformation "Cult of Tudor authority".

A most impressive description of this world picture can be found in an official Tudor sermon of 1547. Published shortly after the succession of Edward VI., it was decreed that this homily amongst others had to be read in every church and chapel throughout England at least once a year. "Almighty God," the opening passage stressed, "hath created and appointed all thinges in heaven, yearth and waters in a moste excellent and perfect ordre." The lowest part is knit together with the highest in due proportion. Biblical descriptions of the heavenly states of archangels and angels demonstrate that in heaven degrees are well observed. Correspondingly, on earth, the sermons says, God "hath assigned kynges, princes, with other governors under them" to preserve "all in good and necessary ordre" and to hinder mischief and forestall chaos. Political relationship - the *subiectio civilis* of man to man which is necessary for the attainment of the common good - is not a consequence of sin but effected as an aspect of order. Since kings are representatives of God on earth and therefore subject to divine will, man, for conscience's sake, has to be obedient to God's lieutenants on earth. Furthermore the homily teaches that "[e]very degree of people, in their vocation, callyng and office, hath appoynted to them their duetie and ordre. Some are in high degree, some in lowe, some kynges and princes, some inferiors and subjectes, priestes and laimen, masters and servauntes, fathers and chyldren, husbandes and wifes, riche and poor" ("An Exhortation", 161). Truly, this homily is a conjuration of the eternal order and an adjuration to stick right fast to it. Shakespeare, amongst many others, echoed the homily in Ulysses' truly famous degree-speech in *Troilus and Cressida*:

> The heavens themselves, the planets, and this centre,
> Observe degree, priority, and place,
> Insisture, course, proportion, season, form,
> Office, and custom, in all line of order (I, iii, 87-90).

2. Processions and Procedures: Parliamentary Ceremony

Parliament was an ordered institution as well as a display of order. As Sir Thomas Smith defined in a text to be taken as the official statement of government, it is to be regarded for "the most high and absolute power of the realme of Englande, [...] where the king himself in person, the nobilitie, the rest of the gentilitie, [...] the bishoppes [...] and the knightes, esquires, gentlemen and commons for the lower part of the common wealth" are present for consultation and deliberation. Although the active participation through voting was considered essential, there was a belief that the Commons was nonetheless representative. "For everie Englishman is entended," as Smith expressed, "to bee there present, either in person or by procuration and attornies, of what preheminence, state, dignitie, or qualitie soever he be, from the Prince (be he King or Queene) to the lowest person of the Englande" (Smith, 78-79). The same idea can be found in the oration of an unknown speaker in 1594. Parliament, he said, is "an epitome of the whole realm [...] . They eyes of the poore are upon this parliament" and members must take account of their grievances (Hartley III, 220). It was the essence of parliament to observe and preserve hierarchies and yet to represent the whole body of the realm.

The opening ceremonies of parliament are of revealing significance. They were staged in public as an occasion to instruct the many spectators, gazing at the procession as it rolled through the streets, and to reinforce the values of monarchy by law. The significance of the procession lay in that as an emanation of vertical order it actively grew out of the private household of the monarch and into the public sphere with the Lord Chancellor, carrying the Great Seal of England, the ultimate symbol of the God given right to make law, at the head, followed by the nobility framing the monarch according to rank. Once the divine service at Westminster Abbey was over, the monarch and the lords spiritual and temporal met the elected representatives of the people in the House of Lords. There, in the name of the monarch, the Lord Chancellor or the Lord Keeper declared the reasons for the summoning, and invited the Commons to elect their speaker to effectively become a body. As the last act of the opening procedure the Commons would present their speaker to the sovereign on the third day. Thus, the monarch in due observation of preeminance and appropriate participation of every rank recreated the full representation of the realm for councel and established its legal capacity as the highest court of England.

The Lord Keeper's opening speech itself reinforces once more this respect for order. It was the learned humanist oration of the Lord Keeper Nicolas

Bacon in 1559 which set the pace for the rest of the reign (Hartley 1995, 19-20). In the beginning it is stressed that it was the monarch's pleasure to summon his "high courte of Parliament" for important matters, affecting the nation. The opening parallels the emergence of the sovereign as the fountain of all good, acting on behalf of God and to ensure the wellbeing of his people. After the introductory part, Bacon, firstly, suggested that of all matters to be discussed the most important is religion, "the chief pillar and buttres" of the realm. Only through a continual striving for the advancement of God's glory the commonwealth "is continually to be sustained and maintained." As God's lieutenant on earth and in conjunction with the people represented in parliament the king carries out his responsibility to provide for good ecclesiastical order. Then the Lord Chancellor allowed, in the name of the monarch, secondly, a legislative review. The privilege of this parliament would be "reforming and removing all enormities and mischeifes that doe, or might, hurte or hinder the civill orders of pollices of this realm" (Hartley I, 34). Recent revisionist accounts have stressed the importance of this legislative activity as the "prime function" of parliament (Elton, Graves). Admittedly, most of the time in both Houses was spent with "private matters." Yet, the assumption that contemporaries valued parliament primarily as an institution to pursue their self-interest probably goes too far. Though it cannot be denied that interested groups like the fishmongers' guild or the London merchants effectively lobbied parliament, their agents, "men of business" such as Thomas Norton, Thomas Digges, Robert Bell or the parliamentary outsider Robert Hitchcock, kept an eye on the common interest of the realm or even valued that common interest above private concern. As the third and last item on the agenda the Lord Chancellor touched the matters of state and introduced the quest for the necessary provisions to meet the costs for the administration and the defence of the realm (Hartley I, 33-39, 185-187). This does not mean that matters of state came after private matters. In his account on the *Order and Usage how to keep a Parlement in England in these dayes* the Exeter MP John Hooker stated unmistakably that according to convention religion always comes first, followed by vital secular matters relating to the state, and, at the last, "the making and establishing of good and wholesome laws" (Hooker, 146-147). In consideration of such a general statement, the modification in the opening speech indicates a rhetorical device that, in fact, reinforces the basic concept. Acting in behalf of his monarch, the orator honoured the concerns of the representatives 'above degree' to oblige them most politely the more to respond generously if asked for taxes and subsidies.

Apart from such artistic devices of the Lord Chancellor, the opening speech made one thing abundantly clear: The function of the king in the parliamentary process, while not central to the lawmaking process, was essential. Due order and polite respect for the restrictions, put forth by the Orator to mark the limits of agreeable debate, have to be observed. True, "there are sundreye orders which of him [the monarch] are to be observed, or els the Parlement surcesseth to be a Parlement and taketh not his effect," notably free elections after due warning and the granting of immunity to all lawful elected members and several other ancient customs, freedoms and privileges. Yet, "without him and his authoritie: nothing can be doon, and with it: all things take effect." Monarchical authority is necessary to initiate the summons and convene the component parts. It is vital, too, to bring parliamentary matters to an end. The king is "the beginning and the ending of Parliament, [...] upon whome resteth and dependeth the effect and substaunce of the whole Parlement" (Hooker, 178-179). This elevated position is, last but not least, expressed in the final act of royal approval or rejection of bills at the end of the parliamentary session. The king is like

> [...] the glorious planet Sol
> In noble eminence enthron'd and spher'd
> Amidst the other; whose med'cinable eye
> Corrects the influence of evil planets,
> And posts like the commandment of a king,
> Sans check, to good and bad.
> (*Troilus and Cressida*, I, iii, 91-6).

3. Preconceptions and Prejudices: The Quandary of the Queen

So far masculine nouns and pronouns, such as king, his, and he or the more neutral abstraction of monarch, sovereign or prince, have deliberately been used. This is legitimised by the gist of most formidable descriptions of the laws and conventions of parliament, written by the public servant Sir Thomas

Smith, the Exeter MP John Hooker, the antiquarian William Lambarde or the minister William Harrison. Despite the fact that a woman sat on the throne, all of them tried hard to avoid the word "queen".

We have already come across the reason for such dodging and ducking. The definition of the homily *An exhortation to Obedience* leaves the conclusion in no doubt: women are inferior to man. The male body was presented as the "epitome or compendium of the whole Creation", whereas the female body was defined as "the weaker vessel." The latter phrase - also common to Shakespeare (*Love's Labour's Lost* I, i, 275, 2; *Henry IV* II, x, 5; *Romeo and Juliet* I, i, 19) - originated with William Tyndale's translation of the New Testament in English in 1526 and quickly became an established proverb (Fletcher, 60). Pointing to St Peter (1 Pet 2), too, the official sermon *Of the State of Matrimonie* confirms: "[T]he husband [...] ought to be the Leader and Author of Love [...] for the Woman is a weak Creature, not imbued with like strength, and constancy of mind, therefore they be sooner disquieted, and they be the more prone to all weak affections and dispositions of mind, more than Men be, and lighter they be; and more vain in their fantasies and opinions." And somewhat later the same homily - personally inspected and approved by the Queen and ordered by the Convocation to be regularly read in all churches in England in 1563 - exhorts all married men: "But consider thou again, that the Woman is a frail Vessel, and thou art therefore made the Ruler and Head over her, to bear the weakness of her in this her subjection." Revealingly, the sermon compared the relation man to woman with "king" to nobles, to drive home his argument of the stronger honouring the weaker, whereas the weaker has to pay obedience to the stronger (*Certain Sermons* 307, 312).

Within the given frame of order of the Elizabethan world a woman on the throne was an open contradiction to the eternal laws of cosmic order. How could the moon, traditionally equated with woman, dare to prescribe the glorious sun, usually likened to the man, *his* orb? In his furious attack on the rule of women the misogynist John Knox cried out what most Englishmen had fully internalised: "To promote a woman to bear rule, superiority, dominion or empire above any realm, nation or city is repugnant to nature, contumely to God, a thing most contrarious to His revealed will and approved ordinance, and finally it is the subversion of good order, of all equity and justice." But in his eyes to accept a woman-ruler is not only a matter of order but also of expediency: "[T]heir sight in civil regiment is but blindness, their strength weakness, their counsel foolishness, and judgement frenzy, if it be rightly considered" (Knox, 8-9). The same discrimination can be found in the confession of love-ridden Troilus, who feels himself unable to join the battle: "The Greeks are strong and skilful to their strength, [...] But I am weaker than a woman's tear, [...] Less valiant than the virgin in the night, And skilless as unpractis'd infancy" (*Troilus and Cressida* I, i, 7, 9, 11-12). This is one of the very rare self-assessments in this play that proves to be right. When the victorious Trojans came back from the battlefield, the valour and vigilance of the heroic fighters can be measured by the upright posture whereas effeminate Troilus is "creeping" home.

With a woman on the throne, quite obviously, the joy of creation and the delight in plenitude were at odds with the more austere demands of a male-conceived mundane world. Significantly (not to say ironically), Knox's prejudice about a woman's inherent weakness was reinforced in John Aylmer's defence of Queen Elizabeth. In order to counter the zeal of the Scottish clergyman, Aylmer - who later became Bishop of London - used a similar argumentative strategy. First he pointed out that God likes to work through the weakest of his creatures. To demonstrate his greatness the Almighty employs even such inferior instruments as women (Aylmer, sign. B 4). If, then, it is the will of the Almighty that England should be ruled by a woman, Englishmen must in obedience submit. Secondly, he suggested that it is less dangerous to have a female ruler in England than elsewhere in the world, because "[t]he regiment of England is not a mere Monarchie as some for lack of consideracion thinke, nore a meere Oligarchie, nor Democrate, but a rule mixte of all these wherein ech one of these have or should have like authoritie [...] [and in which], if the parliament [Senate and Commons] use their privileges: the King can ordain nothing without them. [...] She maketh no statutes or laws, but the honourable court of Parliament: she breaketh none, but it must be she and they together or else not." The moral spelt out is that it is not "she that ruleth but the laws, but the executors whereof be her [male] judges, appointed by her, her justices of peace and such other officers" (sign. H 2-H 3).

The three elements in the defence of Elizabeth demand closer scrutiny. First of all, monarchy is not taken to be an indelible and sacred property of a dynasty but a public and localised office. One can find the same tenor in Smith's description of monarchical authority, where "it is the office, not the person, to whom Englishmen give their reverence" (McLaren, 220). This sounds somewhat modern but was in fact a medieval conception of the magistrate as a Vicar of Christ. Ascribed exclusively to temporal princes after the Reformation, the monarch was regarded as the administrator of God's laws. Protestant thinkers never surrendered the thought that law, by its divine origin, is above the state and does not depend on the state for its existence. Peter Wentworth, quoting Bracton, said in his parliamentary speech in 1576: "The king ought not to be under man but under God and under the law, because the law maketh him a king. Lett the king therefore attribute that unto the law which the law attributeth unto him, that is, dominion and power" (Hartley I, 429). Secondly - and again based on medieval precursors -, there was the idea that man was incapable of attaining full knowledge of God's order due to the darkening of his rational capacities as a consequence of the fall. To restrain the prince from falling foul to his own will and lusts he was taken to stand in the need of the advice of an informed conscience, not of another single man but of all the wisest and most honourable persons of the realm. It is the duty of all sage councillors, said Peter Wentworth, to inform her Majesty faithfully as "it is both trayterous and hellish through flattery to seeke to devoure our naturall prince" (428). Thirdly, it is not to be denied that Aylmer, Hooker, and Smith as well as most other leading men in Elizabeth England adhered to the principle of a mixed government, an idea taken from Polybius. According to this theory, the essential feature of the most stable form of government was some sort of constitutional system in which the principles of monarchy, aristocracy and democracy were combined, and the prince was made dependent on the rule of law as the expression of the collective wisdom of the system (Smith 52, 78-88; Hooker 105). Put in such a light, parliament fulfilled not just the function to 'bridle' the potentially tyrannical monarch, but also to mend the permanent insufficiencies of a woman ruler. The importance of parliament in the Elizabethan period was greatly enhanced by the fact that a female was at the helm of the state (McLaren, 161-197).

4. The Crisis of Authority and the Reactionary Response

Throughout the first years of Elizabeth's reign parliament tried to solve the paradox of having a woman ruler in a patriarchal world by pressing the marriage - an abortive design mainly due to Elizabeth's constant evasions. Elizabeth herself, too, knew very well about this problem, but tried to present herself as above the weakness and frailty of her sex because of her appointment by God to be Queen. This was her justification when, in 1563, she mused, in a speech to the House of Commons, about whether "being a woman, wanting both wit and memory" she should be silent.

> I cannot attribute these haps and good success to my device without detracting much from the divine providence [...], nor challenge to my private commendation what is only due to his eternal glory: my sex permits me not. [...] And as for those rare and special benefits [described by the Lord Keeper] which have many years followed and accompanied my happy reign, I attribute to God alone the prince of rule, and count myself no better then his hand maid. (Hartley I, 472)

Later the same year, she told a parliamentary delegation "though I be a woman yet I have as good a courage answerable to my place as ever my father had." Seemingly more self-confident but, implicitly, accepting the inferiority of women, she claimed in 1581: "I have the heart of a man, not of a woman and I am not afraid of anything" (Haigh, 21-22).

The problem of the 'masterless woman' boiled hot in the crisis around the plotting of Mary Stuart and permeated the parliamentary discourse upon that topic. The attempt to put things right in patriarchal terms can be observed in a dossier drafted by the bishops in a parliamentary committee in 1572. Because Elizabeth hesitated to execute her cousin, Mary Stuart, for high treason, she explained her own indecision with "[the] nearness of the blood." The bishops likened her to the biblical figure David. When Absalom rebelled against the godly king, they said, David did not fulfill his office as King. Instead of prosecuting the traitor he gave himself wholly to his passions and wept "effeminately" about his insolent son. In such a moment of utmost danger for the kingdom, able men close to the womanish king like David's general Joab would have to take initiative to safeguard the kingdom irrespective of the Queen's will (Hartley I, 278). In the Commons men eagerly grasped the hint and its implications. Thomas Digges intimated in his speech before the lower house that "the preachers have plentifully poured out vehement reasons, urgent examples and horrible menaces of sacred scriptures concerning the execution of justice and shunning of that sugared poison bearing in outward show the countenance of mild pity" (294-295). Others harped on the same string. According to Thomas Norton, Elizabeth was disabled because she was "naturally enclined [to mercie]" (326). And Job Throckmorton informed the assembly that "when yt came to the upshotte that her Majestie should ratifie the whole by her royal assent, then a man might easely see where mercy and lenitye hadde taken up theire seate. It was so contrarye to her nature to sheade bloude that (notwithstandinge the thinge were proposed devysed for her owne safety) shee woulde none of yt [...]" (Hartley II, 230). If Elizabeth proved unable to take appropriate action, Robert Snagg cried out in the House of Commons, they should do it themselves and execute the traitorous wretch Jezebel, namely Mary, "without much adoo" (cf. Metzger).

But whereas reason had failed King David just temporarily during Absalom's rebellion, Queen Elizabeth's defect was constant, because she was a woman and, consequently, "the weaker vessel." This understanding of gender meant that in Elizabeth no recovery of normatively male rationality could be expected. In the last analysis, the men of the age tried to resolve their problem with a female ruler through the development of a "quasi-republican" statement, the "Bond of Association". Men would collectively supply right reason. Unfortunately, with this particular type of a "quasi-republican" statement discourse transcended parliament in pledging that every signatory would in case of a plot against Elizabeth act like Joab and kill the conspirators without waiting any more for direction from authority (Collinson 50). The "Bond" promised to defend the legitimate order of gender and of a Protestant Nation with recourse to illegitimate means and in open contradiction to the fundamental hierarchies. "Bifold authority", to use Shakespeare's expression (*Troilus and Cressida*, V, ii, 144), seemed to establish itself to confront most stunningly the official pathos of order. But, as the elite soon realised, the prompting of such irreverent reverence of order was uncalculable. Here, indeed, lurked the possibility of an even far greater danger than the violation of the order of gender: social anomie. In parliament Thomas Digges pointed out the de-stabilising paradox of the "Bond":

"Breefly me thought I did behowld a confuesed company of all partes of the Realme of all degrees and estates then rising in Armes at such a tyme as there is now cowncel of estate in Lyfe, no Lawfull generall, no [...] presidente, no Judges, no sherriffes, no justices, breefly no officers" (Collinson 51). During the last two decades of the century such contradicting discourses were responsible for growing uncertainties and widespread fears, voiced by Shakespeare, too. "Take but degree away," Ulysses warned in *Troilus and Cressida*, "untune that string / And hark what discord follows! each thing meets / In mere oppugnancy [...]" (I, iii, 109-111).

With the "Bond of Association" the discourse about the capabilities of the woman ruler traversed Parliament, to vagabond through streets in town and country. As long as "the gravest heades under the sun" could contain the discourse within parliament, the foundations seemed stable enough to carry the somewhat impaired hierarchical edifice. However, as soon as "meane men" thought themselves called to "shrincke not" to deliver their opinion and "young headdes grew venterous" inside and outside of parliament because they assumed that the "honourable, [...] wyse, [...] grave and grayheadded" had failed to take the heed of the nation, as the ardent Puritan and author of the rebellious Marprelate Tracts, Job Throckmorton, claimed (Hartley II, 311), the elite closed ranks. After the nightmare of a Catholic plot was over - Mary executed, Philipp's Armada dashed - and the Puritan threat contained through the rigorous persecutions of Archbishop Bancroft - nicknamed "Elizabeth's little black husband" - the elite slyly came to terms with having a woman ruler, hiding their somewhat spoiled Tudor reproduction of the cosmic order with a moon at the top of the firmament instead of a bright shining sun behind a screen, painted with the gender neutralising icon of Elizabeth as the "Virgin Queen". But that mainly happened in the years after 1588, when parliamentary politics lost momentum, and a more "scurvy" type of politician, like Ulysses (Harold Bloom), entered the stage, demagogically exploiting the pathos of order without really believing in the intrinsic value of the concept any more.

5. Traditional Precepts and Contemporary Rhetorical Principles

The rise of English as a national standard language in the 16th century, when portrayed in histories of the language, is often seen as a regional process with London and the East Midlands as its centre: "ye shall therefore take the vsuall speach of the Court, and that of London and the shires lying about London within lx. Myles" (Puttenham 157). It is also presented as a socio-economic process of post-Reformation liberation with members of the nobility and gentry at the Tudor Court and upper middle class citizens in London as focal points and linguistic yardsticks. These social strata acquired a new national consciousness which is directly expressed by the high-master of St. Paul's School, Richard Mulcaster, in 1582:

> For is it not in dede a mervellous bondage, to becom servants to one tung for learning sake, the most of our time, with losse of most time, whereas we maie have the verie same treasur in our own tung, with the gain of most time? our own bearing the joyfull title of our libertie and fredom, the Latin tung remembring us of our thraldom and bondage? I love Rome, but London better, I favor Italie, but England more, I honor the Latin, but I worship the English.
> (*The First Part of the Elementarie*, cited from Baugh and Cable 203-204)

Finally the new vernacular norm is frequently depicted as a cultural process with the new print medium and book production as driving forces and the formation of a national literature as its chief result. It is true variation in time, regional and social variation do play a major role in the development of standard English and the codification process runs parallel to the formation of poetic norm and literary canonization. However, discourse rules and textual organisation in factual prose in its various genres were equally important as formative forces. Very little attention has been paid in histories of English to functional variation, to the language of written documents in everyday life, such as contracts, wills, public records and notices, to the language of textbooks, diaries and educational manuals as well as to written language for oral delivery in church and parliament.

English was very much an institutional language, an establishment variety involving the Crown and Parliament, the Anglican Church, Oxbridge, the Chancery and the Inns of Court. The Palace of Westminster was close at hand, and the seat of ecclesiastical power at Canterbury was not far from the City. Puritans among the citizenship attached particularly high esteem to religious discourse and the sermon as central part of Sunday service, which was more or less compulsory, was also valued by the non-puritan Anglican community. The university towns of Oxford and Cambridge were not only near geographically, but also politically as training grounds for successive Lord Keepers, Lord Chancellors, Lord Chamberlains, Speakers of the House of Commons, Privy Councillors, secretaries of state as well as archbishops, bishops, deans and other spiritual advisers to the Crown.

To give an example: Sir Nicholas Bacon (1509-1579) immediately after Queen Elizabeth's accession to the throne in 1558 was made Lord Keeper of the Great Seal, admitted to the Privy Council and given a knighthood. He had received his early education at the abbey school of Bury St. Edmunds and between 1523 and 1527 went to Corpus Christi College, Cambridge, where he graduated B.A. In Cambridge he made friends with William Cecil, later Lord Burghley (1520-1598), who was at St John's College, Cambridge, aged 15 and already highly accomplished in the classical languages. On her accession Queen Elizabeth made him chief secretary of state, a post that gave him power as her most influential political adviser. Bacon and Cecil also made friends with Matthew Parker (1504-1575), who was educated at St. Mary's Hostel, Cambridge, and also went to Corpus Christi College, Cambridge. Early in 1559 he was consecrated archbishop of Canterbury. In this high church office he advocated and advanced Queen Elizabeth's third way in the middle between Romanism and Puritanism.

The Anglican church in abbey schools and grammar schools and the universities in their faculties, adapting to post-Reformation conditions and fashionable humanist influence, were busy exploiting classical educational traditions when

> through the apostleship of Humanists like Roger Ascham, Sir John Cheke, and Sir Thomas Elyot, there came a revival of interest in the pagan literature produced by the classical authors. When Aldus, in 1503, published the works of the chief Greek rhetoricians, classical rhetoric was assured of its share of this renewed interest. The cause of rhetoric was further aided [...] by the direction that men like Erasmus and Vives gave to the curriculum of the English schools. It was not long before rhetoric became the dominant discipline in the Tudor grammar schools and universities. (Corbett and Connors 502)

Due to the influence exercised by Continental scholars like Erasmus, who spent five years in England and among other things prepared rhetorical textbooks for Dean Colet's new school at St. Paul's Cathedral, published in 1512, and the Spaniard Juan Luis Vives, who also lived and worked a few years in England as a lecturer in rhetoric at Oxford, instruction in the first three decades of the century was in Latin. Vives also helped establish the new approach to an English rhetorical curriculum, which gave prominence to *elocutio*, the third part of the rhetorical canon, and to sermons and oratory at the expense of letter-writing.

This was very much in line with the concepts of Pierre Schade alias Petrus Mosellanus (1493-1524), a professor of Greek at Leipzig University, who, with his book *Tabulae de Schematibus et Tropis Petri Mosellani*, "during the first half of the sixteenth century [...] became the standard author on *elocutio* in the English grammar schools" at Eton as early as 1530 (Corbett and Connors 501).

In the same year the first contribution to English vernacular rhetoric was made by the Berkshire schoolmaster Leonard Cox: *Arte or Crafte of Rhetoryke*. He relied heavily on Philippus Melanchthon's *Institutiones Rhetoricae* (1521), which was also widespread in English schools as a textbook with a traditional outlook. As a matter of course Cox followed Melanchthon in putting emphasis on *inventio* and arrangement of the material in contrast to the figurist school which gained some influence in the second half of the century.

The figurist school was represented by the unsuccessful headmaster of Magdalen College School, Richard Sherry, who tried to control the market for school textbooks on schemes and tropes, but found himself thwarted in his efforts by the continuing production of Latin books of continental authors, e. g. Mosellanus and above all others Joannes Susenbrotus's *Epitome Troporum ac Schematum* (Zurich 1540), reprinted eleven times in London between 1562 and 1635 (cf. Plett, *English Renaissance Rhetoric*, 139).

A real success among the vernacular rhetorics, acknowledged to the present day, was Thomas Wilson's *The Arte of Rhetorique* (1553). The three books are characteristic of the best of classical and medieval tradition, convincing in rhetorical doctrine, enriched by personal observation and perceptive comment and written in a straightforward, easily comprehensible and clear language.

Another contemporary success story was George Puttenham's *The Arte of English Poesie* (1589). In the third book of his treatise Puttenham makes a major contribution to rhetorical theory by dealing briefly with the history of rhetoric and linking to it detailed comment on the practical application of rhetorical rules in figurative speeches. He advocates a classification of figures of speech into three groups:

> And that first sort of figures doth serue th'eare onely and may be therefore called *Auricular:* your second serues the conceit onely and not th'eare, and may be called *sensable,* not sensible nor yet sententious: your third sort serues as well th'eare as the conceit and may be called *sententious figures* [...]. (Puttenham 171)

The first group is only important for the poet, whereas the second and third groups are important for the orator. Puttenham warns the public speaker of abuse, but at the same time recommends the sparing and purposeful use of ornamental figurative language to distinguish the language on special occasions from its ordinary use in everyday life.

> Bvt as it hath bene alwayes reputed a great fault to vse figuratiue speaches foolishly and indiscretly, so is it esteemed no lesse an imperfection in mans vtterance, to haue none vse of figure at all, specially in our writing and speaches publike, making them but as our ordinary talke, then which nothing can be more vnsauourie and farre from all ciuilitie. (Puttenham 151)

He mentions Parliament and office holders expressly and allows the printer Richard Field to dedicate the treatise

> TO THE RIGHT HONO
> RABLE SIR VVILLIAM CECILL
> KNIGHT, LORD OF BVRGHLEY, LORD
> HIGH TREASVRER OF ENGLAND [...]

Field continues in his dedication

> [...] and seeing the thing it selfe to be a deuice of some noueltie (which commonly giueth euery good thing a speciall grace) and a noueltie so highly tending to the most worthy prayses of her Maiesties most excellent name (deerer to you I dare conceiue them any worldly thing besides) mee thought I could not deuse to haue presented your Lordship any gift more agreeable to your appetite [...]. (Puttenham 18)

Puttenham also recalls Sir Nicholas Bacon in his book, who had died ten years before its publication, and praises him and Lord Burghley for their rhetorical skill:

> [...] wherein I report me to them that knew Sir *Nicholas Bacon* Lord keeper of the great Seale, or the now Lord Treasorer of England [Lord Burghley], and haue bene conuersant with their speaches made in the Parliament house and Starrechamber. From whose lippes I haue seene to proceede more graue and naturall eloquence, then from all the Oratours of Oxford and Cambridge...I haue come to the Lord Keeper Sir *Nicholas Bacon,* and found him sitting in his gallery alone with the works of *Quintilian* before him, in deede he was a most eloquent man, and of rare learning and wisedome, as euer I knew England to breed [...]. (Puttenham 152)

No doubt the Queen, her ministers and the parliamentarians of the ten Elizabethan Parliaments between 1559 and 1601 must have known and used rhetorics to prepare their orations and other contributions. Opening speeches and speeches at the close of parliament exist in several copies, in shorter and longer versions, in drafts based on briefs by Lord Burghley. Most of them contain alterations, revisions and corrections. The most reliable source with all the alternative readings is Hartley's three volume edition *Proceedings in the Parliaments of Elizabeth I*.

The figurists among the English rhetoricians concentrated on the study of schemes and tropes. In some cases it was their exclusive interest as the long lists of figures in their books demonstrate. Puttenham dealt with 107 figures, Henry Peacham in his *The Garden of Eloquence* (1577) distinguished 184 figures (cf. Corbett and Connors 502ff.).

Modern stylistics tends to concentrate on a smaller number of widely used figures avoiding intricacies and overlappings in classification as much as possible. For a stylistic analysis Nash (1989) suggests the following broad nomenclature for figures of speech:

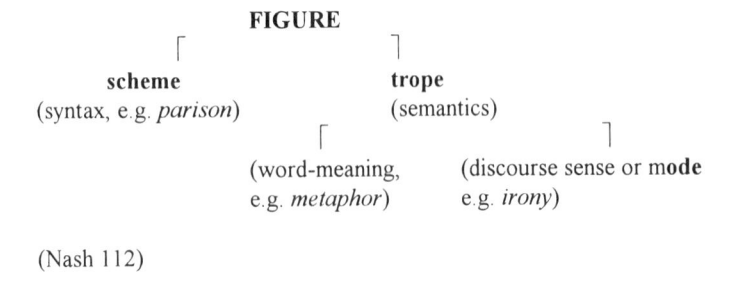

```
                    FIGURE
        ┌─────────────────────┐
      scheme                 trope
 (syntax, e.g. parison)    (semantics)
                   ┌─────────────────────┐
              (word-meaning,       (discourse sense or mode
              e.g. metaphor)        e.g. irony)
```

(Nash 112)

6. Ceremonial Proceedings and Rhetorical Practice

Special occasions and special settings require special language. The opening ceremony of a new parliament is such a special communicative situation. The Queen is present and both houses are assembled to receive her policy instructions for the forthcoming sessions. The herald's account of the opening proceedings of the fourth parliament on 8 May 1572 bears witness to the grandeur and splendour:

> The Quene's Majeste did take her coche at the garden dore of St James and was conveyed thoroughe the parke by her nobles, prelates and gentlemen and ladies *etc.* to White Hall where her Majeste stayed the space of one hower and there put on her robes and a diadeame of gowld with riche stones and jewelles on her hed. This done, she came from her pryve chamber in White Hall with her nobilite thorough the chambers to the hall and so to the common brydge called the Water Gate where her Highenes toke her barge and was rowed to the Kinge's Bridge at Westminster, wheras her coche was reddywith all her nobles and bushops in theyre robes on horsback, all men in order placed. (Hartley I, 267)

A detailed description follows of the Royal household in order of precedence, complete with robes and insignia, proceeding to prayers at the cathedral church of St. Peter in Westminster, choirsinging and a sermon by the Bishop of Lincolne.

In parliament house the Queen was taken to the royal seat, which was prepared with carpets and cushions under a rich cloth of estate.

> Thus her Majeste beinge sett in her chayre of estate th'Erle of Kent with the Hatt standinge on the right hand and the Lord Chamberlen with him, th'Erle of Ruttland and th'Erle of Worcester with the sword and rodd on the left hand, *viz* all placed, the lower howse cam into the same place. The Lord Keeper stode up on the right hand of her Majeste['s] clothe of estate, havinge a place there made for him, began an oration declaringe the cause of her Majeste's sommoninge of this highe court of Parliament: which done the knightes and burgesses beinge appoynted to repayre to the lower howse to chose theyre Speker. (268)

Sir Nicholas Bacon's oration at the beginning of the first parliament on 25 January 1559 is an excellent example of the carefully composed and richly ornamented language fit for the occasion. The form of address and the introduction are conventional:

> My lordes and maisters all: the Queene's most excellent Majestie our naturall and most gratious soveraigne Lady, having as you knowe summoned hether her high courte of Parliament, hath commaunded me to open and declare unto you the chiefe causes and consideracions that moved her Highnes thereunto. (Hartley I, 33)

The orator uses the usual exordial topoi ("circumstances") prescribed by rhetorical doctrine for deliberative speeches: he acts according to orders (*"the Queen has commaunded me"*), he points out the significance of the subject matter (*"the great weightines and worthines of the matter"*, *"the greatnes of such a cause"*), he expresses his inability to treat the matter fairly (*"mine imperfections to do it justice"*, *"mine imperfect and disordered speaking"*) and he demonstrates his determination to do his best (*"good will shall not want in me"*). Giving reasons for calling the parliament is another *locus communis*. The combined knowledge of the assembled parliamentarians on the subject matter must be conveyed to the Queen (*"the immediate causes of this sommons and assembly be consultacion, advise and contentacion"*).

The second paragraph outlines the general plan and composition of the oration, reflecting the arrangement of ideas (*dispositio*) in brief and informative remarks (*propositio*).

> Now the matters and causes whereupon you are to consulte doe chieflye and principally consist in three poyntes. Of theis the first is the well making of lawes for the accordinge and unitinge of the people of this realme into an uniforme order of religion, to the honour and glorie of God, the establishment of his Church and tranquilitie of the realme. The seconde for the reforming and removing of all enormities and mischeifes that doe, or might, hurte or hinder / the civill orders or pollices of this realme. The thirde and last is advisedly and deepely to wey and consider the state and condicion of the realme, and the losses and decayes that have of late happened to the imperiall crowne thereof, and thereuppon to devise the best remedyes to supplie and relieve the same. (34)

The third and the following paragraphs refer back to the three points, with the orator arguing in favour or against aspects in more detail (*confirmatio, refutatio*). Sir Nicholas mentions causes of rejoycing and causes of sadness and discomfort and proceeds to suggest remedies for the latter. The conclusion (*peroratio*) is an appeal to the representatives to do duty:

> Now to make an end, the Queene's Majestie's pleasure is that you, her trustie and welbeloved knightes of her shieres and burgesses, according to your laudable custome shall repayre to your common howse, and there [...] selecte one both grave and discreete, who [...] shall then occupie the office and roome of your common mouth and speaker. (38-39)

Throughout the speech, schemas and tropes are used to establish textual unity, coherence and intrinsic continuity or to emphasize rhetorical organisation, formal cohesion and general ornate presentation. Cross reference and linkage by conjunction and subjunction as well as presentational and psychological sequencing are among the explicit cohesive devices. There is a clear preference for schemas. Quotes and metaphoric imagery are almost totally missing in the Lord Keeper's matter-of-fact approach to the country's problems and the fulfilment of the Queen's wishes and intentions.

The schemas he uses are frequently linear figures of a formal phonological, morphological and syntactic structure:

Progression (repetition, serial links)

On the sound level alliteration and assonance occurs in all word classes:

nouns: *weightines and worthines* (33), *names and nurces* (35), *indeavor and diligence, lawe and ordinaunce, lawes and orders* (192), *tumultes or sturres* (36), *fear and dreade* (33), *honour and glory, order and sorte* (33), *lande, lymme, yea, and lyfe* (37) (with a climax in the three parts);

adjectives and verbs: *pernicious and pestilent* (36), *great and weightie* (38), *abashed and astonied* (33), *hurte or hinder* (34), *sustained and maynteyned*;

collocations: *to be meetest medicine* (33), *forreigne power or potentate* (36), *it must breed in his breast two contrary effectes* (36), *faynte freindes* (37).

On the word, word-group and clause level anaphora and epistrophe are used to convey the three-fold unity of God, Queen and the realm/the individual:

> [...] *ffirst and principallye for the dutie you beare to Gode whose cause this is, and then for the service you owe to her Majestie and your countrie, whose weale it concerneth universallye, and for the love you ought to beare to yourseves whom it toucheth one by one particularly*[...]. (34)

> *Thus forced to this by your duties to God, feared thereto by his punishmentes, provoked by his benefittes, drawen by your love to your countrye and your selves, incouraged by so princely a patronesse, let us in God's name goe about this worke* [...]. (35)

> [...] *I thinke no man so blinde but seeth it, no man so deafe but hath heard it, nor no man so ignorant but understandeth it.* (37)

Opposition (contrast, parallel links)

The creation of opposites, thesis and antithesis, is a very important and frequent operation in Elizabethan parliamentary rhetoric. It is also practised in the essays of Sir Nicholas Bacon's younger son Francis, and its overwrought and bombastic formations are ridiculed in Shakespeare's dramas, e. g. in the linguistic mannerism of the schoolmaster Holofernes in *Love's Labour's Lost*. These figures of counterpoise are semantically linked with figures of equipoise and synonymic linking (coupling). On the word level the encoding devices are antonyms (to express contrariness) and other forms of lexical opposition (to express complementation, direction, etc.), mainly as pairs of two (parison):

whether any lawes be to severe and to sharpe or to softe and to gentle (35), *comforte [...] and discomforte, joy and sadness* (36), *so deare [...] so odible* (36).

On the word-group and clause level the syntactic cohesive devices are corresponding forms such as *more ... than, for one thing ... for another, both ... and, neither ... nor* combined with contrastive conjunctions such as *but, whereas, yet*:

> *[...] meeter for ostentation of witt then consultacion in weightie matters, comelyer for schollers then for counsellors, more beseeminge for schooles then for parliament / houses [...].* (34)

> *But as the causes of our reioysing for such respectes be (thankes be to God) both many and great, so for other respectes the causes of our sadnes and discomfort be neither few nor little.* (36)

Hyperbaton (inversion and insertion, unusual links)

In order to catch or retain the audience's attention, orators in Parliament often use interjections such as *Marye!* (36, 86) *Marry!* (37), *yea* (37), *the more pittie* (38). Another device is the interrruption of the normal flow of speech by parentheses containing

- comments on the subject matter: (*a marvailous matter*) (36), (*a straunge matter and scarse credible*)(38), (*thinges standing as they do*) (38);

- wishes and hopes: *(which our Lord long preserve)*(38), *(for that I can hardly hope of)* (83), *(for I cann hardlie hope of that)* (192);
- exhortations: *(trowe yee)* (85), twice repeated and directed to the audience, *(ye knowe)* (84), *(your wisdomes and good inclinacions considered)* (187);
- hedges and gambits: *I say* (37, 191), *(I truste)* (80, 85), *(as I knowe commonlye they be)* *(as I thinke commonly they be not)* (82), *(I must confesse)* (83), *(me thinkethe)* (81), *Plainelie to speake* (190);
-thanks: *(thankes be to God)* (36), *(God be thanked)* (85, 187), *(God be praised)* (186).

Insertions from a wider intertextual point of view include Latin quotations from classical authors, which are interspersed in the ceremonial addresses by successive Lord Keepers and Speakers. In the pragmatics of quotation (cf. Plett, *Intertextuality* 12 ff.) they answer conventionalised demands and could be classified as both authoritative and erudite, even as ornamental. In a social institution such as parliament the quote often has a ritualised ideological character, i.e. it represents historical and/or political doctrine. The orator Bacon claims authority for authors like Seneca and Juvenal and uses them to prop up his persuasive arguments as chief representative of the Queen. However, he is also a scholar who relies heavily on his academic sources, such as Cicero and Quintilian. Like the authoritative quote it is never attacked or questioned by Bacon; it is normative and always positively contextualised:

Acriores sunt morsus intermissae libertatis quam retentae (83) refers to Cicero *De officiis* II, 24 *(acriores autem morsus sunt intermissae libertatis quam retentae* – 'the sting of temporarily lost freedom is more painful than that of retained freedom'). When he uses the quote again in the third parliament it is changed and partly mutilated *(remissae?)*.
[...] *recti facti merces est fecisse tantum* (86) goes back to Seneca's *Epistolae ad Lucilium* 81, sect. 19/20 'to have done the right deeds is reward enough' and is also changed; *tantum* is added. The rare bird in *rara avis in terris* (86) is proverbial and correctly quoted from Juvenal's *Satires*, VI, 165 (cf. also Horace *Satires* II, 2, 26 where it is the peacock).

Sometimes, one may suspect, the Latin quote is purely ornamental and serves no other purpose than to delight the audience, because an English paraphrase follows or precedes the Latin decoration, e.g. Cicero's *dare verba* (86) – 'empty words, wind'. The quote loses ist persuasive force when it is used again and again in differing contexts, e. g. *gladius gladium iuvabit* (82) – 'the sword will support the sword' in 1562 in the second parliament and in 1571 in the third parliament: *gladius gladium iuvaret* (183); *ultra posse non est esse* (86) – 'nothing exists beyond capability' in 1562 and again in 1571. Obviously all the quotations are commonly known and widely employed tags. The orators are not accurate in rendering their sources. Word order is freely changed, adverbs dropped or added and morphological endings adapted to personal whim.

Semantic linking is restricted to the use of figures that do not transfer concepts by comparison or metaphor but rather emphasize an idea by giving semantically similar or contingent structures coupled in pairs of two (*hendiadys*) or in pairs of three (*oratio trimembris*). The Elizabethan age makes full use of the abundance of new vocabulary from Latin directly or from Latin via French which arrived during the 15th and 16th centuries. The culmination point of lexical importation was reached at the end of Elizabeth's reign. Tropes, which play on the sense of words, are the most frequently applied, perhaps also the most powerful and certainly the most characteristic figures in Elizabethan prose. The amassing of synonymic variants, words of native Germanic origin and Norman French and late Latin borrowings occurs in all content word classes. Hendiadys is used both to paraphrase new and less familiar vocabulary with well-known everyday counterparts and to emphasise important concepts by repetition in coupled or tripartite combinations.

Paired nouns: *some comfort and encouring* (33), *this sommons and assembly* (33), *the accordinge and unitinge of the people* (34), *contentacion by assente and suertie by advise* (34), *chaunge and alteracion* (34), *your assemblye and conference* (34), *disorder and offence* (35), *the inclination and disposition of the people* (35), *any bondage or servitude* (35), *sores and woundes* (36), *decaye and waste* (37), *griefe and torment* (38).
Paired adjectives: *neither unmindfull nor uncarefull* (34), *most certaine and stable* (34), *her trustie and welbeloved knightes* (38).
Paired verbs: *abasshed and astonied* (33), *to be erected and builte, to be directed and governed, to be sustayned and maynteyned* (34), *meaneth and*

intendeth (34, 36), *to breede or nourishe* (35), *lament and bewayle* (36), *hath preserved and guarded* (37).
Paired adverbs: *sufficiently and fully* (34), *chieflye and principally* (34), *deliberately and advisedlie* (38).

Triads for amplification:
Nouns: *majestie, honor and understanding* (33), *consultacion, advise and contentacion* (33), *fidelities, wisedomes and discretions* (34), *honour, rule and soveraignetie* (34), *profitt, pleasure or ease* (34), *witt, learninge or knowledge* (34), *humblenes, singlenes and purenes of minde* (34), *causers, continuers and increasers of displeasure, hate and malice* (35).
Adjectives: *sophisticall, captious and frivolous arguments* (34), *contentious, contumelious or opprobrious wordes* (35).
Verbs: *debated, examined and considered* (34).
Adverbs: *soe lovingly, carefully and prudentlie* (38).

In contrast to ceremonial addresses normal speeches depend much more on personal conviction; they have emotional and ethical appeal rather than rational persuasive force. Excellent examples are the speeches made by the Puritan opposition in the Commons on controversial subjects such as Peter Wentworth's oration on freedom of speech in 1576, for which he was imprisoned in the Tower, Job Throckmorton's speech against Mary Queen of Scots in 1586, his speech on the Bill and Book (religious freedom) in 1587, and Henry Jackman's speech on the bill against foreigners in England in 1589.

The schemes in quantity are more or less the same as in speeches on formal occasions. Tropes, particularly similes and metaphors, are far more frequent. However, the character of the speeches in general is different. Throckmorton acts like the counsel for the prosecution in court or a clergyman giving a passionate sermon to a Sunday congregation using very frequently quotations from the Bible and allusions to Biblical events. These quotes are mainly authoritative; a wide scope of validity and legitimacy is claimed by the orators. Some others are erudite or purely ornamental. Pathos, ethos and logos alternate in Jackman's very fervent personal speech (cf. Hartley II, 480ff.). The design of the often bitter and sharp speeches against Mary Queen of Scots demanded different stylistic ways and means from ceremonial addresses. The atmosphere in the House was often emotional: "Proceedings could be noisy and disorderly. Unpopular speeches were subjected to loud chatter, 'hemming', laughing, coughing, hawking and even spitting" (Graves 67). Ornate orations and well-mannered, decorous assemblies had their unpleasant and undesirable counterparts in sharp and bitter speeches with naming names in personal attacks on individuals, irrelevant, tactless remarks and riotous interruptions or deliberate and mindless filibustering.

To the Elizabethan orators and parliamentarians "language was God's great gift, the capacity for eloquent speech the property that made men and women, of all creatures, the most nearly divine. All their debates were essentially variations on the problem of power, discussions of how the possibilities of the word might most effectively be harnessed" (McDonald 29). Rhetoric is a political instrument, not in the first place to encourage and promote free debate and useful discussion, but rather to impress, control, manipulate and ultimately vanquish rivals and antagonists. Wayne A. Rebhorn very nicely sums it up: "At its core, then, Renaissance rhetoric is animated by a fantasy of power in which the orator, wielding words more deadly than swords, takes on the world and emerges victorious in every encounter" (15).

Works Cited

"An Exhortation to Obedience." *Certain Sermons or Homilies. A Critical Edition.* Ed. Ronald B. Bond. Toronto: U of Toronto P, 1987. 161-73.

Aylmer, John. *An Harborowe for Faithfull and Trewe Subjects Against the Late Blown Blast Concerning the Government of Women.* Strassbourg [i.e. London: John Day], 1559.

Baugh, Albert C., and Thomas Cable. *A History of the English Language.* [1951] 3rd and rev. ed. London: Routledge, 1978.

Carter, Ronald, and Walter Nash. *Seeing Through Language.* Oxford: Blackwell, 1990.

Certain Sermons or Homilies Appointed to be Read in Churches In the Time of Queen Elizabeth. London: Published by Authority for the Use of Churches and Private Families, 1757.

Collinson, Patrick. "The Monarchical Republic of Queen Elizabeth I." Patrick Collinson. *Elizabethan Essays.* London and Rio Grande: The Hambledon Press, 1994. 31-58.

Corbett, E. P., and R. J. Connors. *Classical Rhetoric for the Modern Student.* New York: Oxford UP, 1999.
Elton, Geoffrey Rudolf. *The Parliament of England, 1559-1581.* Cambridge: Cambridge UP, 1989.
Fletcher, Anthony. *Gender, Sex & Subordination in England 1500-1800.* New Haven: Yale UP, 1995.
Gelfert, Hans-Dieter. *Shakespeare.* München: Beck, 2000.
Gilkes, Rosslyn Kaye. *The Tudor Parliament.* London: London UP, 1969.
Graves, Michael A. R. *Elizabethan Parliaments 1559-1601.* London: Longman, 1987.
Haigh, Christopher. *Elizabeth I.* London: Addison Wesley Publishing Co., 2000.
Hartley, Terry E., ed. *Proceedings in the Parliaments of Elizabeth I.* 3 vols. Leicester: Leister UP, 1981-1995.
Hartley, Terry E. *Elizabeth's Parliaments: Queen, Lords and Commons, 1559-1601.* Manchester: Manchester UP, 1995.
Hooker, John. "Order and Usage." *Parliament in Elizabethan England. John Hooker's Order and Usage.* Ed. Vernon F. Snow. New Haven, CT: Yale UP, 1977. 145-204.
Knox, John. "The First Blast of the Trumpet" [1558]. *John Knox. On Rebellion.* Ed. Roger A. Mason. Cambridge: Cambridge UP, 1994. 3-47.
Lovejoy, Arthur O. *The Great Chain of Being.* The William James Lectures Delivered at Harvard University, 1933. [1936] 2nd print, Cambridge, MA: Harvard UP, 1942.
McDonald, Russ. *Shakespeare and the Arts of Language.* Oxford: Oxford UP, 2001.
McLaren, A. N. *Political Culture in the Reign of Elizabeth I. Queen and Commonwealth, 1558-1585.* Cambridge: Cambridge UP, 1999.
Metzger, Hans-Dieter. "David und Saul in Staats- und Widerstandslehren der Neuzeit." *David.* Ed. Walter Dietrich and Hubert Herkommer. Fribourgh: Universitäts-Verlag (forthcoming).
Nash, Walter. *Rhetoric.* Oxford: Blackwell, 1989.
Plett, Heinrich F., ed. *Intertextuality.* Berlin: Walter de Gruyter, 1991.
Plett, Heinrich F. *English Renaissance Rhetoric and Poetics: A Systematic Bibliography of Primary and Secondary Sources.* Leiden: Brill, 1995.
Puttenham, George. *The Arte of English Poesie.*[1589] Carefully edited by Edward Arber. London: 87 St. Augustine Road, Camden Square, N.W., 1869.
Rebhorn, Wayne A.. *The Emperor of Men's Minds: Literature and the Discourse of Rhetoric.* Ithaka: Cornell UP, 1995.
Ronan, Clifford J. "Daniel, Rainolde, Demosthenes, and the Degree Speech of Shakespeare's Ulysses." *Renaissance and Reformation.* N.S. 9 (1985): 111-18.
Smith, Sir Thomas. *De Republica Anglorum.* Ed. Mary Dewar. Cambridge: Cambridge UP, 1984.
Suerbaum, Ulrich. *Das elisabethanische Zeitalter.* Stuttgart: Reclam, 1989.
Tillyard, Eustace M. W. *The Elizabethan World Picture.* Harmondsworth: Penguin, 1979.

Man's View of His World in *Beowulf*

Annemarie Hindorf

Much has been written about *Beowulf*, the longest heroic poem in Old English, in the last hundred and twenty-five years; and it is doubtful if anybody could read everything there is to be read, and if it is still possible to think or say anything about *Beowulf* that has not been thought or said before. Nevertheless, an attempt will be made here to show how the unknown *Beowulf*-poet presents man's view of the world in which he lives. According to Robinson

> Understanding literature from another time and land is an exercise in projecting ourselves imaginatively into other people's minds and lives and language. It is this exercise that constitutes one of the greatest rewards of literary study, as one thinks one's way into a different time and a different world from one's own. The world of *Beowulf* is worth the effort. (51)

The world the *Beowulf*-poet describes must even at that time have been remote for his contemporaries and is even more remote and strange in comparison with the world in which we live.

What then did the poet see as characteristic of that world?

1. God's Gifts to Man

We are told by the Anglo-Saxon poet that Beowulf and his contemporaries believed that the world was created by God (although not necessarily by the Christian God), who erected heaven as a vault (*heofones hwealf*, 576) above the beautifully bright plain of the earth, which he surrounded by a ring of water:

cwæð þæt sē Ælmihtiga   eorðan worhte,
wlite-beorhtne wang,   swā wæter bebūgeð; (Wrenn, *Beowulf* 92-93)

While telling of the creation of the world, the *scop* in Hrothgar's hall mentions that God made everything beautiful:

ond gefrætwade   foldan scēatas
leomum ond lēafum   (96-97)

But God's most important gift to the world was light, especially that of the sun, 'heaven's candle' or 'God's beacon':

gesette sige-hrēþig   sunnan ond mōnan
lēoman to lēohte   landbūendum, (94-95)

...   Lēoht ēastan cōm,
beorht bēacen Godes;   ... (569-570)

God is the giver of everything, he is the creator (*scyppend*) and the life-giver (*līf-frēa*). He is the father of all creation (*fæder alwalda*):

...   līf ēac gesceōp
cynna gewhylcum,   þāra ðe cwice hwyrfaþ. (97-98)

He regulates the seasons of the year:

ðonne forstes bend   Fæder onlǣteð
onwindeð wǣl-rāpas,   sē geweald hafað
sǣla ond mǣla;   þæt is sōð Metod.. (1609-1611)

God is the king and protector of the heavens (*heofona cyning, heofena helm*), a wise god (*wītig god*) and the eternal liege-lord of man (*ēce drihten*). He is also the judge of all actions (*dǣda dēmend*):

Wolde dōm Godes   dǣdum rǣdan
gumena gewhylcum,   swā hē nū gēn dōið. (2858-2859)

God rewards the good (*woruld-āre forgeaf,* 17) and punishes the evil (*hē him ðæs lēan forgeald,* 114).

Throughout the poem God and the old Germanic fate (*wyrd*) seem to be parallel forces. On the one hand, God is said to be *ælmihtig* and the one who metes out fate (*metod*), e.g. when he does not allow Grendel to commit more atrocities:

    ... *swā hē hyra mā wolde,*
 nefne him wītig God wyrd forstōde (1055-1056)

On the other hand, equal or possibly even greater power is sometimes ascribed to *wyrd*:

    ... *Wyrd oft nereð*
 unfǣgne eorl, þonne his ellen dēah. (572-573)

    ... *hine wyrd fornam.* (1205)

Life is only a temporary loan, and when a man comes to the end of his life on earth (*ende gefēred lǣnan līfes*, 2844-2845), he gives himself up into God's keeping, but he does so at a time predestined by fate (*gescæp-hwīl*):

Him ðā Scyld gewāt tō gescæp-hwīle,
fela-hrōr, fēran on Frēan wǣre. (26-27)

2. The Achievements of Man

God has created the world and peopled it with animals and human beings. The achievement of man is the creation of useful artefacts, and these man-made things are always spoken of with approval, even with love and reverence, because they are reassuring signs of man's ability to tame nature and impose order on a former wilderness.

Although men have begun to build roads to get more quickly and safely from one human habitation to another, in Anglo-Saxon times paved streets are still rare, and the seemingly endless Roman roads still a thing of wonder.

Strǣt was stān-fāh, stīg wīsode
gumum ætgædere. (320-321)

The hall is not only the centre of community life, but also a place of security for the people inside. The halls of kings are, of course, more imposing than others and Hrothgar's hall the most splendid of all:

    ... *oþþæt hȳ sæl timbred,*
geatolīc ond gold-fāh ongyton mihton;
þæt wæs fore-mǣrost fold-būendum
receda under roderum, on þǣm sē rīca bād;

līxte sē lēoma   ofer landa fela. (307-311)

Inside the hall the warriors sit down to their meals or banquets (*symbel*), and the poet dwells lovingly on the beautiful beakers and other drinking-vessels in which mead and beer are served.

As Anglo-Saxon society was a warrior society, which was based on the concept of voluntary companionship rather than subservience, weapons were of tremendous importance, and the poet's Anglo-Saxon audience fully understood this angle of Beowulf's world.

Every warrior possessed a spear and shield. Spears made of ash-wood were especially prized (*æsc-holt ufan græg*, 330). Shields were necessary for defence, and their metal buckles shone like gold in the sun (*beorhte randas*, 231; *fætte scyldas*, 333).

Swords, helmets and mail-shirts were worn only by the noble or wealthy warrior because they were very valuable, as they had often been made by famous smiths (*smiþes orþanc*, 406; *Wēlandes geweorc*, 455) or even by some long-departed giants (*eald-sweord eotenisc*, 1558), and they were handed down from generation to generation (*Hrædlan lāf*, 454; *ealde lāfe*, 795; *yrfe-lāfe*, 1053). The damascened swords (*hyrsted*, 672; *āter-tānum fāh*, 1489; *wǣg-sweord*, 1489) were certainly *dēor* and therefore often given names. Unferth's sword is named *Hrunting*, the sword with which Beowulf fights the dragon *Nægling*.

The valuable helmets were gold-adorned, and there were also those with mask-protection (*grīm-helmas*, 334) or with protective animal ornaments:

```
        ...         Eofor-līc scionon
ofer hlēor-bergan:    gehrōden golde,
fāh ond fȳr-heard,    ferh-wearde hēold:  (303-305)
```

Protection against all kinds of antagonistic forces was a necessity. Streets, halls and weapons were a defence on land. To conquer the sea, man needed ships. The crossing of the sea was a dangerous but necessary undertaking, and the ships had to be strong enough to withstand the turbulent waves and the storms at sea. Those were the days when a leader of men had to be a *lagu-cræftig mon* (209). Ships as symbols of human skill and endurance feature prominently in the poem. Apart from near synonyms, such as *scip*, *bāt*, *flota*, *naca*, *stefn*, *fær*, other more picturesque and reverential descriptions and kennings are used, such as *ȳð-lida* (wave-traverser), *sund-wudu* (sea-wood), *wudu bundene* (joined / adorned wood), *bront cēol* (high keel), *wunden-stefn* (curved prow), *hringed stefn* (ring-prow), *flota fāmī-heals* (foamy-necked floater*), wudu wunden-heals* (wood with curved neck). Even the dead were sometimes put on board funeral ships and consigned to the care of the sea (*on flodes ǣht*, 42):

> ālēdon þā   lēofne þēoden
> bēaga bryttan   on bearm scipes,
> mǣrne be mǣste;   ...   (34-35)

3. The Threat of Untamed Nature

Man had enforced order only on a very small part of his world, and nature outside this small circle of human habitation was still untamed and mysterious and therefore to be feared by man:

> [...] the *eormengrund*, the great earth, ringed with *garsecg*, the shoreless sea, beneath the sky's inaccessible roof; whereon, as in a little circle of light about their halls, men with courage as their stay went forward to that battle with the hostile world and the offspring of the dark which ends for all, even the kings and champions, in defeat. (Tolkien 18)

Their earth was surrounded by the vast and dangerous sea. Descriptions of the sea deal with the waves (*ȳþas*), the ocean streams (*lagu-strēamas*) and the flood (*flōd*). The ships ride on the back of the sea (*ofer geofenes begang*, 362; *ofer wæteres hrycg*, 471), but as the sea is the realm of sea animals, the sea is also called *hron-rād* (whale-road) or *swan-rād* (swan-road) or compared to a warrior with white foam spears (*gār-secg*). How much the sea appeared to be a threat to mankind - especially in winter, with the cold North wind blowing - becomes evident in Beowulf's swimming contest with Breca, son of the chief of the Brondingas:

>   ...   Geofon ȳþum wēol,
> wintrys wylmum;   ... (515-516)
>
> wado weallende,   wedera cealdost,
> nīpende niht,   ond norþan wind
> heaðo-grim ondhwearf.   Hrēo wǣron ȳþa,
> wæs mere-fixa   mōd onhrēred. (546-549)

But not only sea-animals including such awe-inspiring beings as *hron-fixas* (whale-fish) live in the sea, there are also sea-monsters, such as *niceras* (water-demons), *wyrm-cynnes fela* (a multitude of races of serpents) and *sǣ-dracan* (sea-serpents).

On land, the moor is eerie. Everything there is enshrouded in mist (*mistige mōras*, 162). What is hidden from sight is mysterious (*dȳgel lond*, 1357), and the shapes looming out of the mist engender fear. But the dread of the unseen and unknown is not the only reason to fear the moors and the fens - it is here that the monsters, the ancient and timeless enemies of mankind, have their haunts. The poet says of Grendel:

> *Wæs sē grimma gǣst   Grendel hāten,*
> *mǣre mearc-stapa,   sē þe mōras hēold,*
> *fen ond fæsten;   fifel-cynnes eard*
> *won-sǣlī wer   weardode hwīle.* (102-105)
>
> *Ðā cōm of mōre   under mist-hleoþum*
> *Grendel gongan,   Godes yrre bær;* (710-711)

We are told that all the monsters are the offspring of Cain (*Caines cynn*, 107):

> *Þanon untȳdras   ealle onwōcon,*
> *eotenas ond ylfe   ond orcnē-as,*
> *swylce gīgantas,   þā wið Gode wunnon*
> *lange þrāge;   ...* (111-114)

Ever since Cain slew Abel, they have all been banned from the paths of mankind. In their various forms as *untȳdras* (wicked offspring, evil progeny), *eotenas* (giants, monsters), *þyrsas* (demons, giants), *orcnē-as* (evil spirits of the dead), etc. they have to live in the wastelands (*wēsten warode*, 1265), in the fens and on the moors. And when they are finally banned from the world of men, their heathen souls will go to *dēop hell*, as we are told when Grendel dies for his sins:

> *...   syðða dreāma lēas,*
> *in fen-freoðo   feorh ālegde,*
> *hǣþene sāwle;   þǣr him hel onfēng.* (850-852)

The darkness is the only friend of the monsters, who shun the light and hide from it (*sē ellen-gǣst, ... sē þe in þȳstrum bād*, 86-88). But during the absence of light, at night, they venture out of their dwellings to threaten and kill. Therefore it is only at night that the murderous, sinister Grendel dares attack the hall:

> *Gewāt ðā nēosian,   syþðan niht becōm,*
> *hēan hūses*   (115-116)

> *dēogol dǣd-hata   deorcum nihtum*
> *ēawed þurh egsan   uncūðne nīð,*
> *hȳnðu ond hrā-fyl.*   (275-277)

As Grendel's mother and the dragon only sally forth upon their vengeful raids after the sun has set, it seems that the powers of all the monsters are restricted to the hours of darkness (*niht-bealwa mǣst*, 193). With the coming of light in the morning their powers wane, and they have to retrace their steps to wherever they can hide.

As mentioned before, the world outside the small circle of human civilization is still unexplored and widely unknown, and is therefore a constant threat. This dread of untamed nature is revealed first by the taciturn reference to the child Scyld Scefing being sent on his way to face the forces of nature alone:

> *... þe hine æt frumsceafte   forð onsendon*
> *ǣnne ofer ȳðe   umborwesende.* (45-46)

It is even more forcibly expressed by Hrothgar's tale of the Grendel mere:

> ...   *Hīe dȳgel lond*
> *warigeað, wulf-hleoþu,   windige nǣssas,*
> *frēcne fen-gelād,   ðǣr fyrgen-strēam*
> *under nǣssa genipu   niþer gewīteð,*
> *flōd under foldan.   Nis þæt feor heonon*
> *mīl-gemearces,   þæt sē mere standeð*
> *ofer þǣm hongiað   hrinde bearwas;*
> *wudu wyrtum fæst   wæter oferhelmað.*
> *Þǣr mæg nihta gehwǣm   nīð-wundor sēon,*
> *fȳr on flōde;   nō þæs frōd leofað*
> *gumena bearna   þæt þone grund wite.*
> *Ðēah þe hǣð-stapa   hundum geswenced,*
> *heorot hornum trum   holt-wudu sēce,*

feorran geflȳmed,   ǣr hē feorh seleð,
aldor on ōfre,   ǣr hē in wille,
hafelan hȳdan.   Nis þæt hēoru stōw;
þonon ȳð-geblond   ūp āstīgeð
won tō wolcnum,   þonne wind styreþ
lāð gewidru,   oðþæt lyft ðrysmaþ,
roderas rēotað.   ... (1357-1376)

> [They live in a land of mysterious secrecy, slopes haunted by wolves, wind-swept headlands, a terrifying region which crosses the fenlands where the mountain torrent goes deep down neath the mist-covered rocks, in a flood under the earth. It is not far from thence in measured miles that there stands the mere, above which there overhang thickets of bushes covered in hoar-frost: and the water is shadowed above by densely-rooted forest. At that place every night is to be beheld a mysteriously terrifying sight, fire upon the water. There is none of those wise in age among the children of man who knows its depth. Even though the stag who traverses the heath strong in his horns may seek the forest when hard pressed by hounds from afar in flight, he will give up his life on the mere's bank before he will dive in to hide his head. That is not a place of pleasantness. From there the swirling of the waves rises up beneath the clouds when the wind stirs up horrible storms, till the air becomes choking mist and the skies weep.] (Wrenn, *Literature* 114-115)

Safety on earth is still precarious and the life of man always threatened by malignant nature.

> A light starts - *lixte se leoma ofer landa fela* - and there is a sound of music; but the outer darkness and its hostile offspring lie ever in wait for the torches to fail and the voices to cease. (Tolkien 33)

4. Dualism and Contrast

The world of *Beowulf* is characterized by dualism and contrast. Throughout the poem the contrast between man-made order and untamed nature appears as an opposition of light and darkness, sound and silence, society and solitary existence.

Home is safe and sweet (*swǣsne ēðel*, 520) because it is in that part of the world where man has imposed order. Whatever is familiar and known, be it the way back from the Grendel mere (*cūþe strǣt*, 1634) or the welcome sight of the cliffs of the Geats' homeland (*cūþe næssas*, 1912), is often seen as

bright (*beorht*), intrinsically good, desirable and useful. That part of the world, however, where the rule of man is not yet accepted, is usually described as dark, evil, or at least useless.
Light and the gold-shining beauty of *Heorot* are contrasted with the dark:

> *sinc-fāge sel   sweartum nihtum* (167)

As soon as Grendel rules in *Heorot* the golden hall becomes *īdel ond unnyt* (485) for men.

Beowulf's world is full of sounds.
We hear the roar of the burning funeral pyre (*wæl-fȳra mæst, hlynode for hlāwe,* 1119-1120) and listen to the terrible noise attending Beowulf's fights with the monsters. During his fight with Grendel the hall groans (*Dryht-sele dynede,* 767; *Reced hlynsode;* 770), and during his fight with the dragon the earth itself resounds (*hrūse dynede,* 2558).
Armour and weapons give off bell-like sounds, as they ring and sing:

> ...   *byrnan hringdon,* (327)
> ...   *hring-īren scīr*
> *song in searwum.*   ... (323-324)

Even more space in the poem is given to elaborate conversations and the description of all kinds of communicative sounds, whether it is the merry noise of feasting in the hall:

> ...   *þǣr wæs hæleða drēam* (497)
>
> *Ðǣr wæs hælepa hleahtor,   hlyn swynsode,*
> *word wǣron wynsume.   ...* (611-612)

the voice of Beowulf calling forth the dragon to the fight:

> *Let ðā of brēostum,   ðā hē gebolgen wæs,*
> *Weder-Gēata lēod   word ūt faran,*
> *stearc-heort styrmde;   stefn in becōm*
> *heaðo-torht hlynnan   under hārne stān..* (2550-2553)

or voices raised in a sad lament for the loss of loved ones:

> ... *wōp ūp āhafen,*
> *micel morgen- swēg.* (128-129)

> ... *ides gnornode,*
> *geōmrode giddum.* (1117-1118)

Yet this need for communicative interaction seems to be restricted to mankind; the monsters, apparently, can do without. It is only when mortally wounded and despairing of life, that Grendel cries out in pain and terrifies the listeners outside the hall with his frightening death-song:

> ... *wōp gehȳrdon,*
> *gryre-lēoð galan   Godes andsacan,*
> *sige-lēasne sang,* .... (128-129)

Grendel's mother never utters a word, nor does the dragon.

As all Cain's offspring were condemned to flee whatever man delights in (*man-drēam flēohan*, 1264), Grendel cannot bear the merry voices and the music in the hall:

> *þæt hē dōgora gehwām   drēam gehȳrde*
> *hlūdne in healle;   þǣr wæs hearpan swēg,*
> *swutol sang scopes.* (88-90)

A monster obviously keeps to himself and leads a solitary and cheerless existence devoid of companionable sound.

Man, however, is a social being. The joys of shared companionship are mentioned several times. Beowulf is a mighty hero, but he still sets out on his voyage *fīf-tȳna sum* (207) - as one of fifteen. Even a born leader, a lord or king, must have his following (*wil-gesīþas*, 23; *swǣse gesīþas*, 29); and the lives of his followers are centred on their lord (*lēof land-fruma*, 31; *lēof þēoden*, 34). Only a king who upholds order and provides places of safety for his people is a *gōd cyning*.

Men share food and drink in the lord's hall:

> ... *hū hit Hring-Dene*
> *æfter bēor-þege   gebūn hæfdon.* (116-117)

Grendel, on the other hand, is the *atol ān-genga* (165), who lives and eats alone. He carries his loathsome food back to his lair:

>   ... *þanon eft gewāt*
> *hūðe-hrēmig   tō hām faran,*
> *mid þǣre wæl-fylle   wīca nēosian.* (123-125)

The one exception is his hasty and solitary meal within the hall of men, when he gulps down one of the warriors before he meets his well-deserved end at Beowulf's hands.
Anyhow, the basic isolation of Grendel and the dragon is made clear to us by their being mentioned as *ān*, before we learn who this *ān* is:

> *Swā ðā driht-guman   drēamum lifdon,*
> *ēadiglīce,   oððæt ān ongan*
> *fyrene fremman   fēond on helle.* (99-101)

>   ... *oððæt ān ongan*
> *deorcum nihtum,   draca ricsian*
> *sē ðe on hēaum hofe   hord beweotode,*
> *stān-beorh stēapne;*   (2210-2213)

The fact of Grendel's being a solitary enemy of all men is again emphasized when his nightly reign over Heorot is mentioned:

> *Swā rīxode   ond wið rihte wan*
> *āna wið eallum,   oððæt īdel stōd*
> *hūsa sēlest.*   ..... (144-146)

The oppositions of light and darkness, sound and silence, society and solitude are elaborated on, whereas other contrasts can only be understood by inference.
Light as God's gift to mankind is beautiful, but the light of Grendel's eyes is horrible (*ligge gelīcost lēoht unfǣger*, 727) as it stands for the ancient evil.

The cold outside is hateful to man, but there is never any reference to a warming fire in the hall. The only fires referred to are the fire that will eventually destroy Hrothgar's hall Heorot (*heoðo-wylma bād, lāðan līges*, 82-83), the fire under the flood in the sinister mere (*fȳr on flōde*, 1366), the fire of the dragon (*sē ðe byrnende biorgas sēceð, nacod nīð-draca, nihtes flēogeð fȳre befangen*, 2272-2274), the funeral pyre (*Hēt ðā Hildeburh æt Hnæfes āde ... bān-fatu bærnan ond on bǣl dōan.* 1114-1116) and the hell-fire awaiting the souls lured away by the devil (*Wā bið þǣm ðe sceal þurh slīðne nīð sāwle bescūfan in fȳres fæþm*, 183-185), all signifying threatening and anguishing experiences.

5. Man's Acceptance of His Fate

Again and again we are told that limits are set upon the knowledge and understanding of man, that people do not know the bottom of the Grendel mere (*nō þæs frōd leofað gumena bearna þæt þone grund wite.* 1366-1367), nor the way into the dragon's lair (*stīg under læg eldum uncūð;* 2213-2214). Of course, men may hazard a guess, but they cannot know the truth or speak truthfully about what is hidden from them, as e.g. where hell's councillors (*hel-rūnan*) wander (*men ne cunnon hwyder hel-rūnan hwyrftum scrīþað.* 162-163); and least of all do they know their own fate or that of other people (*wyrd ne cūðon*, 1233).

But even if people cannot know what will happen after Scyld's death to him and his funeral ship:

>   *Men ne cunnon*
> *secgan tō sōðe,   sele-rǣdende,*
> *hæleð under heofenum,   hwā þǣm hlæste onfēng.* (50-52)

there is still hope that his soul and their own souls will finally be safe in God's keeping:
>   *Wēl bið þǣm þe mōt*
> *æfter dēað-dæge   Drihten sēcean*
> *ond tō Fæder fæþmum   freoðo wilnian!* (186-188)

Death is the fate of man and the reward of heroes - this seems to be the generally accepted view in Beowulf's world and perhaps even in the Anglo-Saxon world.

> [...] we may remember that the poet of *Beowulf* saw clearly: The wages of heroism is death. (Tolkien 26)

It is only the hero's impressive deeds that live on in the memory of later generations, his fame that survives after he himself has died.

God has ordered the lives of men in the past and will go on doing so in the time to come:

   ... *Metod eallum wēold*
   gumena cynnes, *swā hē nū gīt dōið.* (1057-1058)

Since God has created this world and rules there as seems best to him (*swā him gemet þince*, 707), all that is left to man is acceptence of his fate and of life in all its manifestations (cf. Alexander 28):

Gǣð ā wyrd swā hīo scel! (455)

The *Beowulf*-poet tells of man's joy in God's gifts and his acceptance of God's judgement, of man's pride in his own achievements and his dread of the hostile wilderness.

Remote and strange as Beowulf's world may be found to be, any attempt, however limited, at gaining further insight into how Beowulf and his contemporaries might have perceived their own world, unveils another layer of the intricately woven tapestry of the poem - and this is probably a reward in itself (cf. Robinson 51).

Works Cited

Alexander, Michael. *Beowulf. A Verse Translation.* Harmondsworth: Penguin Books Ltd., 1984.
Beowulf. With the Finnesburg Fragment. Ed. Charles Leslie Wrenn. London: Harrap, 1953.
Robinson, Fred C. *The Tomb of Beowulf and Other Essays on Old English.* Oxford: Blackwell, 1993.
Tolkien, James R.R. *The Monsters and the Critics.* Edited by Christopher Tolkien. London: George Allan & Unwin, 1983.
Wrenn, Charles Leslie. *A Study of Old English Literature.* London: Harrap, 1967.

Black Vernacular English and the Feature of Ethnicity

Werner Plehn

Black Vernacular English (BVE) has always been felt to be different from other dialects of English in many respects. To a large extent, this has to do with the social role its speakers have had to play on the American continent since their first arrival. As slaves in colonial times, black people were treated differently from white servants and their inferior position in comparison with that of the whites gave room to the development of a special racial feeling, which Howard Zinn describes as a "combination of inferior status and derogatory thought" (23). Thus, attitudes towards this race also mark its language and they are hardly based on the physical differences of its speakers but rather on aspects of racism connected with the low social status of this ethnic group.

Since research on BVE began on a large scale about 40 years ago it has not lost its attractiveness. Topics like the origin of this linguistic variant, aspects of its present development in terms of convergence or divergence from standard English, or the support of the Oakland Unified School District Board of Education in 1996 (cf. Wolfram 18) to use BVE at school as a bridge to learning standard English have led to heated and controversial debates which are still going on. In all of these discussions, the ethnic identification of this dialect takes a prominent position.

1. Terminology and Ethnic Reference

Starting with different designations of this variety, an ethnic reference, though mainly aiming at skin colour, is quite obvious. This extralinguistic factor is chosen over and over again to name this dialect. In older publications on this subject, terms like *Negro dialect, Negro English, American Negro English* or *Non-standard Negro English* (cf. Ewers 11;

Rickford, AAVE xxi) were applied, emphasising the ethnic component by using the word *Negro* besides marking this variety as non-standard. Designations like these contain connotations which very clearly reflect social attitudes. The term *Negro* itself, although used with pride by black people during the Civil War and Reconstruction periods, is strongly associated with slavery and thus connected with a negative connotation (cf. Gester 55; Dillard, *Black English* 190-191). Combinations with dialect as in *Negro Dialect* often amplify this connotation, for dialect is a loaded term and often used for varieties with a very low prestige.

The switch to *black* as an element in designations of this variety marks a further stage in an ethnic identification. Here, we find terms like *Black Dialect*, *Black Folk Speech*, *Black Language*, *Non-standard Black English* or *Black Vernacular English*. Of these, the shortened form *Black English* is still popular. The change from *Negro* to *black* may be seen as a development in attitude. Especially in the 1960s, caused by a changing social climate in regard to African-Americans in the USA, the word *black* gained a positive connotation. Slogans like *Black Power* or *Black is Beautiful* contributed to this development. However, *Black English* is far from being an accepted term for this variety. First, the direct reference to the skin colour is sometimes felt as an abuse and second, it is still misleading as there are also standard Black English varieties (Weber 419).

Afro-American English or *African-American English* and *Ebonics* (a blend of ebony and phonics) are other designations of this variety nowadays. Here, an ethnic reference is very obvious, too. The assignment of African-Americans to Africa, however, is often rejected too, for not all see their origin on that continent. *Ebonics*, on the other hand, is nothing more than a metaphorical reference to the skin colour. It became popular with the discussion of the Oakland School Board decision, but does not seem to be a more appropriate substitute for older designations as it does not denote anything new or more objective. In our study, we will use BVE as a term for this variety. It is used by many others in a similar way and is intended to be understood as a neutral term.

2. Origins and Ethnicity

The ethnic reference to BVE is also well reflected in debates about the origin of this variety. With the development of research on BVE in the 1960s a number of scholars presented a Creole hypothesis claiming a Creole past for this dialect (Stewart, Dillard, Rickford). They see the origin of BVE in linguistic forms that resulted from contact situations between colonists and black people. On the one hand, such assumptions are based on similarities to well-known English-lexified Creoles still spoken on islands off the coast of South Carolina and Georgia, or in the Caribbean and West Africa. In the course of history, these linguistic variants were modified in a process called decreolisation and finally resulted in present-day features of BVE. On the other hand, further evidence for this hypothesis was derived from characteristics of BVE which do not, and probably did not, occur in English dialects spoken by whites or are used differently or less frequently by them (Fasold 211, Wolfram 175). One of these typical features, for instance, is *copula-dropping*, which will be discussed below. Opponents of the Creole hypothesis claim that BVE developed in a social environment similar to that of other dialects of American English. These opponents became known as representatives of the Anglicist hypothesis (Schneider, Ewers). The advocates of this theory ground their evidence on historical data about living conditions which are said to have not been so different from other non-English speaking people, and thus black people should have been exposed to similar contacts with the English as other nationals. Problems, however, occur with features of BVE which cannot be explained by earlier stages of the English language.

Although the Creole hypothesis seems to be well established (Fasold 212), the controversy on this subject is still going on. Other scholars like Wolfram (178) are looking for a compromise that accepts both Creole as well as English influences as driving forces in the development of BVE.
Current changes in progress in this variety and their being different from tendencies in white vernaculars of American English have led to the establishment of a divergence hypothesis. Labov and Harris (20) and, independently, Bailey and Maynor (cf. Wolfram 179) conducted studies in black communities and found out that BVE seems to diverge from other varieties of American English. They pointed out that features like the use of verbal *s* as a marker of a narrative past or the use of invariant habitual *be* are

spreading, above all among younger African-Americans, and may be interpreted as a new direction in the development of BVE. If so, this variety may be enriched by further ethnic features or existing markers will become a regular element. However, one has to consider, as Rickford stated, that "Black teenagers are less assimilationist than their parents [...] and more assertive about their rights to talk and act" (AAVE 274). This could mean that changes are an age-grading socio-linguistic feature and those speakers may return to general linguistic habits when the grow older. Ongoing changes in BVE may also be taken as evidence against the Creole hypothesis for they seem to contradict a process of decreolisation leading to a step by step convergence with standard English or white vernaculars. According to Fasold, however, divergence is "far from incompatible" (216) with this hypothesis. A new divergence trend could involve a Creole that has already reached an advanced state of decreolisation (215).

3. The Role of Ethnicity

The discussion so far has already shown that different issues of BVE cannot be separated from its ethnic characterisation. Ethnicity has played a central role in the description of this dialect and has become a significant parameter in sociolinguistics and modern dialectology. It is, however, not easy to define what is covered by this notion. Forms of culture, religion, food, dress and language are all ways of expressing people's ethnicity, of signalling a certain togetherness in a group. Even in language, as Wolfram states (165), it is difficult to say what can be identified as ethnicity. Language forms a continuum and generally combines different types of variation. Thus, BVE in particular contains regional, common social and socio-ethnic markers. It originated in the south of the USA and it is spoken by African-Americans who belong to the lower classes. These regional-ethnic and social-ethnic colourings of the dialect make it difficult to draw a borderline between ethnicity as such and other social factors.

It is certainly true to conclude that "in communities where the local lore acknowledges more than one ethnic group, we would expect ethnicity to be a factor of language variation" (Laferrier 603). People use a distinctive language associated with their ethnic identity, but the extent to which this ethnic feature occurs can differ widely from one social group to another.

While the scope of linguistic markers expressing ethnicity within minority groups in the USA like the Italians, Jews, Vietnamese, Germans or Hispanics is often rather limited or restricted to single fields of language, BVE seems to be a prototype of an ethnolect. It "represents the paradigmatic case for examining the role of ethnicity in dialect diversity" (Wolfram 169). This means that many linguistic features in different areas of language have developed and, according to the divergence hypothesis, are still developing. They set BVE apart from other varieties in American society. Reasons for this strong ethnic marking can probably be found, as mentioned above, in the social situation. De-facto segregation and a low social status have been a fertile soil for cultivating feelings of togetherness and solidarity among black Americans and this has been manifested in language. The use of specific pronunciation and intonation patterns, of deviant grammar forms, or of marked lexical items can all be interpreted as expressions of such an ethnic awareness, as linguistic ways to distinguish African-Americans from standard English speakers in society.

4. Ethnic Markers of BVE

Looking for ethnic features of BVE, it is, as already mentioned, not easy to separate them from those which are also characteristics of other regional or social varieties. Such overlaps probably explain why many authors list features of BVE without distinguishing what might be ethnic. Hansen et al., for instance, compile eleven phonological, eight grammatical and seven lexical peculiarities of this dialect, among them are widespread features like 'g-dropping', 'monophthongisation of diphthongs' or the use of 'gonna' (115-116). Rickford mentions 18 main distinctive phonological and 36 main distinctive grammatical (morphological and syntactic) features of BVE (AAVE 4ff.). This detailed description offers a good survey of possible characteristics and so includes features of many non-standard varieties, regional as well as ethnic markers which are, however, not marked as such. Wolfram (171), on the other hand, bases his description of BVE on distinctions by Fasold. He confines himself to just eight features and identifies them as unique. According to him they cannot be found among Anglo, lower-class southerners. This selection could qualify as an inventory of ethnic characteristics of this variety as their uniqueness sets them apart from other dialects. But this again depends on how far one goes with such a classification. If one accepts that ethnic properties of this variety do not just include unique features but also peculiarities that occur much more frequently than in other varieties, then the range of ethnic markers must be extended. Considering this, features of pronunciation, grammar as well as lexis should be included. There is no doubt that, for instance, a simplification of consonant clusters, the deletion of the plural suffix *s*, or double and multiple negation are frequent markers of BVE, and yet authors above all emphasise differences in grammar as the most significant. In particular, verbal markers have been a central focus in this variety. Fasold, for example, points out that "it is the features of the verb system that are the most remarkable" (208). Consequently, he concentrates on such aspects in his characterisation of this dialect. His list contains the following features:

- A. Habitual or distributive *be*.
  (But the teachers don't *be* knowing the problems like the parents do.)
- B. Remote time *been*
  (I *been* knowing that.)
- C. Completive or perfective *done*.
  (I *done* forgot to turn off the stove.)
- D. Future completive or future perfective *be done*.
  (I'll *be done* bought my own CB waitin on him to by me one.)
- E. Aspectual *steady*.
  (Your mind is *steady* workin'.)
- F. Semi-auxiliary *come*
  (She *come* going in my room – didn't knock or nothing.)
- G. Absent form of *be*.
  (She _ real nice.)
- H. Absent verbal *s*.
  (He walk_ to school every day.) [208 ff.]

5. Empirical Evidence

5.1 The Database and the Objectives

The characteristics, distinguished by Fasold, can be considered as the most typical features of BVE in the sense of ethnic markers and will be chosen as the basis of the following empirical analysis. The purpose of it is to investigate what role these ethnic features play in three American novels in which BVE is a significant element of the text structure. The books chosen as a database are Mark Twain's *Adventures of Huckleberry Finn* (*HF*, 1884/85), Zora Neale Hurston's *Their Eyes Were Watching God* (*EWG*,

1937) and Alice Walker's *The Color Purple* (*CP*, 1983). They cover a time span of one hundred years and may reveal tendencies of usage.

The emphasis in this short study will mainly be laid on quantitative analyses which are one major component of dialect research. Rickford, for instance, underlined such an approach when he recommended considering "not only what occurs and where, but also how often" (Principles 39f.).

The analysis will first concentrate on the occurrence of those ethnic features to find out if and how often they are used by the authors. Comparing those data possible preferences might be revealed. Then the linguistic environment of each relevant ethnic marker will be examined to show differences in usage and to uncover semantic functions in the text. Where appropriate, quantitative comparisons with standard English forms will be included to underline the functional role of the ethnic markers. Finally, conclusions will be drawn on how these literary texts by means of vernacular usage can transport an ethnic awareness of language.

To use written evidence for an analysis of a dialect may be problematic as it is often unknown how far an author has been capable of giving a real reflection of the language, how far authentic linguistic features have been chosen. While Ewers believes that such databases are "inappropriate" and "not comparable with real language data" (8), they are supported by Dillard who states that literary representations are often more reliable than some scholars assume ("Nova Scotia" 269).

The problem of authenticity in regard to BVE is often discussed quite controversially. Twain claims in his introductory note to his novel *Huckleberry Finn* that besides others the Missouri Negro dialect is used (6) and Tidwell believes "that Mark Twain was both sincere and competent in his representation of Nigger Jim" (176). Sewell, on the other hand, contradicts this and thinks the very fact "that Twain's slave Jim does not speak the exaggerated farcical dialect of the blackface minstrels has misled critics into describing his speech as 'realistic' black dialect. It is, in fact, romanticized folk speech" (95). However, from Twain's correspondence we know that he worked hard on practising this dialect:

I amend this dialect stuff by talking & talking it till it sounds right - & I had difficulty with the Negro talk because a Negro sometimes (rarely) says 'goin', & sometimes 'gwyne', & they make just such discrepancies in other words - & when you come to reproduce them on paper they look as if the variation resulted from the writer's carelessness. But I want to work at the proofs & get the dialect as nearly right as possible. (Paine 26)

As far as Hurston is concerned we know that she not only grew up in an all-black social environment but also worked as an anthropologist and even did research on the subject of BVE. Critics confirm her competence with ratings like "careful representation of dialect" (Johnson 57), "brilliant use of dialect" (Meese 61) or "an example of dialect writing at its best" (Holton 125). The very fact that Hurston's use of dialect enraged other African American writers such as Richard Wright, who accused her of exploiting "those 'quaint' aspects of Negro life that satisfied the tastes of a white audience" (cf. Washington viii) also speaks for her ability to reflect this dialect realistically.

In a similarly positive way critics refer to Walker's BVE in *The Color Purple*. They praise "the beautiful voice in the book and Walker's ability to capture an authentic black folk speech without all the caricature that usually typifies such efforts" (Harris 155). They also underline that "Walker explores the richness and clarity of black folk English in such a way that the reader understands the inner core of a person who cannot be truly known except through her own language" (Christian 185). Comments like these seem to justify the use of literary evidence in general and, concerning these three novels, in particular as a basis for a linguistic analysis.

5.2. Non-core and Core markers

The empirical study of the ethnic markers chosen with regard to their occurrence and frequency in the novels yielded quite different results as shown in the following table:

	Habit. *be*	Remote *been*	Completive *done*	future compl. *be done*	Asp. *steady*	Semi -aux. *come*	Absent *be*	Absent verbal *s*
HF	-	-	-	-	-	-	14	22
EWG	2	2	79	2	-	-	50	85
CP	23	2	20	-	-	-	818	2676

A first look at the distribution of those features reveals that some markers do not occur at all, others only in some novels and often with a low frequency, and others again are quite regular features of the texts. This different part they play may depend on the authors' preferences or the structure of the novels; however, it seems that one should distinguish between core and non-core ethnic markers.

5.2.1. Semi-auxiliary *Come*, Aspectual *Steady* and Future Completive *Be Done*

The study shows that both *steady* as an intensified continuative marker and *come* as a semi-auxiliary expressing a person's indignation would qualify for the non-core category. They are aspectual markers and seem to be very special and infrequent in use. Such an assumption can also be derived from other linguistic research. Neither Wolfram referring to unique features of BVE (171) nor Rickford selecting classic features of the dialect (AAVE 263) include them.

Be done can also be classified as rather rare. It occurs just two times and only in one of the corpora. In linguistic studies, it is referred to as evidence of the divergence hypothesis for it seems "to have arisen only in recent decades" (Wolfram 179). If this is assumed to be, it is no wonder that this feature does not figure prominently in our texts. The two instances we found are of the following kind:

> If Ah wuz, you'd be done woke me up callin' me. (*EWG* 50)
> De man wid his switch blade will be done cut yuh tuh death while you foolin' wid uh razor. (*EWG* 190)

In both sentences a resultative or completive aspect corresponds to a conditional or future perfect tense in standard English.

5.2.2. Remote *Been*

Remote *been* functions as another aspect marker. In linguistic studies, it is regarded as one of the central features of BVE and often taken as a piece of evidence for the Creole hypothesis. Dillard characterises it "as the most easily diagnostic feature of the Creole stage of the Black English Vernacular" ("Nova Scotia" 72). It is a stressed form of *been* which indicates an action in a distant past and is, because of this aspectual function, restricted from co-occurring with time adverbials (Rickford, "Principles" 20). The important role which is assigned to this feature, however, cannot be confirmed in this study. It occurs in two corpora only and with a very low frequency. In most cases where *been* is used in the analysed texts, it has an adverbial in its linguistic environment and corresponds to an unstressed form:

> Pheoby, we been kissin' friends for twenty years. (*EWG* 19)
> Ah been waitin' a long time. (*EWG* 32)

To interpret these examples as remote time *been* would mean to express a similar feature twice. The stressed form, however, occurs in examples like the following:

> Ah been prayin' fuh it tuh be different wid you. (*EWG* 29)
> Anyhow, I say, the God I been praying and writing to is a man. (*CP* 164)

In these sentences the actions "been prayin" and "been praying and writing" are characterized by the remote time aspect *for a long time* and correspond to present perfect tense in standard English.

5.2.3. Habitual *Be*

Invariant forms of *be* are another ethnic feature in BVE and they occur in two variants. On the one hand, *be* is used as an infinitive and is the result of will/would deletion as in "By time I git back from the well, the water be warm" (*CP 4*). On the other hand, *be* represents a finite form and is a main verb. Here, it expresses another aspectual differentiation in BVE underlining a habitual activity. This ethnic marker appears as quite a regular characteristic in *CP*; it could, however, be found only twice in *EWG* and Nigger Jim in *HF* does not use it at all. *Be* in this function occurs in different linguistic environments. First it is followed by a verb-*ing* construction:

> A. Folks be making soup out of everything but shoe-leather trying to kill off the yam taste.(*CP* 213)
> B. The children be making mud pies on the edge of the creek, they don't even look up. (*CP* 30)

In sentence **A** a certain regularity of the action is expressed; it occurs repeatedly. In example **B**, however, invariant *be* seems to reflect a progressive aspect, an action which is taking place over time. This instance seems to support the statement put forward by Ewers that there are two aspectual meanings of *be*, "namely habitual and (to a lesser extent) progressive aspect" (74).

In other examples *be* is preceding a nominal phrase:
> And now I feels sick every time I be the one to cook. (*CP* 3)
> It bees that way sometime. (*CP* 10)

Here, the habitual aspect is also emphasised by the use of the adverbials "every time" and "sometime". Such a habitual aspect can also be expressed by constructions where *be* is followed by a locative:

> Mr....be in the room with her all the time of the night or day. (*CP* 43)

A characteristic marker of habitual *be* is that it takes the auxiliary *don't* for negation. This use is reflected twice in the material:

> And don't lemme ketch none uh y'all dumpin' white folks, and don't be wastin' no boxes on colored. (*EWG* 253)
> But anyhow, watch yo'self, Janie, and don't be took advantage of. (*EWG* 170)

In the first sentence "don't be wastin" probably refers to repeated events where blacks treated dead blacks in the same way as white ones, while in the second example "don't be took advantage of" seems to be a warning about younger men who take advantage of older women.

5.2.4. Completive *Done*

Another quite regular ethnic marker is the verbal construction *done + past/past participle* which denotes a completed action or perfective aspect. With it the whole event and the fact that the event is over is expressed, or as Comrie puts it the "whole of the situation is presented as a single unanalysable whole, with the beginning, middle, and end rolled up into one" (3). This feature occurs as a consistent element in *EWG* as well as in *CP* although the ratio is almost four times higher in the former. The use of this construction reveals that a certain continuous relevance is emphasised by the speaker. This aspectual feature, however, may occur with different shades of meaning. First, it may refer to an action that was finished or completed but still affects the present. Often a certain result is underlined by it:

> Ah done scorched up dat lil meat and bread too long to talk about. (*EWG* 13)
> So round four o'clock Ah done cleaned 'em out complete – (*EWG* 190)
> Done been worked tuh death; done had his disposition ruint wid mistreatment. (*EWG* 89)

Second, completive *done* emphasises an action that took place in the prepast:

Dat school teacher had done hid her in the woods all night long, and he had done raped mah baby and run off just before day. (*EWG* 36)

Third, a process completed in the past and still having a certain impact on the present is referred to:

Don't you set dere pointin' wid me after all Ah done went through for you. (*EWG* 28)

Tea Cake had done gone crazy. (*EWG* 282)

Fourth, *done* marks a completed state. Here, the conditions continue to hold up to the present:

Grandma done been long uh few roads herself. (*EWG* 43)
Ah done been tuh de horizon and back and now Ah kin set heah in mah house and live by comparisons. (*EWG* 284)

It is interesting to note that the database also contained one example with a past tense marker:

Somebody done spoke 'bout you long time ago. (*EWG* 27)

This use may serve as a counterexample to Green's statement that *done* "is excluded from occurring with adverbials that indicate past tense" (48).

5.2.5. Absent Verbal *s*

Absent verbal *s* belongs to those ethnic markers which have received extensive attention in linguistic literature. Several studies have shown that it amounts to high percentages among lower-class African-Americans. It also occurs as a frequent marker of black speakers in the database, but, above all, is a high-ranking feature in *CP*. On the one hand, this underlines the low and uneducated status of the protagonist Celie, on the other hand, it can be put down to her habit to represent the past in present tense. The prominent role absent verbal *s* plays as an ethnic indicator becomes apparent when it is compared with standard forms used by the same speakers. In none of the texts do standard verbal *s* forms prevail. "Nigger Jim" in *HF* uses absent *s* forms 22 times in contrast to 8 standard forms. In *EWG* the proportion between absent and present suffix *s* is relatively balanced with a ratio of 85/77, but even here absent *s* is in the lead. The most dramatic difference, however, was found in Celie's speech where 2676 occurrences of this feature confront only 15 standard forms. The ratios of absent *s* forms in these texts thus amount to 73.3%, 52.4% and 99.44%, respectively. In this comparison it is worth pointing out that standard forms in *HF* and *EWG* are repeatedly applied in a religious context mentioning God, the Bible or the church:

Boun' to git yo' money back a hund'd times, de preacher says. (*HF* 51)
..., as the good book says (*HF* 69)

De sun-maker brings it up in the mornin', (*EWG* 72)
If he buy all dat you talkin' 'bout Mist' Starks, God knows what he do wid it. (*EWG* 114)

The awareness of God's authority seems to make the speakers adapt their speech to standard usage as it is found in the Bible which is preached in Sunday schools and in Sunday services and obviously seems to have had a conditioning effect, so that it is not quite decided whether the choice of word forms is conscious or not. This effort to distinguish between God and man is very clearly reflected in the last sentence of the examples. Celie in *CP*, however, does not follow this pattern. Her use of absent *s* is very consistent.

5.2.6. Copula-dropping

The last feature of the list, absent form of *be* or *copula-dropping*, is probably the most typical of all. It occurs regularly and is considered as ethnically unique and taken as the proof of a Creole past of this variety. *Copula-dropping* also figures quite well in the analysed corpora. Similar to the distribution of absent verbal *s*, there is an increasing occurrence of absent *be* from *HF* over *EWG* to *CP* with 14, 50 and 818 instances. Here again, a comparison with occurring standard forms can provide an insight into the role this marker plays in the characterisation of black people. In *HF* 14 instances found oppose 70 full and 89 contracted forms of *be*. In *EWG* the ratio is 50/304/394 and in *CP* 818/185/176. These figures show that the feature *copula-dropping*, although a significant factor of ethnic marking in all texts, only prevails in *CP*. Here again, it seems that Alice Walker, above all, by means of this ethnic feature intends to emphasise the low social status of her protagonist.

A further finding is that this characteristic feature does not occur in all linguistic environments equally. Some are more favoured by the authors than others. Above all five structures form the direct syntactic environment of absent *be*. These are:

1	V-ing	So what _ you gointuh do now. (*EWG* 140)
2	Adjective	He _ black as the inside of a chimney. (*CP* 27)
3	Noun phrase	It _ not my house. (*CP* 42)
4	Locative	...he _ in my house messing it up. (*CP* 224)
5	gonna /gwyne	You _ gwyne to have considerable trouble ... (*HF* 23)

In the three corpora they occur as follows:

	V-ing	Adj.	NP	Loc.	Gonna/gwyne	Total
HF	-	1	1	1	11	14
TEWWG	40	7	2	1	-	50
CP	194	376	184	63	1	818

As can be inferred from this table, there are significant quantitative differences. The dominant environment in Nigger Jim's speech is *gonna/gwyne* while it is hardly used by speakers in the other texts. *V-ing*, however, is the most significant collocation for *copula-dropping* in *EWG* and only ranks second in *CP* after a frequent use of an *adjective* environment. This high occurrence rate of the *V-ing* in connection with *copula dropping* corresponds to other studies described in linguistic literature (cf. Rickford, AAVE 268; Ewers 216).

Copula-dropping, however, does not concern all forms of *be*. As this study reveals, some forms are deleted regularly while others are only dropped sporadically, or are not affected by this process at all. Relating the five environments of *copula-dropping* to single singular and plural subjects the following distribution was received:

	1ˢᵗ p.sg	2ⁿᵈ p.sg.	3ʳᵈ p.sg.	1ˢᵗ p.pl.	2ⁿᵈ p.pl.	3ʳᵈ p.pl.
V-ing	- - -	- 21 34	- 8 112	- 4 13	- 2 1	- 5 34
Adj.	- - -	- 1 24	1 4 296	- - 2	- - -	- 2 54
NP	- - -	- - 20	1 2 142	- - 2	- - -	- - 20
Loc.	- - -	- - 2	1 1 50	- - 1	- - -	- - 10
Gonna/ Gwyne	- - -	4 - -	5 - -	1 - -	- - -	1 - 1

Each column of the table contains the relevant data in chronological order of the first publication of the novels *HF, EWG, CP*. They reveal very clearly that the *be*-form is mainly deleted with the third person singular followed by the second person singular and the third person plural while there is no occurrence with the first person singular. Only in *EWG* does the second person singular preceding *V-ing* have the highest frequency. Thus it is quite obvious that the forms *is* and *are* seem to be favoured by deletion while *am* is relatively stable and remains unaffected by this process.

6. Concluding Remarks

To sum up, the present study has shown that the feature of ethnicity is directly woven into the fabric of BVE. Due to the socio-economic situation many African-Americans had to face attitudes developed which gave their language a marked ethnic character, which is well reflected in designations of this variety. Socio-economic conditions also led to a strong ethnic awareness among the speakers of BVE which found its expression in unique linguistic features and tendencies of divergence from standard forms of English.

The empirical analysis of literary texts revealed that linguistic features described as unique in linguistic literature are represented quite differently with regard to their occurrence and frequency while a significant change in ethnic markers during that span of time could not be found. Their different occurrence seems to justify a classification of ethnic markers into non-core features like aspectual *steady*, semi-auxiliary *come* or future completive *be done* in contrast to core features like the aspectual markers remote *been*, completive *done* or invariant *be* and frequent characteristics like absent *be* or absent verbal *s*. The last two figure prominently in all three corpora and may be regarded as ethnic markers par excellence . They, together with the other core features, serve to transport an ethnic awareness in language and help to mark BVE as a prototypical ethnolect.

Works Cited

Bailey, Guy, and Natalie Maynor. "Decreolization." *Language in Society* 16 (1987): 449-74.

Christian, Barbara. *Black Feminist Criticism: Perspectives on Black Women Writers.* The Athene Series. New York: Pergamon Press, 1985.

Comrie, Bernard. *Aspect: An Introduction to the Study of Verbal Aspect and Related Problems.* Cambridge: Cambridge UP, 1976.

Dillard, Joey Lee. "The History of Black English in Nova Scotia: A First Step". *African Language Review* 9 (1970-71): 263-279.

Dillard, Joey Lee. *Black English: Its History and Usage in the United States.* New York: Random House, 1972.

Ewers, Traute. *The Origin of American Black English: Be-Forms in the Hoodoo Texts.* Berlin/New York: Mouton de Gruyter, 1996.

Fasold, Ralph. *Sociolinguistics of Language.* Cambridge/Oxford: Blackwell, 1990.

Gester, Friedrich Wilhelm. "Negro, Afro-American oder Black? Zu einer aktuellen sprachlichen Auseinandersetzung in den USA." *Die Neueren Sprachen* (Neue Folge) 20.2 (1971): 53-63.

Green, Lisa. "Aspect and Predicate Phrases in African-American Vernacular English." *African-American English: Structure, History and Use.* Ed.Salikoko Mufwene, John Rickford, Guy Bailey, and John Baugh. London/New York: Routledge, 1998. 37-68.

Hansen, Klaus, Uwe Carls, and Peter Lucko. *Die Differenzierung des Englischen in nationale Varianten.* Berlin: Erich Schmidt, 1996.

Harris, Trudier. "On the 'Color Purple', Stereotypes, and Silence". *Black American Literature Forum* 18.4 (1984): 155-61.

Holton, Sylvia. *Down Home and Uptown: The Representation of Black Speech in American Fiction* London: Associated University Presses, 1984.

Hurston, Zora Neale. *Their Eyes Were Watching God.* London: Little, Brown and Company, 1999.

Johnson, Barbara. "Metaphor, Metonymy and Voice". *Zora Neale Hurston's Their Eyes Were Watching God: Modern Critical Interpretations.* Ed. Harold Bloom. New York: Chelsea House, 1987. 41-57.

Labov, William, and Wendell Harris. "De Facto Segregation of Black and White Vernaculars." *Diversity and Diachrony.* Ed. David Sankoff. Philadelphia/Amsterdam: John Benjamins, 1986. 1-24.

Laferrier, Martha. "Ethnicity in Phonological Variation and Change." *Language* 55 (1979): 603-17.

Meese, Elisabeth. "Orality and Textuality in *Their Eyes Were Watching*

God." Zora Neale Hurston's Their Eyes Were Watching God. *Modern Critical Interpretations.* Ed. Harold Bloom. New York: Chelsea House, 1987. 59-71.

Mufwene, Salikoko S. "The Development of American Englishes: Some Questions from a Creole Genesis Hypothesis." *Focus on the USA.* Ed. Edgar W. Schneider. Philadelphia/Amsterdam: John Benjamins, 1996.231-64.

Paine, Albert Bigelow, ed. *Mark Twain's Letters.* 2 vols. New York: Harper & Brothers, 1917.

Rickford, John R. "Some Principles for the Study of Black and White Speech in the South". *Language Variety in the South: Perspectives in Black and White.* Ed. Michael B. Montgomery, and Guy Bailey. Tuscaloosa, AL: U of Alabama P, 1986. 38-62.

Rickford, John R. *African American Vernacular English.* Malden/Oxford: Blackwell, 1999.

Schneider, Edgar Werner. "On the History of Black English in the USA – Some New Evidence." *English World-Wide* 3.1(1982): 18-46.

Sewell, David R. *Mark Twain's Languages: Discourse, Dialogue and Linguistic Variety.* Berkeley: U of California P, 1987.

Stewart, William A. "Sociolinguistic Factors in the History of American Negro Dialects." *Florida Foreign Language Reporter* 5 (1967): 11-29.

Tidwell, James Nathan. "Mark Twain's Representation of Negro Speech". *American Speech* 17:3 (1942): 174-76.

Twain, Mark. *The Adventures of Huckleberry Finn.* London: Orion Publishing Group, 1997.

Walker, Alice. *The Color Purple.* Reading: Cox and Wyman, 1992.

Washington, Mary Helen. "Foreword." Zora Neale Hurston. *Their Eyes Were Watching God.* [Perennial Library]New York: Harper & Row, 1990. vii-xiv.

Weber, Klaus. "Some Facts About 'Black English' Spoken in the USA." *Wissenschaftliche Zeitschrift der Humboldt-Universität* [Gesellschaftswiss. Reihe 33] 4 (1984): 419-420.

Wolfram, Walt. *American English –Dialects and Variation.* Malden/Oxford: Blackwell, 1998.

Zinn, Howard. *A People's History of the United States – 1492- Present.* Revised and Updated Edition. New York: HarperPerennial, 1995.

Denotational Incongruencies: A Very Short Introduction and Typology

Olaf Jäkel

1. Introduction: Denotational Incongruency

This paper outlines a major research project (Jäkel, *Bedeutungs-Inkongruenzen*) currently in progress. The overall aim of that project lies in the attempt to combine traditional structural semantics in a modified version of field theory with a cognitive linguistic approach in the investigation of alternative semantic construals within one and the same conceptual domain.

The basic heuristic method employed is that of the theory of semantic fields, or rather the field approach (cf. Lehrer x), which goes back to the German linguist Trier (*Wortschatz*), and was introduced into English linguistics and elaborated mainly by Lehrer (*Semantic Fields*), Lyons (*Semantics*), and Lehrer & Kittay (*Frames*). At the centre of this approach to lexical semantics is the structuralist tenet that "the single words determine each other's meaning by their number and position in the overall field" (Trier 7, transl. O.J.). In the words of Lehrer & Kittay (3-4), "the meanings of words must be understood, in part, in relation to other words that articulate a given content domain and that stand in the relation of affinity and contrast to the word(s) in question."

In his discussion of Jost Trier's (*Wortschatz*) theory of semantic fields, John Lyons (*Semantics*) introduces a distinction between *lexical field* and *conceptual field*, explicating that different lexical fields may "cover the same conceptual field" (253). Using the conceptual field of colours as an example, Lyons states that "the *denotational boundaries* between roughly equivalent colour terms in different languages are often *incongruent*" (246; italics O.J.).

This is where I have borrowed my central term: I speak of *denotational incongruencies* when roughly equivalent lexemes in different languages are used without full synonymy in the sense of *denotational equivalence* (cf. Lyons 213), or when the use of even one and the same term in different varieties of the same language displays differences in denotation.

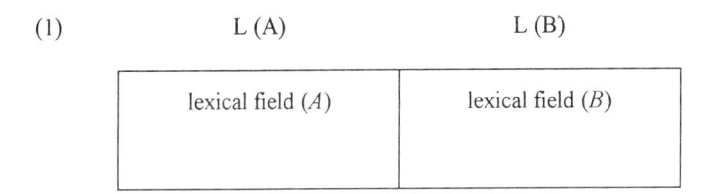

(1)   L (A)   L (B)

lexical field (*A*)	lexical field (*B*)

I hope to show that such differences can be brought out best by studying the different patterns of internal boundaries displayed by the lexical fields (*A* vs. *B*) of two languages, varieties or lects, L (A) vs. L (B), within one and the same conceptual field (see 1).

While this modified field semantic approach is rooted in the almost forgotten tradition of Trier (*Wortschatz*) and Lehrer (*Semantic Fields*), this is anything but a traditionalist enterprise. Taking lexical differences as indicators of different construals or cognitive models is not only in line with the latest cognitive semantics in the manner of George Lakoff (*Women*; "Cognitive Semantics"; "Cultural Theory"). It also follows the lead of the classic approach to linguistic relativity by Benjamin Lee Whorf (*Language*).

For linguistic examples and paraphrases of meaning I have mainly drawn on recent, corpus-based monolingual dictionaries (CED, DCE, WDW; see appendix). For descriptive purposes, sense components or semantic features are employed at some stages during the investigation, but only as diagnostic components (Nida 112) or distinctive features (Lipka 115), without subscribing to any of the more controversial tenets of componential analysis of the Katz and Fodor ("The Structure") type.

The main part (section 2) of this paper is devoted to distinguishing seven different subtypes of denotational incongruency. These types are introduced on the basis of typical English examples, which in some cases are compared with their German equivalents. The paper ends with a short summary and conclusion (section 3) pointing out some theoretical issues as well as some possible fields of application.

2. Types of Denotational Incongruency

Due to limitations of space, the following account of seven different types of denotational incongruency is anything but exhaustive. The selection of examples should rather be taken as illustrative of the general approach, which relies on a much more comprehensive treatment of theoretical points (see Jäkel, *Bedeutungs-Inkongruenzen*) as well as on more data-rich studies (such as Jäkel, "Morning").

2.1 Staggered Incongruency

In one common type of incongruency, the denotational boundaries between the lexemes in question do not meet head-on, but face each other in a 'staggered' way (examples 2, 3).

(2)   English   German

pupil	*Schüler*
student	*Student*

While the German lexeme *Student*, incompatible with *Schüler*, denotes only a person who has entered university, its English cognate *student* is used for young people at an earlier stage of their educational carreer. With *pupil* denoting mainly the very young children at school, already juveniles in their final years (like Sixth Form) of secondary school are called *students*.

A second example of *staggered incongruency* comes from a comparison between different expert languages (3):

(3) Philosophy   AI

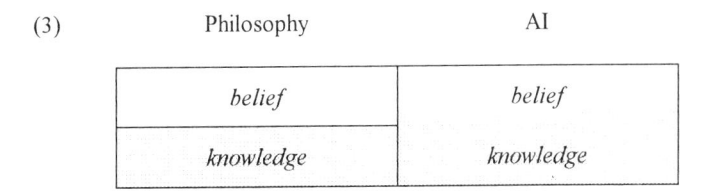

belief	belief
knowledge	knowledge

In the context of Cognitive Science, philosophers clinging to their traditional criteria of *knowledge* [+SUBJECTIVE CONVICTION, +OBJECTIVE VALIDITY] as opposed to simple *beliefs* [+SUBJECTIVE CONVICTION, -OBJECTIVE VALIDITY] confront researchers with a background in Artificial Intelligence (AI), who use the two terms almost synonymously, speaking of *belief systems* as well as of *knowledge systems*. As the decisive criterion for them is [+FUNCTIONAL RELEVANCE] within the system, they simply disregard the issue of 'outside' objectivity, allowing a more unrestricted – and by most philosophers' standards quite shocking – use of the term *knowledge*, which leaves the denotational boundary towards the field neighbour *belief* fuzzy if not completely open.

2.2 Diagonal Incongruency

Whereas in cases of staggered incongruency there is at least a denotational overlap of the lexemes compared (Jäkel, "Morning", uses the label of *overlapping incongruency*), there is another type of incongruency without any such overlap. If the same word form is used with a completely different denotation, the resulting structural pattern in the lexical fields compared motivates the technical term of *diagonal incongruency*. This type is most frequently found between dialectal varieties of one language, so that the following examples come from comparing the two main "dialect families" (cf. Strevens 16-20) of British English (BrE) vs. American English (AmE).

(4)

British English	American English
1st floor	*2nd floor*
ground floor	*1st floor*

While the counting of floors may not be a strictly 'lexicological' case, this example (4) most graphically represents the typical 'diagonal' structural pattern displayed by quite a number of other lexical fields. These include the following cases, which for brevity's sake are simply listed under (5), with the 'diagonally related' lexemes in bold print:

(5) British English American English

cot // camp bed – crib // ***cot***

chips // crisps – french fries // (**potato**) ***chips***

vest // waistcoat – undershirt, T-shirt // ***vest***

football // American football – soccer // ***football***

apartment // flat – 'large and expensive flat' // ***apartment***

bug // 'small insect' – bedbug // ***bug***

pavement // 'road surface' – sidewalk // ***pavement***

truck // lorry – 'open railway vehicle' // ***truck***

In all of these cases, the denotation of the first lexeme in the BrE pairs (e.g., *cot*) equals that of the first of the two AmE expressions (e.g., *crib*), while the denotation of the second AmE lexeme (e.g., *cot*) equals that of the second of the two BrE terms (e.g., *camp bed*). In cases where a variety lacks a proper lexicalization I have provided a paraphrase instead.

2.3 Crosspiece Incongruency

If there is this denotational incongruency with a *diagonal* pattern, could we not expect there to be even cases of *double* diagonal incongruency? The answer is yes, although this *crosspiece incongruency* must be the rarest of all types, and may indeed be best regarded as a special subtype of *diagonal incongruency*. The following is the only example I was able to find from comparing British English with American English:

(6)   British English   American English

trapezium	trapezoid
trapezoid	trapezium

Within the conceptual field of geometrical forms, the lexical fields of the two varieties display a full crosspiece pattern, with BrE *trapezium* equalling AmE *trapezoid* in its denotation of 'a shape with four sides, of which only two are parallel' (DCE), and BrE *trapezoid* equalling AmE *trapezium*, both denoting 'a shape with four sides, of which none are parallel' (DCE). However, *crosspiece incongruency* may be regarded the least interesting of all types, not only because it is very uncommon, but also because this type is unlikely to influence in any way the thinking of speakers. On the other hand, it is very likely to cause misunderstandings in topical encounters between speakers of the two varieties unaware of the nature of these truely 'false friends'.

2.4 Granularity Differential

In a much more common type of denotational incongruency, one of the two fields compared is split up into smaller lexical sectors than the other, resulting in a *granularity differential*, like in the following example:

(7) English   German

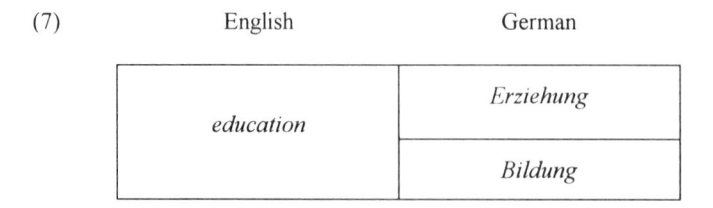

| education | *Erziehung* |
| | *Bildung* |

Here, two lexemes in the German field divide the same denotational space between them that is occupied by only one lexeme in English. The general pattern exemplified in (7) will yield an even 'steeper' differential when a single lexeme in one language faces as many as three in another, as is the case with, e.g., English *knowledge* as against German *Wissen* // *Kenntnis* // *Erkenntnis*, or with German *Glück* versus English *happiness* // *luck* // *fortune*. While examples like these show that one language can be richer than another in its choice of lexical items within a certain field, granularity differentials are also to be found between different theories, as in (8):

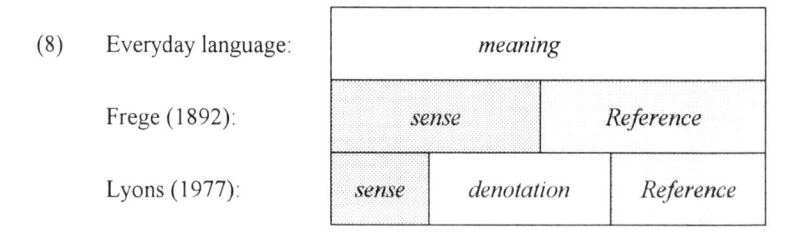

(8) Everyday language: | *meaning* |||
     Frege (1892): | *sense* || *Reference* |
     Lyons (1977): | *sense* | *denotation* | *Reference* |

Where everyday language uses the pretty vague term *meaning*, semantics after Frege ("Sinn") distinguishes between *sense* and *reference*, and Lyons (206-215) introduces a third term *denotation*. This example shows how the need of more finegrained distinctions may lead experts to introduce and employ technical terms to differentiate within a given field. It also shows how the introduction of a new term reduces the denotational extension of the other field members.

2.5 Alternative Classifications

Moving on to larger sectors of conceptual fields, we find cases in which the lexical fields of different languages or lects express *alternative classifications*. In example (9), it is the classification of the English lexeme *thumb* in relation to *finger* which differs from the field pattern in German:

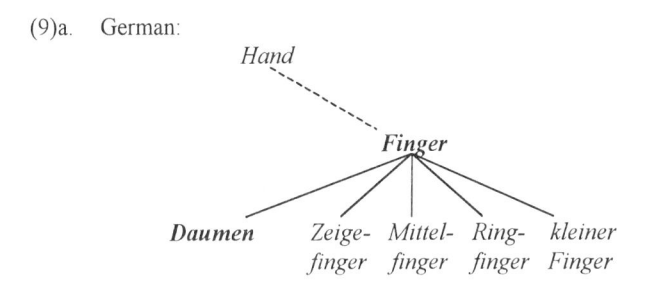

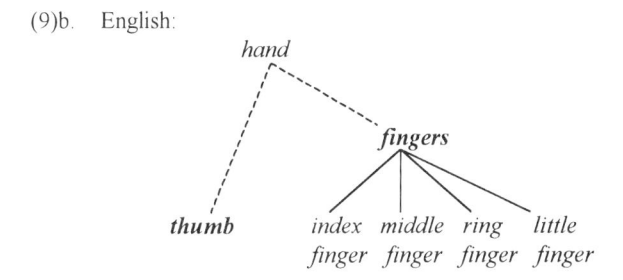

(9)a. German:

```
                    Hand
                      ˙˙˙˙˙˙˙˙˙
                              Finger
              ┌──────────┬────┼────┬──────────┐
          Daumen     Zeige-  Mittel-  Ring-   kleiner
                     finger  finger   finger  Finger
```

(9)b. English:

```
                   hand
               ⁄       ˙˙˙˙˙˙˙
             ⁄              fingers
           ⁄            ┌────┼────┬──────┐
         thumb        index middle ring  little
                      finger finger finger finger
```

Though sense relations like hyponymy and meronymy (see Cruse 159-62; cf. Saeed 70) are situated in lexical fields, lexical hierarchies can be more clearly arranged in the shape of tree diagrams like those above (cf. Lehrer 20), with continuous lines representing relations of hyponymy, and broken lines representing relations of meronymy.

Whereas in the English field the lexeme *thumb* is commonly classified not as a hyponym of, but as incompatible with *finger* (cf. the DCE paraphrase of *finger* as 'one of the four long thin parts on your hand, not including your thumb'), we find an alternative classification in the German field, where the lexeme *Finger* denotes 'each of the five mobile individual end sections of the hand' (WDW, transl. O.J.), with *Daumen* as one of its hyponyms.

The following example (10) shows that alternative classifications are not only found between languages, but also between lects like, e.g., everyday language versus expert languages. The scientific taxonomy of heavenly bodies devised by astronomers (10b) borrows some of its central terms from the 'folk taxonomy' as expressed in everyday language (10a). In the process, however, the whole field undergoes a complete reorganisation, so that most of the lexical items find themselves in different places within the taxonomy.

(10)a. Everyday language / folk taxonomy:

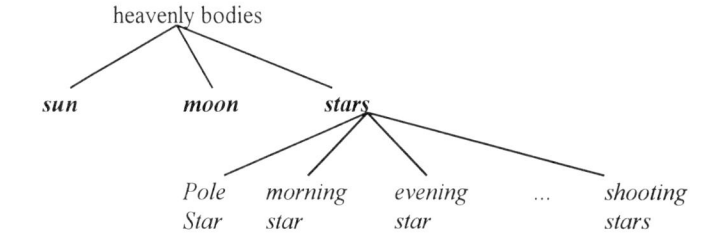

```
                    heavenly bodies
                   /       |        \
                 sun      moon      stars
                                   / | | \
                               Pole morning evening ... shooting
                               Star  star    star         stars
```

(10)b. Astronomy:

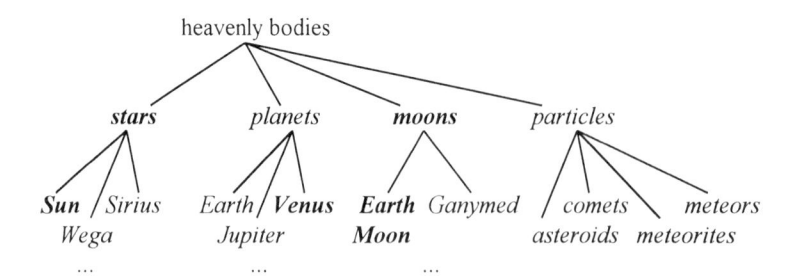

```
                        heavenly bodies
                    /        |       |        \
                stars     planets  moons    particles
                / | \     / | \     / \     / | \  \
           Sun /Sirius Earth/Venus Earth Ganymed /comets \ meteors
              Wega       Jupiter    Moon        asteroids meteorites
               ...         ...        ...
```

Whereas the folk taxonomy represents an unsophisticated classification of 'lights in the earth's sky', which is geocentric, based on unaided perception, and probably rooted in mystical origins, the expert taxonomy applies objective criteria such as true size of the object and type of its motion within a system of coordinates to determine its classification. The most interesting details of that reorganisation, though, will have to be discussed elsewhere.

2.6 Lexical Gaps

The comparison of lexical fields between languages may also reveal one language's lack of an equivalent to a certain lexeme present in the other. Although there may be a certain amount of overlap with some cases of *granularity differential* (see 2.4), the phenomenon of *lexical gaps* represents one more subtype of denotational incongruency. But as *lexical gaps* have a long tradition in semantics and lexicology, the presentation in this section can be kept to a minimum.

(11) German English

Ohr	Ohrmuschel	∅	ear
	Ohrläppchen	earlobe	

Once more, example (11) comes from an English-German comparison, this time in the conceptual field of body parts. The lack of an English equivalent to the German *Ohrmuschel* ('upper part of the outer ear') constitutes a *co-meronym gap* in the meronymic hierarchy under the holonym *ear* – depending on their position within the lexical network of sense relations, *lexical gaps* may also appear as *hyperonym gap*, *co-hyponym gap*, *holonym gap*, and maybe even *antonym gap* (for further discussion and examples, see Jäkel, *Bedeutungs-Inkongruenzen*). The fact that this sort of denotational incongruency appears not in a highly abstract domain, where traditional lexicology would expect it, but even in the most concrete as well as the most basic of all fields, is interesting in itself.

2.7 Contested Concepts

The last type of denotational incongruency is not about yet another structural field pattern, but about a certain kind of *contested concepts* (Lakoff, "Cultural Theory"), cases in which the field patterns themselves are under dispute. Such 'boundary disputes' occuring between different interest groups, parties, or ideologies, are a reminder of the fact that denotational boundaries are in general open to change over time (cf. Trier). Here are some examples:

(12)

marriage	heterosexual couples
	homosexual couples

Should marriage be open to homosexual couples? While the liberal-minded and some of those concerned are in favour of extending the denotational boundary of *marriage* (12), conservative forces like the Catholic church defend the traditional boundary which excludes homosexual couples.

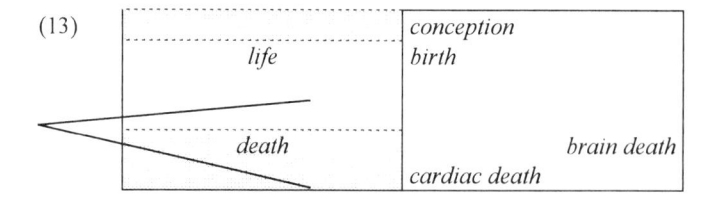

(13)

life	conception birth
death	brain death cardiac death

When does human life start? And when does it end? In recent years, debates about the ethics of abortion on the one hand, and of organ transplants on the other hand have left both entrance and exit boundaries of *life* (13) contested. Opponents of abortion, e.g., favour *conception* instead of *birth* as the start of life. Some advocates of organ transplants argue their case by 'wedging in' a relatively new concept of *brain death* to replace the old definition of *cardiac death*.

(14)

drugs	hard drugs	LSD
		heroin
		cocaine
	soft drugs	marijuana
		...
		tobacco

The final example (14) concerns the classification of *drugs*. Does tobacco count as a drug? Should cocaine be legalized because it is only a 'soft' drug? Contested issues like these can be analysed as 'boundary disputes' over the denotations of some crucial lexical items, in which the diction used by opposed parties or interest groups gives voice to alternative classifications.

In all of these and many more cases of *contested concepts*, what is at issue is the dislocating or relocating of denotational boundaries. From a linguistic perspective, examples like 12, 13, and 14 provide a brilliant chance to witness the natural diachronical change of field patterns happening 'in quick motion'.

3. Summary and Conclusion

What has been achieved, apart from suggesting a couple of new technical terms for the classification of semantic and lexical differences? Though highly selective, and presenting only a small sample of semantic fields, this comparative investigation has confirmed the view that "field theory is particularly helpful in the area of contrastive linguistics" (Lipka 157). The phenomenon that "the boundaries between the meanings of what at first sight appear to be semantically equivalent words in different languages may be, and very often are, incongruent" (Lyons 236), however, is even more general and widespread than traditional field theorists believed. Using the different field patterns displayed as a heuristic method, it makes sense to distinguish various subtypes of incongruencies that appear not only in the comparison of quite different languages, but even on a much smaller scale.

The approach has a number of possible fields of application. Apart from contrastive semantics as such, it affects issues of translation (cf. Jäkel, "Morning") as well as foreign language teaching, where denotational incongruencies may be responsible for native language interferences. The approach may also contribute to research on languages for specific purposes as well as to comprehensibility research. And with the analysis of contested concepts it might even provide a more solid basis for critical linguistics.

Some theoretical issues that have only been touched upon include the evaluation of different approaches to lexical semantics: While cognitive semantics typically investigates categorization and prototype phenomena, structural semantics seems more suitable when it comes to describe semantic fields, including sense relations as well as lexical gaps. The question in what way componential analysis can contribute remains to be discussed elsewhere, just as the interdependence of diachrony and synchrony in field structures, the interdependence of lexical semantics and pragmatics in the study of usage and collocations, and matters of linguistic philosophy revolving around Whorf's famous "linguistic relativity principle" (214).

As to linguistic relativity, it is worth noting that denotational incongruencies are found not only between "Standard Average European (SAE)" (Whorf 138) languages such as English versus German, but already between regional dialects (British vs. American English), between different social registers or lects like everyday language and various scientific expert languages, and even between the jargon employed by different theories as well as the diction of different interest groups, parties, or ideologies. One conclusion to be drawn here is that in order to find examples of relativity we do not have to go to comparisons of distant, 'exotic' languages: Linguistic relativity starts at home.

Appendix: Sources of Linguistic Data

CED: *Collins Cobuild English Dictionary.* Ed. John Sinclair. London: Harper Collins, 1995.
DCE: *Longman Dictionary of Contemporary English.* Ed. Della Summers. München: Langenscheidt-Longman, 1995.
WDW: *Wahrig: Deutsches Wörterbuch.* Ed. Renate Wahrig-Burfeind. Gütersloh: Bertelsmann, 1994.

Works Cited

Cruse, David Alan. *Lexical Semantics.* Cambridge: Cambridge UP, 1986.
Frege, Gottlob. "Über Sinn und Bedeutung." *Zeitschrift für Philosophie und philosophische Kritik* 100 (1892): 25-50. Reprinted in: Frege, Gottlob, *Funktion, Begriff, Bedeutung.* Ed. Günther Patzig. Göttingen: Vandenhoeck und Ruprecht, 1994. 40-65. English translation: "On Sense and Reference." *Translations from the Philosophical Writings of Gottlob Frege.* Ed. Peter Thomas Geach and Max Black. Oxford: Blackwell, 1960. 56-78.
Jäkel, Olaf. "'Morning, Noon and Night': Denotational Incongruencies between English and German." University Essen: LAUD Series A, Paper No 519, 2001. Also to appear in: *Text Transfer: Metaphors, Translation, and Expert-Lay Communication.* Ed. Cornelia Zelinsky-Wibbelt. Berlin/New York: Mouton de Gruyter, 2001.
Jäkel, Olaf. *Bedeutungs-Inkongruenzen: Anwendungsfelder struktureller und kognitiver Semantik.* [*Denotational Incongruencies: Fields for Applied Structural and Cognitive Semantics*] Unpublished manuscript, University Halle.
Katz, Jerrold J., and Jerry A. Fodor. "The Structure of a Semantic Theory". *Language* 39 (1963): 170-210.
Lakoff, George. *Women, Fire, and Dangerous Things: What Categories Reveal about the Mind.* Chicago/London: U of Chicago P, 1987.
Lakoff, George. "Cognitive Semantics." *Meaning and Mental Representations.* Ed. Umberto Eco, Marco Santambrogio, and Patrizia Violi. Bloomington/Indianapolis: Indiana UP, 1988. 119-154.
Lakoff, George. "Cognitive Cultural Theory." Plenary Lecture at the *3rd International Cognitive Linguistics Conference.* Leuven, 18th-23rd July 1993.
Lehrer, Adrienne. *Semantic Fields and Lexical Structure.* Amsterdam/London: North-Holland Publishing Company, 1974.
Lehrer, Adrienne, and Eva Feder Kittay, eds. *Frames, Fields and Contrasts: New Essays in Semantic and Lexical Organization.* Hillsdale, NJ: Lawrence Erlbaum, 1992.
Lipka, Leonhard. *An Outline of English Lexicology.* Tübingen: Max Niemeyer, 1990.
Lyons, John. *Semantics.* Vol. I.& II. Cambridge: Cambridge UP, 1977.
Nida, Eugene A. *Language Structure and Translation.* Stanford, CA: Stanford UP, 1975.
Saeed, John I. *Semantics.* Oxford: Blackwell, 1997.
Strevens, Peter. *British and American English.* London: Cassell, 1978.
Trier, Jost. *Der deutsche Wortschatz im Sinnbezirk des Verstandes: Die Geschichte eines sprachlichen Feldes.* Heidelberg: Carl Winters Universitätsbuchhandlung, 1931.
Whorf, Benjamin Lee. *Language, Thought, and Reality.* Cambridge, MA: M.I.T. Press, 1956.

Expressive Adjectives and Their Semantic-Syntactic Patterning - A Corpus-Linguistic Study of Newspaper English

Hans-Dieter Schöne und Dietmar Schneider

In Britain the attention paid to language and style in day-to-day politics is increasing to the same degree as the media's influence is increasing on the outcome of elections, opinion polls and popularity ratings. Party-appointed producers of soundbites and slogans, spin doctors, task forces, focus groups and special advisers and their rhetoric seem to be playing a more prominent role on both sides of the House of Commons than traditional parliamentary committees and their elected members. The press reflects every movement on the linguistic front between the Labour Government and the Conservative Opposition. Even before its publication in 2000 Norman Fairclough's book *New Labour, New Language?* was commented upon with eager journalistic anticipation. Fairclough is a Professor of Language in Social Life at Lancaster University, who devoted his study to the language of the 'Third Way', to Tony Blair's personal rhetorical style and to the widespread demand *Bin the spin!* The issue arising from the book and similar publications is the delicate relationship between rhetoric and reality, presentation and practice, 'spin'make and policy matter.

The latest accusation came from William Hague at the Republican National Convention in Philadelphia. His target was New Labour: "They made a systematic attempt to occupy the centre ground of politics by imitating our language, adopting our issues, and pretending to be parties of the right" (*Guardian*, 01.08.2000, 9). Language comes first, but Hague's particular wrath was directed at the alleged occupation of Conservative territory, in the attitude of caring and sharing, and the newly adopted

American-style compassionate conservatism: "The left talks of compassion but often opposes the main things that compassionate politics should be about" (*Guardian*, 01.08.2000, 8). Hague argued that parties of the right were much better at both compassion and fairness in practice.

A Corpus-Analytical Approach to Evaluative Adjectives

If a neutral observer, who can afford to step back and view the British situation from a distance, wants to find reliable linguistic data on the subject, detailed studies of large corpora of language material are inevitable. It is true such extensive corpora do not provide factual evidence, but may give tentative answers to relevant questions such as: How are the values of decency, compassion and social justice conveyed to the public? What is the real meaning behind political discourse as it is reflected in the press?

The following brief considerations attempt to point out a potential approach by presenting a corpus-linguistic analysis of three evaluative/emotive adjectives, which are likely to play a prominent role in expressive speech acts when viewing past experiences, the present state of affairs or plans of the policies of the future: *afraid, anxious* and *sorry*. This is the area of "evaluation" (Thompson 65f.) or "attitudinal predicates" (Kreidler 252ff.) on the borderline of grammar. There are, however, a number of formal structures which are regularly used to convey general feelings retrospectively on past experiences (*mental reviewing*) or prospectively on possible future performances (*mental rehearsing*). Among them, first and foremost, are comment clauses and embedded clauses, both containing attitudinal predicates with the aforementioned adjectives plus their complements.

The analysis of the three emotive adjectives during John Major's premiership is based on a complete year's issues of the right-of-centre paper *The Times* (1992) and the left-of-centre daily/weekly *The Guardian/The Observer* (1996), with about 38 million words each. Similar comparative studies should also be made of the period after 1997. The number of expressions of worry and concern has slightly increased under New Labour and so has the variety of topics causing worry and concern. Moreover, there is a diversity of participants involved, either directly or indirectly, in a general state of anxious and apprehensive political expectation. *The Times* in 1999 e.g. has 1124 instances of *afraid*, 1223 instances of *anxious* and 1453 instances of *sorry*. The computer programme that was used in each case is *Microconcord* (1993), developed by Mike Scott in collaboration with Tim Johns.

A breakdown of the inquiry into the uses of the three adjectives should focus on the following semantic, syntactic and pragmatic issues, some of which cannot easily be answered:

1. What is the total number and the relative frequency of attributive and predicative uses? Which are the nouns characterized by adjectival attributes? To which participants or syntactic subjects do predications refer?

2. Which complements occur in predicative uses? Which semantic differences result from different or competing syntactic patterns? Does affirmative or negative polarity play a role?

3. Which are the verbal and nominal collocates of the adjectives? Which semantic groups and fields are involved? Is personal or temporal deictic nearness or distance signalled? Are there impersonal, general, vague or semantically empty forms?

4. What is the discourse function of the adjectives in pragmatic and rhetorical terms? Are there adverbial modifiers and other collocations with typical stylistic or rhetorical effects (figures of speech, conversational gambits and similar devices)?

The three adjectives as expressions of interpersonal meaning do not only have basic denotations but serve other communicative purposes as well:

> In addition to communicating propositional content, speakers and writers commonly express personal feelings, attitudes, value judgments, or assessments; that is, they express a 'stance'. (Biber et al. 966)

They point out a stance relative to another proposition, i.e. they are part of an overtly evaluative (introductory) comment clause and show the attitude of the writer to the proposition in a (subsequent) subordinate or embedded clause.

Evaluation, like modality, is more a semantic than a grammatical category.

> With evaluation, we are even more on the edge of grammar: much of evaluation is expressed by lexical choices and there are few grammatical structures which can be seen as having evolved with a primarily evaluative function ...(evaluation) is, in a sense, parasitic on other structural elements. (Thompson 65)

A functional-systemic analysis of attitudinal adjectival predicates should thus point out their semantic parallelism to verbal structures: *be afraid* – 'fear, concern oneself'; *be anxious* – 'worry, desire'; *be sorry* – 'regret, repent'. The natural consequence of these considerations is an analysis which does not separate lexical denotation (attributed quality) from grammatical structure (modification and complementation). The functional approach is lexico-grammatical, based on Firth's and Halliday's theory of collocation:

> Not only does collocation provide important evidence for the semantic classification of adjectives, it also constrains possible output in many cases of lexical and grammatical structuring. (Tucker 58)

For the sake of clarity and brevity concordance data in tables will form the starting point of a subsequent discussion of the syntagmatic relations. Fig. 1 to 3 (at the end of the essay) show the concordance findings in detail, i.e. absolute numbers and the relative frequency of the occurrence of the three adjectives, their syntactic patterning (phrasal and clausal complements), and collocating adverbial modifications.

Concordance Findings on *afraid* (cf. fig. 1, p. 187)

The emotive adjective *afraid* is not a prototypical adjective; it goes back to the Middle English past participle *af(f)rai-ed* of the obsolete verb *affray* 'frighten'. Three basic meanings can be registered: (1) fear and anxiety; (2) regret and apology of past action; (3) alarm and worry about possible results and consequences in the future. It is only postpositively used.

Attribution does not occur, with the exception of a very rare pre-modified form (cf. Quirk et al 409: *a somewhat afraid soldier*). Although there is no morphological inflection with *-er*, *-est* the adjective is fully gradable with analytical forms and phrasal intensifiers and emphasizers (intensifying and emphatic degree adverbs). Relative degree of the strength of emotion can be expressed on a scale ranging from high to low (cf. Tucker 184):
high: very, very much, sore(ly), somehow, etc.
low: not so much, a bit, a little bit, a little, etc.

In detail the following forms are used:
Simple intensity: *sore, very,* rarely *very much* (cf. Swan 29, who, strangely, does not permit *very* in front of *afraid*)

```
1 ery far. Everyone is very afraid now that they will start
1 oap opera, I am very much afraid. >THE RUSTLERS OF WEST F
1  -     only to be made sore afraid by angels - would likely
```

Hyperbolic intensity: terribly, horribly, desperately

```
2 and. I was not terribly afraid of it. One tended to worry
5 ; then she was horribly afraid we'd think she was a tart.
2 The CSU is desperately afraid of the electoral threat
```

Simple affective emphasis: *so*

```
3 An 11-year-old boy was so afraid of telling anyone what ha
3 today. Are you really so afraid of  having to say sorry t
3 of a girl in his car, so afraid was he of exposing his li
```

Insistent affective emphasis: *really, truly* and the pseudo-superlative *most*

```
5 advice. ``They are really afraid the  president is going t
1    only when one is truly afraid can the joys of normality
2   the remainder, I am most afraid of Oneupmanship and King
```

Explicit compared degree and superlative degree: *more, less; most, least*

```
3 wasn't  brave. I was more afraid of doing Frocks On The Bo
1   myself love, to be less afraid,and become more physically
```

```
2    ese Communists are most afraid of is me. China dismisse
3    and early. They are least afraid of looking after themselv
```

Sufficiency of degree: *too*

```
2    though, because I'm too afraid of a budget like that, and
```

The negatives *not* and *never* do not signal absence of emotion but the opposite of fear and apprehension. They are employed by the speaker or writer to give courage and spread optimism and hope.

```
2    ople like. They are not afraid of a bit of bawdiness. >''T
2    , because they're never afraid of failure.'' >Jane Tewson'
```

The essential syntactic function of *afraid* is predication. The most frequent occurrence is in a comment clause without any complements in initial, medial or final position giving the speaker's or writer's attitude to the content of the preceding or subsequent clause.

Examples from *The Times*:

```
1    t in the world, but I am afraid the British are not alway
1    A Judgement in Stone, I'm afraid, but there is a side one
1    brother and his wife, I'm afraid.'' The hard work will re
```

The subjects are the participants affected by the emotive evaluation, describing their own state of mind, expressing sympathy, announcing unwelcome news, declining comment on a decision or politely and apologetically refusing action. The general pragmatic purpose is to lessen or soften the effect of unpleasant information.

Deictic nearness is denoted by the overwhelming majority of the cases, 248 in *The Times*, which on the whole is more reserved, and 312 in *The Guardian*, which is more intimate and personal in its journalistic approach to news (more quotes and direct speech). First person pronouns and tenses of the present time level are predominant, as the collocation lists demonstrate. Examples from *The Guardian*:

```
1    estyles than ours? >I'm afraid we're nearly coming to blow
1    were sacking you: `I'm afraid you're going to have to let
```

Clausal substitution of an affirmative statement (*so* in 7 cases) and of a negative statement (*not* in 9 cases) and elliptical clauses can only be found in

The Guardian, both phenomena being grammatical cohesive devices in spoken rather than in written English.

```
1 g to talk about ex? I'm afraid so. >On The Girlie Show, se
1 it already happens? I'm afraid not!'' >Please send brief p
```

The scope of *afraid* comprises the following types of complementation in relative frequency:

1. The causer/cause of the emotive evaluation is most often specified in complementary prepositional groups with the prepositions *of* or *for*. Copula verbs in the clause structure, apart from the forms of *be* are occasionally *feel, become, grow, seem*.

The causers of fear and apprehension are rarely named. They are individuals, e. g. *Virginia Woolf* in the title of the play, *Pat Buchanan, Gordon Brown*, or groups of people, countries and cities, e. g. *Americans, Bosnia, Azerbaijan, Brussels*. Unnamed groups and representatives of organisations are more frequently mentioned:

From *The Times*:

```
2 slightly retarded and was afraid of  Pierre, the older bro
2 balanced with ``They were afraid of us''. These shafts hav
2 , the public is no longer afraid of  the unions. Union lea
```

From *The Guardian*:

```
2 e territory. But we are afraid of China. We do not like th
2 ons said. ''People were afraid of greens. Then we had a gr
2 s gun frenzy, no one is afraid of the police. The balance
```

Most frequently the scope of the adjective is made explicit by specifying the cause of fear and anxiety. The cause is given after the preposition as a noun group which reflects a nominalised clausal predication in a semantically condensed and syntactically reduced form. The following cases are possible:

- an abstract non-count action noun derived from a verb

```
2 s.  > Young Americans are afraid of commitment, emotional
2 ber 1992  PAGE: 14  Who's afraid of devaluation? Anatole
```

- a countable result noun derived from a verb

```
2 gton and London were both afraid of the implications of le
2 . He said Baghdad was not afraid of allied threats to shoo
```

- an abstract non-count quality noun derived from an adjective

```
2 r a year: ``I think he's afraid of intimacy with the Engl
2 es for thought. He is not afraid of  silence. He is then s
```

- a non-count mass noun, sometimes abstract and derived from a noun

```
2 es so: ``Many coaches are afraid of genius because they ar
2  the remainder, I am most afraid of Oneupmanship and King
```

Concrete count nouns are in a clear minority, e. g. animals (spiders, mice, dogs, wolves, birds) or plants (rotten tomatoes). Illnesses are borderline cases requiring pragmatic interpretation, because it is the contraction of the disease that is meant (HIV, syphilis, skin cancer).

2. The cause of the emotive evaluation can also be expressed by complementary non-finite clauses (gerunds and infinitives). The nominalisation of the original predication has been carried out half-way. Gerundial and infinitive structures are verbal nouns and nominal verbs respectively.

The gerund after *afraid* + preposition (with or without an agent) evaluates situations of a general and habitual nature or reported situations with past time reference. Fear and regret was real, a matter of the past in a factual context.

```
3  To say that a man who is afraid of dying in a war that cl
3 and  Schumann are somehow afraid of having it with voice.'
3 e a sumo wrestler who was afraid of flying. The landings,
```

The *to*-infinitive after *afraid,* on the other hand, refers to particular cases, is forward-pointing and denotes future time reference, very often future activity or behaviour, which is potential and not (yet) real. There is a clear preference of dynamic verbs referring to material processes (doing) or verbal processes (saying).

```
4  has appeared who are not afraid to use guns. ``The gangst
4  I did not, and I was not afraid to tell her so fairly and
```

Static verbs (being) are few and far between (sixteen cases in both papers). The large percentage of negated *not afraid* (101 cases out of 210 in *The Times* and 138 out of 277 in *The Guardian*) reflects the effort to do away with the negative emotion and the basic meaning of the adjective and replace it by hope and courage, i.e. a promise of bold action in the future and in a positive atmosphere.

```
4   Thatcher that   he is not afraid to take up unpopular posi
4 s but Bishop Spong is not afraid to make the connection. H
```

3. The third possibility of using the scope to express the cause of the emotion is explaining it by means of an embedded finite clause. The clause gives the complete situation as an explanation. Wh-clauses after a preposition are comparatively rare:

```
3   said. ``We are now very  afraid of what will happen to ou
3 s his Serbian name. ``I'm afraid of what will   come after
```

That-clauses without preposition are more numerous:
```
5 ious, the writers perhaps afraid that even after death she
5 arnard >Peter Barnard is afraid that he is beginning to l
5 f it was true, but  I was afraid that mud would stick.''
```

In this syntactic expression of scope explicitness *afraid* does not occur in the negative. However, a very large number of the *that*-clauses are modalized (73 out of 134 in *The Times*, 119 out of 186 in *The Guardian*). The explanatory situation is presented as probable or possible, often as remotely possible, because the past tense modals are more numerous:

```
5 s if the kidnappers were  afraid he might be discovered. I
5 cause the authorities are afraid the skies  would be dark
5 e for three years he  was afraid that they may become perm
```

The speaker/writer avoids commitment to truth and prefers vagueness, indeterminacy and irresolution.

Concordance Findings on *anxious* (cf. fig. 2, p. 188)

Anxious is a central adjective which appeared late in the English language (17th century) and goes back to a Latin form *anxius* 'troubled in mind', which in turn is related to the Latin *angere* 'choke', 'oppress'. The basic attributive meaning is 'causing/showing fear and distress', the predicative meanings are either 'showing mental unease, concern or worry about something' or 'feeling the intense desire or eagerness for something'.

The attributive use is fairly widespread in collocations with proper and common nouns denoting persons and groups of persons in various functions, organisations and institutions including whole countries.

```
0 , with loyal backing from anxious Tory MPs, ministers soug
0 o.  > Accompanied by ever anxious bodyguards, Jackson and
0 time for faint hearts. An anxious  electorate was waiting
```

Parts of the human body (face, eye, voice, mind, hands, etc.) appear in a *pars-pro-toto* relationship.

```
0 man with a kind, slightly anxious face,  and very bright e
0  Ascot will be casting an anxious eye skywards in the next
```

A second group of collocations contains abstract nouns, so that the adjective should be analysed as a shifted adverb of manner.

```
0  half in hope and half in anxious expectation. !4011 SOU
0 ilitary operation than by anxious reappraisal of a continu
```

The third major group involves expressions of time (moment, minute, hour, morning, year, etc.):

```
0 ething of a  shock.  > In anxious minutes before half-time
0 dends;Comment >These are anxious days for finance directo
```

There are no attitudinal comment clauses with *anxious*. The predicative clause without complementation is a simple and direct statement of the speaker's/writer's anxiety and concern. Common copula verbs are *feel, look, sound,* the inchoative verbs *get, become, grow* and *make sb anxious.*

```
1 der  must be made to feel anxious again, so that there is
1 ner were beginning to get anxious but, once  Piggott asked
1 ers, parents must be made anxious by the statement in  the
```

Complementation is achieved in three ways:
1. Prepositional groups indicating the cause of anxiety are not so numerous as one might have expected. People are anxious about situations rather than things or persons. So the number of nominalisations by far exceeds that of simple nouns. Causes of concern are:
- non-count actions and processes

```
2 and lawyers alike will be anxious for clarification of  th
2 ultation. The patient was anxious about surgical treatment
```

- count results of actions and processes

```
2    dermatologists have been anxious about the effects of exc
2    Tokyo. Both of them are anxious about the strains on the
```

- quality or lack of quality

```
2 d non-EC  governments are anxious about the secrecy which
2  rubbish there. She is as anxious  for her anonymity as fo
```

Occasionally the preposition *about* is followed by a *wh*-clause, giving the complementary situation in full with a finite predicative:

```
2   either. ``We do not feel anxious about what we  did or th
2   arisen because aides are anxious about whether they will
2   he said that miners were anxious  about how their payment
```

Gerunds in non-finite clauses after a preposition, because of their claim to general validity, habit and factuality of the propositional content, are very rare:

```
2 ar and said students were anxious about securing a job. Li
2 bed with him?''. Boys are anxious about bullying and HIV.
2 e was too  ashamed or too anxious about causing disappoint
```

2. *Anxious* followed by a complementary non-finite infinitive is viewed positively, in contrast to *afraid*, whose negative connotation must be compensated for by *not*-negation. Polarity is characteristically distributed in the following manner:

Evaluative adjective	propositional content	Pragmatic use
Negative: not afraid	positive: to do	Expression of encouragement and optimism
Positive: anxious	negative: not to do	Prevention of adverse effects, avoidance of unwanted action

Not anxious is practically non-existent, whereas the negative infinitive is used in 52 cases (plus 46 cases with the infinitive *to avoid* following) in *The Times*, and in 48 cases (plus 42 with the infinitive *to avoid*) in *The Guardian*.

```
4 tion to one which appeared anxious not to reveal its polic
4 ner in sight. Everybody is anxious not to back a loser and
4 d, a junior doctor who was anxious not to take time off wo
```

The non-factual nature of infinitives, their reference to particular cases and their forward orientation to the future explain the immense popularity of the structure in the press: 58.2 % of the total number of uses in *The Times* and 48.5 % in *The Guardian*.

The lexical meaning of the infinitive is almost always dynamic:
- material action

```
4 data from colleges. She is anxious not to reinvent the whe
4 ifferent lifestyle. We are anxious not to damage the Big I
```

- mental or verbal activity

```
4 a more cautious operator, anxious not to annoy the Britis
4 hidden inside. >Police are anxious to speak to anyone who
```

- locomotion

```
4 , on court one. Stich is anxious to get back on centre co
4 t rom anything else, I am anxious to go home and take care
```

Static verbs of being are rare, 2.1 % and 1.9 % of the total in *The Times* and *The Guardian* respectively.

The infinitive may have an agent/beneficiary of its own in a *for*-construction, 18 cases in *The Times* and 11 cases in *The Guardian*. This is a complex structure, which is close to and an alternative to a fully-fledged finite clause:

```
4 , but it is one he is not anxious for us to grasp. The vis
4 the unfriendly Nineties, anxious for life to take a new t
```

Embedded finite clauses with *that* or rarely *lest* to express the cause for being anxious often contain modal verbs or, in a more formal context, the subjunctive mood. The frequency is about 38 % in *The Times* and 49 % in *The Guardian*.

```
5 iculty with walking I was anxious that he would not  show,
5 disclosed that they were anxious  that the report could b
5 h Gas on July  22. He was anxious that agreement should be
```

Concordance Findings on *sorry* (cf. fig. 3, p. 189)

Sorry belongs to the group of central adjectives, which can be used attributively and predicatively and which can be descriptive and gradable. At the same time sorry is an evaluative/emotive descriptor (Biber, et al. 505-509). It goes back to an Old English adjective *sarig*, Middle English *sory* 'pained at heart' and was finally in the 17th c. assimilated to the unrelated noun *sorrow*.

It is apparent that the attributive use of *sorry* is easily outweighed by predicative structures. The most common nouns used with *sorry* are *tale* and the alliterative *saga, sight, state* and *story*. Even if one includes other collocates, one can conclude that attributive *sorry* is typically followed by abstract nouns and rarely by nouns denoting people. The subject of the sentence can be animate or inanimate. The same applies to the post-modification of the noun described by *sorry*.

The Guardian:

```
0 e was a more familiar sorry story in Melbourne, where all
0 of duds tells its own sorry tale. >It is this background w
0 final chapter in this sorry saga came in March 1995. For m
0 th their feet and the sorry sight of floodlights reflectin
0 10 women over 50. The sorry state of the male can be measu
```

Apart from common predicative structures, we have included the elliptical use of *sorry* (*Times* 199, *Guardian* 397), which is seen as a special case of the predicative pattern with the omission of *I am* . Under this heading we would also like to include a feature that is typical of journalism, the frequent use of ellipsis to 'correct' or comment on the expresssion preceding *sorry*. The device is often used to express humour or sarcasm as illustrated by *The Times*:

```
1 ter >As a woman sorry, differently gendered I am in a bit
```

Zero complementation is a common pattern, in which the first person singular and the present tense dominate. The basic structure 'I'm sorry' can stand on its own as a comment clause. It is, however, frequently followed by a main clause. End position within a sentence is less usual. As ellipsis is generally common with *sorry*, its frequent occurrence in this pattern comes as no surprise.

The last of the examples from *The Guardian* hints at the sometimes subtle difference between *zero construction* (*that* omitted) and the punctuated version. Only the latter comes under the heading of pattern 1.

```
1 her face ashen. `I'm sorry. Bill's been under pressure la
1 n. ''She said she was sorry, and police noticed the smell
1 y, I thought . . .' >`Sorry, John never comments on disput
1  ruck to get in? >I'm sorry, I don't really understand the
```

1. *sorry + preposition + noun group*

In this complement structure the speakers/writers want to say that they feel sorry for a person or a group of people. This accounts for the frequent use of personal/reflexive pronouns, names or other nouns denoting people (examples from *The Times*). *Sorry about* is used more frequently with an inanimate noun group, whereas *sorry at* is rare and used exclusively in this way.

```
2 ery harsh lesson. I feel  sorry for him but it was a bit o
2  never, in any case, feel sorry for myself in a  cinema. I
2 re this time. I feel very sorry for Ian. But you have to b
2 is intellectual equal. > Sorry about your problems Mr Sne
2 to the Queen we all feel  sorry at her loss, our sympathy
```

Both finite and non-finite clauses are rare in the complementary pattern *sorry + preposition + clause*. The *ing form* is comparatively frequent after *for* in *The Guardian*. The non-finite clause refers to the present or a previous event. There is little evidence that this pattern is commonly used to express habit. The gerund with an agent of its own as in the last example, which might describe habitual action, is exceptional.

```
3 hear is the game.'' >SORRY for being thick but, according
3 face. No doubt he is sorry for hitting Sheryl but the cos
3 hout him. I feel very sorry for single people doing it, fo
```

A non-finite clause in this pattern plays a marginal role. Occurrences in which *for* is used (*The Guardian*) represent the largest group in this category. Even in cases where different prepositions are used (at, about), they are followed by *what + (has) happened*.

```
3 me and said: 'We are sorry for what happened.' How can we
2   e wanted to. I'm very sorry for what has happened.'' >Afte
```

2. *sorry + to-infinitive*

The construction is the most usual way to refer to the moment of speaking or to point forward. As the speaker usually wants to apologize for something (s)he is doing or about to do the first-person pronoun in the singular, the present tense and ellipsis dominate.

The most frequent verbs following *sorry + to* are *say* (*Times*:22x, *Guardian* :24x) and *see* (*Times*: 21x, *Guardian*: 23x). There is one group of verbs which stands out, namely expressions which frequently have a negative connotation: bang on, disturb, leave, lose, rant, rub in, ruin, trouble, etc. Quite often the following part of the sentence refers to a person. The last of the examples from *The Times* illustrates rare end position of the structure.

```
4 orresponded with? > I am sorry to spoil his fun. But I ma
4 they are struck off. I am sorry to say we have to leave it
3   r worked with. I will be  sorry to see him go because he h
4  flabby ones  at that, I'm sorry to say.''  > There was a l
```

3. *sorry + that-clause*

As the style used by the papers investigated is generally rather formal, one might have expected a greater incidence of a *that clauses* than *zero construction*. Left of *sorry I am* and *I'm* dominate. Right of *sorry* the past, present and pre-present tense and the third person (frequently referring to people) and first person are the most typical linguistic phenomena. If the present tense is used, then it is usually with verbs which imply little action (be, feel, see). There are also some examples in which the future tense is used and some instances of putative *should* (Ungerer 181).

Sorry that (or zero construction) + subordinate clause implies the lowest level of hedging . The other conjunctions express the speaker's/writer's need for a more expressive explanation as to why he/she or other people are sorry (examples from *The Times*).

```
5 n a bit of a mistake, I'm sorry I bothered you, good   luck
5 said: ``I am  personally sorry he has gone and I wish him
5 finance, said ``I am very sorry that this  should have hap
```

It is worth pointing out that after the elliptical use of *sorry,* as in the example from *The Guardian, that* is not used in the corpus, although it is not rejected by some native speakers.

```
5 e become a journalist. Sorry we can't talk, I don't want t
```

Although they do not introduce complements, a brief note about other conjunctions seems in order. *But* followed by *if* is the second most frequent conjunction after *sorry*. What may come as a surprise is the rare use of *as* and *because*.

In terms of speech acts predicative *sorry* is used in expressive utterances, which spring "from the previous actions – or failure to act – of the speaker, or perhaps the present result of those actions or failures. Expressive utterances are thus retrospective and speaker-involved" (Kreidler 188). Not all expressive utterances are, however, necessarily restrospective (Verschueren 132).

Sorry is predominantly used with the first person, indicating speaker involvement or the "deictic centre along the social dimension" (Verschueren 20) and tenses of present time, implying that the speaker - no matter whether he or she is aware of it - is often influenced by the concept of immediacy. Both components should be interpreted as deictic nearness (Meibauer 13-14).

The degree of expressiveness and thus the effect the proposition has on the reader is to no small extent determined by adverbial modifiers: *intensifiers* or *downtoners*. The most common intensifiers used with *sorry* are *very* and *so*, the latter being twice as frequent in *The Guardian* as in *The*

Times, which is an indication of a slightly more emphatic style. The generally greater incidence of intensifiers before *sorry* in the former newspapers may be seen as a trend towards a more 'caring society'.

Other intensifiers are awfully, deeply, desperately, dreadfully, extremely, frightfully, genuinely, more, most, pretty, quite, rather, really, terribly, truly, too.

The use of downtoners (*almost, slightly, vaguely*) is rare, which clearly shows that one prefers to be rather more sorry than less.

Conclusions

With regard to expressive adjectives there are only differences in degree, not in principle, between the two newspapers.

There is a clear bias in favour of reporting emotional attitudes of males rather than females. The collocation tables show the following average 'he:she' proportions: *The Times* afraid 3:1, anxious 4:1 sorry 4:1; *The Guardian* afraid 2:1, anxious 2:1, sorry 5:2.

The papers generally introduce pathos and ethos at the expense of straightforward rational argument based on factual evidence. The feelings of both government and opposition, right and left, in their "we-they"-interrelationship, are presented in two situational contexts: Firstly as concern about existing conditions and as professed efforts to avoid unpleasant consequences. Secondly as readiness for decisive action to be taken in the future. In the latter context the speakers/writers try hard to exude confidence, courage and keenness for change.

The Guardian, on the whole, is more emotional in its reporting. It has a greater number and variety of expressive means and is more personal and intimate in outlook and more colloquial and informal in register and style.

The choice by both papers of attitudinal expressions in attributive and predicative structures is often conventional and semantically meaningless, particularly in cliché-ridden quoted speech. Writers and commentators seem to shy away from verbal commitment. Definiteness in factual statement based on speaker conviction is replaced by run-of-the-mill modalized and/or evaluative structures indicating epistemic uncertainty, vague promises and the desire to appear balanced and unbiassed.

A Corpus-Linguistic Study of Newspaper English 187

Afraid	The Times 1992	The Guardian 1996
Sum total	976	1231
Attributive + Pred. Uses	0 No complements: 308	1 No complements: 388
Predicative complement	Preposition + noun group: 203 Of: 193 for: 7 about: 2 by: 1	Preposition + noun group: 274 Of: 265 for: 7 about: 1 from: 1
	Preposition + non-finite -ing-clause: 92	Preposition + non-finite -ing-clause: 96
	Preposition + finite wh-clause: 5	Preposition + finite wh-clause: 5
	Non-finite clause (to-infin.): 229 For + to-infinitive: 0	Non-finite clause (to-infin.): 279 For + to-infinitive: 0
	Finite clauses That-clause: 92 zero: 47	Finite clauses That-clause: 101 zero: 87
Mood modaliza-Tion	Will: 26 must: 3 Can: 7 cannot: 5 May: 3	Will: 28 must: 6 Can: 17 cannot: 3 May: 15
	Would: 26 should: 8 Might: 16 could: 4	Would: 35 should: 21 Might: 26 could: 6
Polarity	Negative: not 177	Negative: not 205
	never 49	Never 35
Personal deictics	1st and 2nd person: I: 446 we: 51 you: 40	1st and 2nd person: I: 502 we: 62 you: 56
	3rd person: he: 79 she: 26 they: 78	3rd person: he: 108 she: 53 they: 117
Temporal deictics	Tenses of present time: Am 123 is 135 are 151	Tenses of present time: Am 81 is 141 are 179
	Tenses of past time: Was 109 were 55	Tenses of past time: Was 173 were 74
Adverbial modifiers	Intensifiers: sore - very - very much – most - more - really	Intensifiers: very – most – more – really
	Downtoners: a little – somehow – less – least	Downtoners: less – a lot less – a bit – a little bit – a little – not so much

Anxious	The Times 1992	The Guardian 1996
Sum total	1257	1275
Attributive + Pred. uses	220	292
Predicative complement	No complements: 99	No complements: 141
	Preposition + noun group: 107 About: 66 for: 36 over: 3 at: 2	Preposition + noun group: 140 About: 97 for: 34 at: 7 over: 2
	Preposition + non-finite -ing-clause: 11	Preposition + non-finite -ing-clause: 8
	Preposition + finite wh-clause: 2	Preposition + finite wh-clause: 7
	Non-finite clause (to-infin.): 714 For + to-infinitive: 18	Non-finite clause (to-infin.): 603 For + to-infinitive: 11
	Finite clauses: 86 That-clause: 81 zero: 4 lest: 1	Finite clauses: 73 That-clause: 69 zero: 3 lest: 1
Mood and Modaliza-Tion	Will: 40 must: 3 Can: 5 may: 5 Would: 7 should: 16 Could: 4 might: 3	Will: 38 must: 0 Can: 8 may: 6 Would: 10 should: 12 could: 4 might: 4
Polarity	Negative: not 69 never 0	Negative: not 68 never 3
	Avoid: 45	Avoid: 41
Personal deictics	1st and 2nd person: I: 33 we: 40 you: 7	1st and 2nd person: I: 50 we: 30 you: 21
	3rd person: he: 69 she: 18 they: 52	3rd person: he: 69 she: 31 they: 45
Temporal deictics	Tenses of present time: Am 11 is 205 are 193	Tenses of present time: Am 8 is 181 are 151
	Tenses of past time: Was 109 were 80	Tenses of past time: Was 113 were 69
Adverbial modifiers	Intensifiers: very – most - more – extremely – particularly	Intensifiers: very – most – more – deeply – extremely - particularly
	Downtoners: less – a little – slightly	Downtoners: a little – a bit – less – mildly – slightly

Fig.2

Sorry	The Times 1992	The Guardian 1996
Sum total	966	1504
Attributive + Predicative uses	146	172
	810 no complements: 322	1320 no complements: 683
Predicative complement	Preposition + noun group: 188 For: 166 about: 20 at: 2	Preposition + noun group: 302 For: 255 about: 44 at: 3
	Preposition + non-finite -ing-clause: 4	Preposition + non-finite -ing-clause: 15
	Preposition + finite wh-clause: 1	Preposition + finite wh-clause: 10
	Non-finite clause (to-infin.): 90 For + to-infinitive: 1	Non-finite clause (to-infin.):151 For + to-infinitive: 131
	Finite clauses: 112 That-clause: 49 zero: 63	Finite clauses: 93 That-clause: 36 zero: 57
Mood	Will: 24 must: 3 shall: 5 Can: 13	Will: 22 must: 12 shall: 0 Can: 49
	Would: 15 should : 11 Could: 8	Would: 10 should: 12 Could: 9
Polarity	Negative: not 45	Negative: not 65
	never 5	never 8
Personal deictics	1st and 2nd person I: 453 we: 58 you: 64	1st and 2nd person: I: 805 we: 103 you: 138
	3rd person: he: 80 she 21 they: 34	3rd person: he: 123 she: 46 they: 57
Temporal deictics	Tenses of present time: Am 113 is: 65 are 37	Tenses of present time: Am 124 is 99 are 71
	Tenses of past time: Was 89 were 17	Tenses of past time: Was 127 were 28
Adverbial modifiers	Intensifiers: very-so-terribly-really-extremely-deeply-most-desperately-genuinely-rather	Intensifiers: very-so-terribly-really-truly-desperately-more-too-extremely-awfully
	Downtoners: a bit-slightly-a little	Downtoners: almost-a bit-vaguelyt

Fig. 3

Works Cited

Biber, Douglas, et al. *Longman Grammar of Spoken and Written English*. Harlow: Longman, 1999.
Fairclough, Norman. *New Labour, New Language*. London and New York: Routledge, 2000.
The Guardian and The Observer. Compact Disc Edition. Cambridge: Chadwyck-Healey, 1996.
The Guardian, 1.8.2000.
Hornby, Albert Sydney *A Guide to Patterns and Usage in English*. Oxford: Oxford UP, 1961.
Kreidler, Charles W. *Introducing English Semantics*. London: Routledge, 1998.
Meibauer, Jörg. *Pragmatik: Eine Einführung*. Tübingen: Stauffenburg, 1999.
Quirk, Randolph, Sidney Greenbaum, and Geoffrey Leech. *A Comprehensive Grammar of the English Language*. London: Longman, 1985.
Swan, Michael. *Practical English Usage*. Oxford: Oxford UP, 1990.
Thompson, Geoff. *Introducing Functional Grammar*. London: Arnold, 1996.
The Times and Sunday Times. Compact Disc Edition. London: Priory House, 1992.
Tucker, Gordon H. *The Lexicogrammar of Adjectives*. London: Cassell, 1998.
Ungerer, Friedrich. *Englische Grammatik heute*. Stuttgart: Klett, 1999.
Verschueren, J. *Understanding Pragmatics*. London: Arnold, 1999.

Pupils Reflecting on Languages, Cultures and Perception:

An Account of a Teaching Programme at Primary Level

Andreas Marschollek

This article outlines the conception and the evaluation of a teaching programme that was implemented by the author in two classes of *August-Hermann-Francke Primary School* in Halle/Saale (Germany) in the school years 1997/98 and 1998/99. To raise the children's awareness of linguistic and cultural phenomena and to sensitise them to the limitations of their own perception, a focus on English was combined with a selective consideration of other foreign languages along with references to German as the mother tongue. The programme conceptually drew from a pilot in-service teacher training course offered at *Martin-Luther-University Halle-Wittenberg* in 1997, in which primary school teachers could acquire a teaching certificate on *Encountering Foreign Languages: Focus on English*. In this context the author had offered seminars dealing with the implementation of the course objectives in classes.

Background

Today learning foreign languages is considered a central aspect in children's education that already has to be introduced at primary level. It is frequently argued that the individual increasingly requires the ability to communicate across linguistic and cultural boundaries – especially in the face of the European integration process. The ability to communicate, however, amounts to more than a proficiency in one or several foreign languages. It especially includes the willingness and capability to open oneself to new, unfamiliar and changing situations. Consequently, supporting pupils in this respect constitutes a major educational goal.

In this framework, foreign language learning is significant. For language is not only the most important means of communication, it also touches upon many aspects of the individual's personal, social and cultural life. This is why dealing with foreign languages at primary level promises to be particularly relevant to the pupils' affective and cognitive growth. It is assumed that this may be achieved by a teaching programme that does not exclusively focus on a single foreign language, but that offers the children a field of experience in which they can experiment with languages and explore their manifold functions. This would give them the opportunity to reflect on manifestations of language, on its usage and on the way it influences their ideas, feelings and actions. Such reflections can have their impact on other learning processes. In addition, this may be accompanied by becoming more open in terms of becoming less ethnocentric and less intolerant (Hermann-Brennecke 1993, 60; Hermann-Brennecke 1994, 16-17) – an essential characteristic of the ability to communicate.

While the majority of people concerned with foreign languages at primary level would probably acknowledge the potential outlined above, it is generally not given high priority as far as theoretical considerations, their practical implementation, and the evaluation of teaching programmes are concerned. In particular, proponents of a systematically progressing introduction of a single foreign language into the primary classroom keep warning that chances of fostering the learners' proficiency in that language would be wasted if the curriculum included other foreign languages as well and allowed time for reflective activities (cf. Sauer 3-6).

However, viewing the development of foreign language skills as competing with the fostering of pupils' reflections on language does not concur with psycholinguistic considerations that see language learning and metalinguistic activities closely linked to each other. Furthermore, there is no convincing evidence to date for the hypothesis that early foreign language learning leads to significant long-term advantages in language proficiency (cf. Blondin, et al. 17-19). What is more, some studies even raise doubts as to whether foreign language teaching programmes at primary level actually foster a positive attitude towards foreign language learning in all children (cf.

Burstall, et al. 243). In the light of these considerations, it seems worthwhile teaching a programme that focuses on making pupils' reflect on languages, cultures and perception.

It is important to note that such a programme requires teachers with adequate background knowledge as well as the didactic competence to transfer it to their pupils. Consequently, training teachers accordingly was among the main objectives of the in-service course offered at *Martin-Luther-University* in Halle. To achieve this aim, participants were given the opportunity to expand their theoretical and practical understanding of language awareness and cultural awareness, and to cross their perceptual boundaries. Furthermore, the course aimed at furnishing them with a competence to apply their insights to their daily teaching. For a detailed account of the concept of the course, its intentions, its syllabus, and its evaluation the reader is referred to the concluding report (Hermann-Brennecke and Marschollek 1999).

The final examination showed that though the participants seemed to still have difficulties implementing their syllabus according to the underlying theoretical concepts, they obviously made considerable progress concerning their capacity to reflect on languages and processes of perception. What is more, they did not only consider this an important personal asset, but also wanted to initiate a similar development on the part of the children entrusted to them. During their in-service course they had been shown possible methodological implementations. Furthermore, they had developed their own teaching materials and had successfully planned their lessons accordingly. Whether the teachers would actually carry on in this respect in the long run could only be speculated about at that stage.

Interviews with the ten participants conducted almost two years after the course revealed that only two of them exclusively concentrated on fostering their pupils' language proficiency in English. The eight remaining teachers allowed between ten and thirty percent of class foreign language teaching time to be used for reflections on languages, cultures and perception. It stands out that the two teachers who were most committed to the fostering of these aims were also the ones who considered the requisite extra workload highest. Nevertheless they were willing to accept that – first and foremost because their pupils constantly came up with new questions and ideas

(Hermann-Brennecke and Marschollek 107-108). This indicates that a teaching programme aimed at initiating and fostering primary school children's reflections on languages, cultures and perception does stand a chance. The following study will substantiate this by outlining the concept, the implementation and the evaluation of a teaching programme pursuing these objectives.

Conception

In order to foster the pupils' reflections on languages, cultures and perception, the syllabus described below followed a two-step strategy. Firstly it brought the pupils into contact with a wide range of linguistic and cultural phenomena. Secondly it encouraged them to reflect on these experiences whenever there was an opportunity. This would in turn broaden the pupils' linguistic and cultural experience and make it personally relevant to them. For this strategy to take effect it was necessary to establish an atmosphere of exploration and cooperation in class – a "community of inquiry" in which the children

> listen to one another with respect, build on one another's ideas, challenge one another to supply reasons for otherwise unsupported opinions, assist each other in drawing inferences from what has been said, and seek to identify one another's assumptions. (Lipman 14)

For the pupils' ability to communicate is by no means restricted to an intercultural or interethnic framework. It is closely linked to their ability to interact with others in the classroom and beyond.

The decision as to which languages and which related cultural phenomena would serve best the realization of the strategy outlined above was influenced by two basic considerations. On the one hand, reflecting on languages is triggered by setting out from intensive experiences with the use of one or more foreign languages. This particularly applies to primary school children whose thinking is still very much dependent on concrete observation. With regard to the limited amount of class time this speaks for concentrating on one foreign language only. On the other hand, language awareness can be elicited more easily and become truly metalinguistic if it starts out from experiences with a number of foreign languages and cultures.

As a kind of compromise, the teaching programme did introduce the pupils to a variety of foreign languages, but it put an emphasis on English. Thus the children could acquire a basic proficiency that enabled them communicate with speakers of that language. This feeling of success was not only likely to boost their interest in foreign language learning and their confidence in their own abilities – two important aims of the programme – it also marked an important step in the children's use of language: Most of them would cross the boundaries set by their mother tongue for the first time in their lives and thus experience language in a qualitatively new way. What is more, in the course of acquiring this basic proficiency the pupils would engage in processes that are supposed to be crucial for language learning such as drawing inferences, generalizing, constructing, abstracting and developing hypotheses as well as testing them – procedural knowledge the pupils could fall back on in their future language learning careers. Initiating these developments would have been more difficult or even impossible if several foreign languages had been given equal shares of class time with the likely result that the pupils could not communicate in any of them.

English was chosen for various reasons. It already played an important role in pupils' everyday life. For instance, it frequently finds its way into the German language, occurs in the media and especially dominates the domain of computers. Besides, frequently elder brothers and sisters already learn English at school. Therefore concentrating on English had the decisive advantage that pupils could not only bring their already existing foreign language experiences into the classroom, but they would also have ample opportunity to apply outside school what they would learn in class. This promised to broaden the range of experiences mediated by the teaching programme.

It has to be noted, however, that concentrating on a language that already has a prominent position might be less suited to trigger reflective processes. In people's perception English is so much taken for granted as an integral part of everyday life and has become so closely connected to our culture that it might not automatically challenge the pupils to analyse and exceed their habitual patterns of language use and perception. This further stresses the importance of including a range of additional foreign languages or linguistic phenomena. Besides, coming into contact with a variety of languages at primary level may make it more likely that pupils will eventually opt for less dominant languages later in their career and thus help to pave the way for more than one foreign language.

As a result of these considerations the syllabus aimed at getting the pupils involved in the following activities in order to foster their foreign language competence as well as their ability to reflect on languages, cultures and perception.

Language proficiency
- *in English:* acquiring and applying basic speech acts for communicative purposes
- *in other languages:* acquiring and using selected linguistic phenomena

Reflecting on languages
- reporting on linguistic phenomena occurring outside school
- comparing selected aspects of languages with each other
- exploring family relations between languages
- discussing the potential and the limits of verbal and non-verbal communication
- experimenting with and comparing different writing conventions, discussing their advantages and disadvantages and exploring the origins of the Roman alphabet
- acquiring and applying strategies that support language learning

Reflecting on cultures
- comparing ways of life across different cultures
- putting oneself in other people's position and tolerating differences in perception
- relating information about foreign cultures to one's own culture and reconsidering one's own values and perspective
- talking about traditions in foreign cultures and comparing them with those in one's own culture

Reflecting on perception
- exploring the relativity of perception and speculating about the functions of prejudices

Implementation

The programme was taught by the author as a visiting teacher at *August-Hermann-Francke Primary School* (Halle/Saale) to two parallel classes beginning in grade three and continuing in grade four. With the parents' consent the subject *Encountering Foreign Languages: Focus on English* was integrated into the mandatory schedule of both groups. It comprised 65 weekly periods altogether that were distributed over the two school years 1997/98 and 1998/99 and lasted 45 minutes each. Thus – from the point of view of time – the implementation corresponded with the schedule for foreign languages at primary level required by the Ministry of Education in Saxony-Anhalt.

Altogether, the programme consisted of nine projects. The following table gives a survey of the projects and indicates the estimated amount of time dedicated to each of them (measured in lessons) and their position within the two school years. Three lessons used for the empirical evaluation are not considered.

3rd grade (35)	Wizadora (23)	Children teaching children (8)	Phonetic transcription (6)	Indians (3)
				Japan (3)
				Visit from America (3)
				World Cup in France (3)
				Gingerbread Man (3)
4th grade (30)				Tanzania (10)

Wizadora

Eight episodes of a video English course for primary school children titled *Wizadora* formed the backbone of the teaching programme in two respects. Firstly, the majority of activities in the English language originated with that series. Secondly, the videos formed a recurring element and thus ran like a thread through the two-year programme.

With regard to fostering the pupils' proficiency in English, the video series offered several advantages. The children found its contents interesting and inspiring: The main protagonist is Wizadora – a young wizard whose magic tricks often fail. She shares her home with a number of animated fantasy friends – a scarecrow, a telephone, a mop, a fish, a coat hanger and four glove puppets. In addition, the two primary school children, Katie and Tom, living in Wizadora's neighbourhood appear in most episodes. Thus twelve native speakers with different accents regularly serve as linguistic models for the pupils.

The non-linguistic features of the video allowed the children to grasp the plot quickly and reinforced their feeling of linguistic competence from the very beginning. To supplement the listening comprehension processes, glove puppets were replicated and used in classroom discourse. For instance, magic tricks were acted out, modified or newly invented by the children. Using the background story as a context, the video series covers a range of basic topics and functions such as 'greetings', 'family and relations', 'making suggestions', 'describing people's appearance', 'requesting' and 'asking for and giving reasons for present actions' – to give only some examples. The vocabulary comprised about 450 lexical items.

It is important to note, however, that the work with the video neither adhered strictly to the linguistic progression proposed by its authors nor followed the respective methodological procedures. The episodes were not even dealt with in the given sequence. Selected scenes were used as starting points for classroom discussions. To provide an example, the critical reflection of one protagonist's inconsiderate behaviour initiated a discussion about the manner in which the pupils dealt with each other in the schoolyard. This shows that although much of the time spent in the context of the project *Wizadora* was used to equip the pupils with a basic proficiency in English, activities suitable to foster the reflection on languages, cultures and perception were integrated wherever possible.

Children Teaching Children

In each lesson the children were allowed some time to report on observations and experiences they had made outside school. Frequently, they had occupied themselves at home with what had been dealt with in class. For example, newly acquired foreign language competencies were tried out on other family members and friends, or the pupils just occupied themselves with drawing or colouring worksheets. Consequently, in the course of the two years of the programme the pupils brought to school a variety of books, (computer) games, maps, atlases, dictionaries, songs, audio and video cassettes, and other objects. To support these activities among all children, additional materials were made available in the classroom.

Being thus prepared and motivated, the pupils willingly slipped into the teacher's role. For instance, two girls made a presentation on ancient Egyptian hieroglyphs –setting out with souvenirs brought home from Egypt and referring to additional material provided by the teacher. They made their classmates speculate about the meaning of some "easy" symbols and later asked them to apply this knowledge in a quiz game. On another occasion, two boys organized the repetition of Japanese numerals that had been dealt with in the project *Japan*. In that context, the pupils made the other children recognize and decipher some of the symbols on coke-tins and pencils with Japanese labelling.

Usually the pupils' presentations lasted about five minutes – sufficient time at least to appreciate the extracurricular efforts. On some occasions, however, additional time was required. In two cases the presentations even extended over the complete lesson in which pupils whose parents are foreign born introduced their classmates to select elements of their parents' mother tongue and culture – including greetings, numbers and geographical details. This is how the Hungarian and Russian languages became part of the syllabus.

The activities outlined above turned out to be particularly suitable to sensitise the children to manifestations of foreign languages and cultures in everyday life which they explored autonomously. In the process, they learned to appreciate the variety of linguistic and cultural phenomena and came to see diversity and difference as stimulating instead of ignoring or even debasing them. Moreover, they experienced that what was learned in class could actually be applied outside the classroom. Apart from that, the children encountered, applied and practised strategies important for language learning such as making hypotheses and putting them to the test.

Phonetic Transcription

This project focussed on the introduction to and on the practice of a limited inventory of phonetic symbols. In its context the children were expected to read phonetic transcription on their own and in this way find out about the pronunciation of new words autonomously.

In two introductory lessons, a video with Disney-cartoons (*Magic English 2: Family: Die Familie*, 1997) brought by one of the pupils was (ab)used to familiarize the children with a number of phonetic symbols. The names of the well-known cartoon characters that most of the children could already pronounce correctly – among them *Mickey Mouse, Donald Duck, Simba* and *Goofy* – were put in phonetic script. Together with several other words they were compiled into a list, which the pupils could refer to later when reading phonetic transcriptions – a recurring feature throughout the teaching programme.

Familiarizing the children with phonetic transcription also fostered their language awareness on a different plane in that it sensitised them to the fact that slight deviations in pronunciation can result in semantic change. In addition they discovered that the pronunciation of words in any language can be coded with the help of phonetic symbols.

Indians

The project *Indians* introduced the pupils to pictographs and encouraged them to compare them to the Roman alphabet. The starting point for this was an authentic story of a Native American tribe written in pictographs that the children tried to read by guessing the meaning of the different symbols. Later, they used these symbols to write their own stories and even invented their own pictographs the meaning of which their classmates had to guess. On the basis of these experiments the children ventured into the pros and cons of both writing systems such as the likeliness of being understood by a large number of people, the problem of ambiguities, the potential for representing abstract concepts or the possibility of having them typed on a typewriter. In this context, modern pictographs as they occur on computer desktops or in codes such as Morse and Braille were discussed as well. In addition, the development of the Roman alphabet with its roots in Hebrew and its development through Greek was retraced for selected letters. Thus, the children could not only identify pictographic writing as a step in the development of more advanced writing systems, but were also given the opportunity to understand the functioning of writing systems in general and the Roman alphabet in particular. In this context the newly introduced reform of the German orthography served as a recent example. Reflections like these threw a different light on their own alphabet and enhanced their interest in alternative writing systems at the same time.

Another story dealt with in class offered the children an exemplary insight into its Native American author's way of viewing nature – involving unity, reciprocality, respect, and admiration. This triggered a critical glance at the pupils' own relation to their environment, which meant a further step towards perceptual awareness.

Japan

The 18th Olympic Winter Games in Nagano, Japan, which took place at some stage of the teaching programme, provided the opportunity to introduce to some aspects of the Japanese language and culture. One focus was on the life of Japanese pupils. A television documentary featuring interviews with children in a Nagano primary school (*Die Flötenkinder von Nagano*, 1998) – part of the media coverage on the Olympic Games – allowed the German children to compare their school life with that of the Japanese pupils. Apart from many similarities, a number of differences were discovered. For example, Japanese school children clean their classrooms, schoolyard and toilets. They also wear school uniforms and have lunch together in their classroom.

The documentary also showed children writing in *Kanji*. The German pupils discovered that the *Kanji* symbols – like the pictographs of the Native Americans – originally derive from pictures representing ideas. Hence, they were encouraged to retrace the development of chosen symbols, to guess their meaning and finally to write some of them – following the correct sequence of strokes and writing from bottom to top and from right to left, just as the Japanese children had done in the documentary. Thus they realized that there are options to the Roman alphabet that are still in use today. Although the experiments with *Kanji* naturally remained restricted and incomplete, they succeeded in giving the children the notion that they were capable of acquiring that writing system – provided they invested the necessary effort and time.

To intensify this impression, Japanese numerals were dealt with in more detail. As only ten symbols and a few rules suffice to write numbers from 1 to 99, the children could soon do 'mathematics in Japanese' – something which boosted their self-esteem. What is more, they even practised pronouncing the numerals – supported by some classmates who used them in their Judo lessons. The pupils also insisted on speaking more Japanese so that further basic idioms and phrases were introduced. Interesting enough, they continued 'speaking Japanese' for several days, something which points to the commitment and joy with which they used what they had learned.

Visit from America

Inviting an American teacher into the classroom allowed the children to put their language proficiency in English to a test. The pupils had carefully prepared for the visit. Partly in groups, they had acquired some geographical background knowledge about the USA and Michigan – the visitor's home state. Furthermore, they had drawn up a list of questions. For most of the pupils this native speaker offered the first opportunity in their lives to use the English language in an authentic context.

The visit itself had a tremendous impact on them. After the children first followed the prepared questions, they soon started to introduce themselves individually or ask spontaneous questions in English – helped by their teacher. However, as the wish to learn more about the guest soon exceeded their communicative competence, the conversation was finally continued in German.

Another authentic occasion to converse in English occurred just before the teaching programme ended, when an Iraqi-born child was transferred to the school and participated in the foreign language lessons. The native speaker of Arabic could not speak German yet, but he had some knowledge of English. Like with the American guest before, it soon became apparent that the restricted communicative abilities in English were only sufficient to exchange some basic information. But this time neither the German pupils nor their Iraqi classmate could fall back on their respective mother tongue. They automatically tried to communicate by means of gestures and pictures. At the same time, the German pupils made an effort to learn some bits of Arabic and to teach their new classmate some German – inside and outside the classroom. In this way they learned to cope with a situation in which language boundaries have to be overcome in one way or another. Besides, the children enjoyed watching the Iraqi boy write Arabic letters and numerals and comparing them with their own. What they had learned about Kanji symbols earlier was now applied to the new situation.

World Cup in France

The soccer world championship in France was another major event that attracted the pupils' attention and served as a starting point for a project. Initially, the children had wished to learn the names of the participating nations in English and to collect their flags. The occasion was used to equip the pupils with some basic speech acts in French, Spanish and Italian. A subsequent comparison of the various greetings in these languages as well as in English and German revealed many similarities – e.g. between the expressions 'Hallo', 'Hola' and 'Hello'. Some differences were discovered, too. The fact, for instance, that there is no equivalent for 'Guten Morgen' in Spanish or for 'Good afternoon' in German sensitised the pupils for the limitations of literal translations between languages. When asked to speculate about the reasons for these similarities, the pupils mentioned the geographical vicinity and family relations between languages. With the help of additional information provided by the teacher they could retrace the relations between German and the other languages.

It was among the main objectives of this project to let the pupils discover and explain similarities and differences between German and other languages, so that they could view their mother tongue and other languages from a new perspective. For this could make them curious to find out more about languages and increase their interest in (foreign) language learning.

Gingerbread Man

In the context of this project the children were introduced to an authentic children's story. They were given the chance to improve their listening comprehension abilities, to use visual aids to understand the story and to retell and to modify it later. Moreover, the story was compared with its German counterpart "Der dicke fette Pfannekuchen" in terms of plot, protagonists, setting and the like. In addition, the children could borrow other books from the teacher.

Tanzania

In the course of this project the pupils were given the opportunity to correspond in English with children of *Igogwe Primary School* in Tanzania. While the contact had already been established by the language teachers in the school year 1997/98, it was not until the German pupils entered the fourth grade that they actively engaged in exchanging pictures, photographs, little letters, teaching materials and the like. Even though the teachers provided considerable support – especially with the writing of the letters – the children found many ways of exchanging information.

The African children documented their life at school and in their village – partly in written form, but frequently by pictures and even complete picture stories. Furthermore, photos of the school building, of all classes, of the staff, and of the pupils engaging in various teaching activities were sent to Germany.

In return, the German children made a video in which they presented themselves, their school and their school life, their free time activities and – not to be forgotten – their favourite stuffed animals. Furthermore, they recorded themselves learning in the language classroom – playing with glove puppets and performing magic tricks. In addition, they interviewed their class teachers. When the surroundings of the school were shown, some pupils could point at the nearby high-rise buildings they lived in. The making of the video involved elaborate preparations. It had to be decided, for example, which aspects would be especially interesting for the African children who lived and learned under such different conditions. The pupils considered how they could present themselves and their school as an appropriate reply to the many letters and drawings that had obviously been produced with much commitment and with considerable time.

In the course of this authentic contact the pupils yet again realised that even their restricted competence in English allowed them to communicate with other people. What is more, they received an impressive insight into the life of children who lived under fundamentally different conditions: The African pupils walked to school over long distances – barefoot but in school uniforms. They hardly possessed any books, writing supplies or paper. Apart from subjects such as English and mathematics, the curriculum also included a range of manual activities such as carpentry and laying bricks in the workshop, as well as farming. The pupils cleaned the classrooms and the schoolyard in regular intervals – as did the Japanese pupils. The photographs and reports also illustrated a high level of discipline and diligence on the part of the African children. After school they helped their parents with their work in the household and in the fields. Nevertheless, their letters made it completely clear that they were happy and proud to be able to go to school and learn.

Of course, the German children automatically compared this with their own background and consequently started to see many things they had taken for granted. While they considered the aspects mentioned above surprising and strange, they also recognized many similarities. For instance, the African children loved playing football during the breaks. On the photos the German pupils noticed that the ball was already badly damaged. This is why they decided to collect money to buy a new one as a Christmas present. A missionary took those gifts to Tanzania.

The children's language awareness profited from this particular exchange in another respect as well. The German children wanted to learn some words in the African pupils' mother tongue of Swahili. Apart from greetings that soon found their way into the letters, the interest especially focussed on the names of the wild animals that occurred so frequently in the African children's drawings.

Evaluation

At the end of the first and the second year, questionnaires were distributed to ascertain the pupils' view on the teaching programme as a whole, on the individual projects and on recurring classroom activities. In addition, the children were asked to comment on their proficiency in English as well as on their ability and motivation to learn other foreign languages. When comparing the results it has to be taken into consideration that only about 90 percent of the data come from the same children – mostly due to illness or change of residence.

The Programme as a Whole

On both occasions the pupils were asked to rate the programme as a whole. 28 of the 35 pupils questioned after the first year considered it "good", six chose the option "average" and only one "poor". By the end of the second year, the number of pupils with a neutral attitude towards the programme remained virtually unchanged. The negative evaluations had increased to five. Correspondingly the portion of pupils with a positive attitude had slightly decreased to 27 out of 39. These results demonstrate that the majority of pupils viewed the teaching programme positively throughout its two-year duration.

When asked to classify the programme's level of difficulty in general, more than 60 percent of the children perceived it as "easy", about 30 percent considered it "average" and less than 10 percent "difficult". In this respect there were no significant changes in the pupils' perception between the two surveys.

It is also noteworthy that two thirds of the children would have preferred more weekly lessons – a fact that can be taken as a further reflection of the pupils' positive attitude towards the teaching programme.

The Individual Projects

In both questionnaires the pupils were also requested to evaluate the projects described above on a five-step scale between "very good" and "poor" and to give reasons for their decision. It turned out that all projects were classified above "average", and that seven out of nine were even rated between "good" and "very good".

The project *Visit from America* received the best evaluation of all. The children's reasons for this show that the attempt to communicate with the guest in his mother tongue had made a lasting impression. The project *Tanzania*, which had also offered the opportunity to communicate with foreign people, received a very positive evaluation as well. The pupils provided a diversity of reasons for this. Comments such as "It is interesting to see the African village and to write to the children" reveal that the curiosity to know and understand more about life in the foreign country had been aroused. Other remarks indicate that the pupils considered this contact a good opportunity to widen their horizon. Furthermore, they appreciated the chance to make the African children happy by sending them pictures, letters and little gifts.

This shows that the children had obviously been able to make quite different and unique experiences. It is important to note that a number of them emphasised the extensive opportunities to work autonomously and creatively over longer periods of time – especially when the video was made. Only a few pupils considered this project difficult because of their limited ability to express themselves in English. Most children were not frustrated by that, but instead made extensive use of the means of communication and the teacher's support they had at their disposal.

In the pupils' perception, the project *Phonetic transcription* scored second best. Among the reasons given, two aspects were prominent: For one thing, many children considered the new writing system a challenge. For another, the ability to read some words in phonetic transcription provided them with a feeling of possessing a specific competence. The remark "The writing helps you to learn" can be taken as a hint that the children were aware of the relevance the phonetic spelling had for language learning.

The project *Wizadora* was also rated between "very good" and "good". The pupils liked working with the video, they considered the plot interesting and – especially after the first year – appreciated the ability to play with the glove puppets.

With ratings between "average" and "good" the projects *Indians* and *World Cup in France* received comparatively unfavourable evaluations. As far as the project *Indians* is concerned, the pictographs and the Native Americans' attitude towards nature seem to have aroused their interest most. However, some of the children stated that they did not like Indians. The title of the project had already activated stereotypes when it first occurred in the course of the teaching programme. Even though this phenomenon had immediately been worked at cognitively in class, it obviously still diverted some pupils' attention from the central aspects of the project – at least in their memory.

A similar mechanism seems to have taken effect in the evaluation of the project *World Cup in France*. Although some pupils remembered that they had liked dealing with various foreign languages, comparing them and reflecting on their family relations – activities the project had actually focussed on – other pupils based their judgment on their individual attitude towards soccer. To provide an example, some girls stated that soccer was something for boys.

These responses do not necessarily mean that the teaching activities in the two projects mentioned above proceeded less productively. However, they do indicate that the selection of titles which activate stereotypes can make the achievement of teaching objectives more difficult. If the two projects had been named *Native American language and culture* and *Comparing languages*, the children's memories might have focussed on the topics that had actually been dealt with in class.

No such effect could be observed in case of the project *Japan*. Most pupils could still recall working with the Kanji symbols and Japanese numerals as well as their attempts to speak some Japanese. Consequently, a considerable number of children were rather satisfied with their efforts to decode and read some of the symbols that had initially seemed so strange. Only a few pupils held a less favourable attitude and argued that the symbols and the pronunciation were difficult for them to handle.

The pupils' evaluation of the project *Gingerbread Man* also reflects differences in their abilities and strategies for coping with new foreign language material. Some children explained their less favourable judgment with their difficulty to understand the story. They were probably frustrated by their inability to comprehend every word or sentence. The majority, however, argued that they could grasp the meaning of the story and that they considered it a good opportunity to learn English. They obviously had no difficulties with the non-linguistic aids.

The project *Children teaching children* was evaluated negatively by a quarter of the pupils. A minority argued that their classmates' presentations had been boring and that they would rather have been taught by the teacher. This can be interpreted as a hint that these children did not consider themselves and their classmates equal members of a learning community. However, the majority of comments on this project reflect that the opportunity to teach was considered a welcome enrichment of the lessons and an additional chance to learn. Indeed, for five children the only negative aspect about the project resided in the fact that they would have liked to contribute to it more often.

Recurring Classroom Activities

To supplement the project-oriented evaluation of the teaching programme, the two questionnaires also ascertained the pupils' preferences for thirteen recurring classroom activities by asking them to decide whether they would have liked to engage in them "more frequently", "less frequently" or "at the same frequency". Differences between the results of the first and the second questioning can be taken as a hint that the children's preferences had changed in the course of the programme. However, to some extent these differences might also have resulted from the fact that the frequency at which the activities occurred in the classroom varied over the two years. Consequently, the data can only be interpreted with the reservation that there might be distorting effects.

Apart from reflecting on stories and singing, all classroom activities were approved of by the majority of the pupils. It stands out that those which involved an active use of language(s) were among the most popular after both the first and the second year – dealing with foreign symbols and languages, inviting foreign guests, playing games and playing with glove puppets. Though comparatively passive or predefined activities such as watching videos or working with worksheets had been held in relatively high regard after the first year, they obviously decreased in attractiveness later. This effect is most significant in the case of some *Magic English* videos that had been brought by the pupils in the context of the project *Children teaching children* all of which followed the same pattern: After some words and simple sentences had been presented, the children were expected to repeat them all together and to sing along with songs. When it had been first introduced in the classroom, the pupils were enthusiastic about that procedure. However, their interest soon deteriorated. Commentaries such as "*Magic English* is so boring" indicate that this was due to the fact that the pupils had to remain rather passive and that the somewhat incoherent collection of scenes taken from various famous Disney movies could not capture the pupils' curiosity in the long run.

A positive trend could be observed in regard to comparing languages and reflecting on stories – indicating that the pupils' interest in thinking about what they dealt with in the classroom may have increased. At the same time, the wish to work in groups more frequently points to a greater autonomy and a heightened willingness to cooperate.

This interpretation is in line with a further result. When asked what aspects of the teaching programme they liked most, after the first year the children named working with videos and playing – especially with the glove puppets. One year later, however, these activities only took third and second place respectively, being surpassed by those that involved encountering many languages or linguistic phenomena.

The only aspect of the teaching programme that struck several children as negative both after the first and the second year was that some of their classmates occasionally disturbed the lessons. While almost no such problems occurred in phases during which the teacher did most of the instruction and told the children exactly what to do, this happened predominantly when the pupils were encouraged to reflect and philosophise. Though the majority of children willingly made use of these opportunities, others were obviously rather inexperienced in arguing and discussing in a group. For them, reaching the level of joint reflection and philosophising about languages, cultures and perception proved to be more difficult. Thus it required intensive efforts from all pupils and the teacher to improve communication and cooperation in class – especially in regard to the fact that there was only one lesson a week.

Language Proficiency and Attitudes Towards Foreign Language Learning

When asked to evaluate whether they could communicate in English with a native speaker at the end of the programme, a majority of 21 out of 39 children felt capable of doing so, whereas only two considered themselves unable to do so. Taking into account the limited amount of class time, this result is encouraging – especially because the pupils' estimation of their abilities can be considered realistic as they all spoke from experience. Under the given circumstances, they could not develop a language proficiency beyond a rudimentary level – even if all 63 lessons had been dedicated to that purpose. Thus it is quite understandable that 16 were not sure whether they could manage to communicate in English.

The question of whether the pupils felt confident that they could learn certain aspects of foreign languages autonomously produced a similarly positive result: 26 children answered in the affirmative, whereas six were uncertain and only seven lacked the requisite self-confidence. After all, the majority of the pupils had already shown in the context of the project *Children teaching children* that they were completely capable of 'exploring' languages on their own. Consequently, it is hardly surprising that more than 60 percent reported that they had already used what they learned in class during their leisure time. Moreover, after the first year 80 percent of the children said that they had talked about the contents of the teaching programme with their parents, relatives or friends.

Accordingly, the children's interest in languages and cultures proved to be high. At the end of the second year 96 percent said they intended to learn foreign languages, and 89 percent were interested in visiting foreign countries. In addition, the diversity of languages and cultures that attracted the children's curiosity had obviously increased. This is illustrated by the answers to the question concerning which languages apart from English they would like to learn in the future. After the first year, the pupils named French, Spanish, Chinese, Russian, Japanese, Norwegian, Danish and Swedish as well as Italian, Swahili, Egyptian, "Indian" and Portuguese. While two children stated that they would like to learn all languages, seven proposed either two or three at a time. After the second year, the number of pupils who named more than one language had increased to ten. The list of favoured languages was again dominated by French, followed by Italian, Russian, Japanese, "Egyptian", Polish, "Mexican", Arabic and Turkish. It is also encouraging that the children's interest was not exclusively directed to those languages that had been dealt with in class.

Another remarkable result is that 25 out of 39 pupils questioned at the end of the second year were looking forward to learning foreign languages at secondary level, whereas only two expressed reservations. They did not know, of course, whether the language classes at the secondary school would be comparable to the teaching programme at primary level which they had evaluated positively. However, they were aware of the fact that their achievement would be graded.

In this context it is important to note that though more than half of the children would have liked to receive marks at primary level, one third rejected the idea. Though the reasons were not investigated, it is likely that these children enjoyed learning without the pressure of assessment. Here, it stands out that several pupils with poor achievements in other subjects had shown an intensive commitment in the language classes and had been able to experience success. It is quite conceivable that they especially feared that marks would have reduced these opportunities. Besides, the pupils did receive consistent feedback for their achievements and efforts, both from the teacher and from their classmates. And at the end of each term all children were given a certificate along with their regular report – certifying their participation in the programme and elaborating on their individual abilities as well as on their contributions to classes. This was also intended to give their parents an idea of their children's abilities and interests that had surfaced in the course of this programme.

Conclusion

Several conclusions can be drawn from the account of this teaching programme concerning the introduction of primary school children to different languages and cultures.

Almost all pupils evaluated the programme positively. The opportunities to use the English language in various contexts with speakers of different nationalities fascinated them as much as catching a glimpse of other foreign languages and cultural manifestations. And while reflecting on languages, cultures and perception was already held in esteem after the first year, it was considered increasingly interesting in the course of the second year.

The pupils clearly took advantage of the fact that the programme integrated various approaches to coming into contact with foreign languages and cultures, and to reflect on them. This allowed them to discover and pursue individual ways of experiencing success – an important step towards learner autonomy that obviously nourished their diverse interests in languages and cultures.

From this point of view, current trends in foreign language education at primary level focussing on a single foreign language only and grading the pupils' achievements appear problematic. This interpretation receives further support from a more extensive study conducted by the author that explored the effects of different teaching programmes on the pupils' development with regard to a number of personality factors indicating their disposition to open themselves to new, unfamiliar and changing situations. Compared to a control group that was taught according to approaches exclusively focussing on the proficiency in a specific foreign language, the experimental group that took part in the programme depicted in this article showed a significant increase in tolerance, willingness to change and ability to control aggression in the face of frustration, as well as a decrease in ethnocentrism during the respective two-year period. Moreover, their attitudes towards the teaching programme remained high, whereas those of the control group deteriorated. A comprehensive final report on the study, which was authorized by the Ministry of Education in Saxony-Anhalt and conducted with 708 children in 31 school classes at 14 primary schools, is in preparation.

While these encouraging results seem to confirm the advantages of the teaching concept applied here, the experiences in class also point to measures that should be taken to preserve and intensify its positive effects. If more than one teaching period per week had been allotted to this particular programme, the pupils would have stood a chance of reflecting on languages, cultures and perception more intensively. Consequently, language programmes like this one should cover a minimum of two classes per week – preferably starting in the first year of primary education.

As the experiences with this programme have shown, working on joint and individual projects proved to be motivating and efficient – especially because of their creative and autonomous components. This could be intensified by a more flexible organization of timetables that allows – for instance – epochal teaching and fosters cooperation across subjects.

Apart from helping pupils to establish thematic links between different domains of knowledge, the subjects should also be co-ordinated to develop basic methodological and social strategies required for learning and communication. For instance, it can be assumed that the phases of joint reflection on languages, cultures and perception would probably have proceeded even more effectively if the children had already been acquainted with procedures of "philosophical" arguments and discussions. After all, the pupils did show a pronounced interest in sharing their experiences and thoughts with others as their commitment to the project *Children teaching children* exemplifies.

It is also essential that foreign language teaching programmes at secondary level and beyond continue fostering pupils' reflections on languages, cultures and perceptions along with their language proficiency. Teachers committed to these objectives can only achieve them if they acquire the requisite theoretical background knowledge and – equally important – experience success in putting it into practice. This account wants to encourage teachers to tread this path.

Works Cited

Blondin, Christiane, et al. *Fremdsprachen für die Kinder Europas: Ergebnisse und Empfehlungen der Forschung*. Berlin: Cornelsen, 1998.
Burstall, Clare, et. al. *Primary French in the Balance*. Slough: NFER, 1974.
Die Flötenkinder von Nagano. ARD. 22 Feb. 1998.
Hermann-Brennecke, Gisela. "Drei Positionen zum Fremdsprachenfrühbeginn." *Warum auch Französisch*. Ed. Wissenschaftliches Institut für Schulpraxis Bremen & Bureaux Linguistiques d'Allemagne du Nord. Stuttgart: Klett, 1993. 52-64.

Hermann-Brennecke, Gisela. "Affektive und kognitive Flexibilität durch Fremdsprachenvielfalt auf der Primarstufe." *Zeitschrift für Fremdsprachenforschung* 5 (1994): 1-21.

Hermann-Brennecke, Gisela, and Andreas Marschollek. "Begegnung mit fremden Sprachen: Eine Studie aus Sachsen-Anhalt." *Frühes schulisches Fremdsprachenlernen zwischen Empirie & Theorie*. Ed. Gisela Hermann-Brennecke. Münster: Lit, 1999. 73-116.

Lipman, Matthew. *Thinking in Education*. Cambridge: Cambridge UP, 1994.

Magic English 2: Family: Die Familie. Prod. Disney. Hamburg: Orbis Publishing, 1997.

Sauer, Helmut. "Frühes Fremdsprachenlernen in Grundschulen – ein Irrweg?" *Neusprachliche Mitteilungen* 53 (2000): 2-7.

"I Want to Become a Teacher Because ...":

Future Teachers Between School and University

Julia Semmer & Dirk Thormann

> *A teacher affects eternity; he can never tell where his influence stops.*
> [Henry Adams. *The Education of Henry Adams*, 994.]

Looking Back

125 years of English studies at Martin-Luther-University Halle-Wittenberg mean more than a century of acquaintance with cultural diversity induced by professional teaching. Karl Elze, who happened to become the first full professor of English at the newly founded seminar at Halle University, was a schoolteacher himself. Still complaining about the lack of professional teacher-training he stated in 1864 that language teachers:

[...] der großen Mehrzahl nach Autodidakten in ihrem Fache sind, weil die moderne Philologie noch immer nicht von Staatswegen anerkannt und in den Kreis der akademischen Studien als gleichberechtigtes Glied aufgenommen ist. Es ist unglaublich, aber wahr. -

[...] are in the majority self-taught professionals, because modern philology has not yet been acknowledged by the state and incorporated as an equal member in the circle of academic studies. It is unbelievable, but true. (Elze 82; *our own translation*)

Since then English as a subject in education and teacher-training has undergone far-reaching changes according to political, economic, and social conditions, and of course by the impact of academic research. Whereas before 1880, emphasis had been placed more on language learning as a means of cognitive and affective growth than the utilitarian aspect of language usage, later, in 1882, Wilhelm Viëtor brought communicative objectives into the discussion through his influential essay called "Language Teaching Must Start Afresh" [Der Sprachunterricht muss umkehren. Ein Beitrag zur Überbürdungsfrage]. His work triggered a lively discourse among school professionals and intensified a more research-oriented development of teaching methods.

More than half a century later, the course programmes offered for prospective teachers up from the winter semester 1947/48 at Halle University show that the learning and teaching of foreign languages had become a domain of methodology at the Department of Education. Less than fifty years later EFL-teaching obtained a different profile under the umbrella of *Anglistik und ihre Didaktik*. Now the emphasis is based on foreign language acquisition and referential disciplines such as psychology, neurobiology, philosophy, sociology, linguistics, literature, and cultural studies in order to give a multi-faceted view of language learning. This approach is meant to provide the students up from the very beginning with the notion that their studies programme is an interdisciplinary and interrelated one.

The authors of this article graduated from schools in East Germany in 1989/90. They experienced massive changes in the system of higher education. Both were trained and worked as schoolteachers before becoming members of staff at the English Department of Martin-Luther-University Halle-Wittenberg.

In the former GDR generations of school pupils met *Mike and Anne* dressed in their flares in the TV language course *English for you* (Gericke DEFA Dokfilm) when the revival of the seventies had not yet taken place. The syllabus hardly focused on critical intercultural understanding and thereby seems to have enforced the production of stereotypes. Catching a glimpse of London on a black and white TV screen was the only cultural asset provided in the English classroom. Reading literary texts did not play any significant role, except for small ideologically suitable extracts. Robert Burns, for example, whose works stood for rebelling "against the social order", decorated the otherwise plain appearance of the textbook (Böse 66).

The state-wide curriculum suggested pragmatic texts focusing on everyday life of the politically committed working class, provided identifiable role models and insinuated the universal strife against capitalism. As English teachers and their students experienced foreign culture merely through one textbook and a standard TV course, the teaching units depended very much on the power of imagination. The fact that the GDR populace had only a very limited access to authentic sources of the English language, instruction centred on grammar and its internalisation, cut off from original discourse. It comes as no surprise then that eventually a sort of GDR "classroom pidgin" evolved over nearly half a century. The dilemma that arose between the difficulty of maintaining political correctness and avoiding "inappropriate" intertextual links caused the language to dry up. In spite of this, foreign languages still contained the flavour of keeping up with the world outside and spread a taste of the exotic and cultural diversity.

In the former GDR, English could only be studied at university in combination with Russian or German as a school subject. The state-wide curriculum, which prescribed contents as well as the amount of courses to be taken per semester, was centrally enforced by the Ministry of People's Education and the Ministry of Universities and Colleges. In comparison with literature, linguistics and cultural studies language practice and methodological training were clearly dominant (Ministerrat, *Studienplan* [...] *Deutsche Sprache und Literatur/Englisch* 36-38). A didactic approach to the study of teaching English as a foreign language based on the disciplines mentioned above did not exist. Instead, the study programme in which we were enrolled at the beginning of our studies at Martin-Luther-University immediately after the Wall came down, focused exclusively on practical issues of language teaching. This is amazing in so far as there was research in the GDR which dealt with issues such as the relation between language and thought (Buchbinder/Strauß 51). The understanding at Halle University, however, was a purely practical one and therefore could not come up with satisfactory solutions to methodological and instructional problems arising in the classroom. The ensuing lack of flexibility neither encouraged the students to take a critical view concerning the teaching subject nor questioned conventional approaches.

Past Instruction and Expectation

Are we going to find our academic future 125 years in the past? Karl Elze, who built his courses around eight students, who all had access to the lecture rooms and the library of the English Department, is most likely to have addressed his students holistically. Nowadays with crowded courses abounding with students trying to assert themselves, it is difficult to do justice to their individual needs.

Since the beginning of our studies at the English Institute some ten years ago, the teacher-training programme has changed considerably. When we returned as members of staff, we were first striving for a one-dimensional teaching manual. But we soon realized that there is no such thing as a homogeneous group of learners and that it is impossible to apply a single uniform approach only.

With this insight in mind, we carried out an empirical study with 80 students enrolled at the English Institute, studying to become teachers. On entering university, students are relatively free to choose from a variety of courses and to determine the focus they want to adopt. Consequently, the integration of the course programme and the extent to which it actually serves teaching purposes depends on the students themselves. Recognizing individual needs and choosing suitable aspects is decisive for the quality of their studies. How can this be managed without neglecting individual requirements? We became interested in how far participating in academically guided practical teaching may change the attitudes towards the study programme and subsequently the way students opt for, process and store information in the course of their studies. The study was guided by these two questions:

What do students expect when they begin their studies?
To which extent do students redefine their focus?

We used questionnaires and conducted qualitative interviews before and after the students embarked on their practical teaching phase to see whether their attitudes had changed or not. Over the last two years (1999-2001) we asked first year students in their first week of studies to answer questions on their own school experience, on what they think makes a good language teacher, on their perception of current school life, on prospective changes within education, on their own future plans, and on social and economic trends.

After their first attempts at teaching a class themselves and after a month-long compact practical teaching phase another row of interviews was carried out, in which students had to comment on their individual lesson planning, their difficulties while standing in front of a class, and their view of our approach to FLT. The survey was supplemented with the analysis of the students' videotaped lessons and reports. This allowed for a comparison of the way the students perceived their own teaching and the way we had assessed it.

Before starting their practical teaching first year students had answered the question: *What do you expect from the teacher-training programme?* Some of the reasons for studying the students had given at the beginning of their courses were:

"I like kids."
"I want to improve my English."
"English is a world language."
"We didn't like our teachers. I want to be a better teacher than they were."
"I had a very good teacher, and I want to be like him."
"I want my pupils to like the English Language as much as I do."

The frequency is represented in the following table:

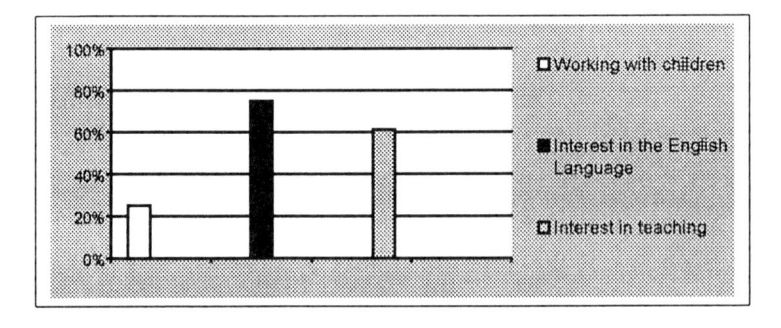

[Bar chart showing: Working with children (~20%), Interest in the English Language (~75%), Interest in teaching (~60%)]

It is amazing that motives such as interest in foreign cultures, getting to know foreign literatures and cultures, understanding the foreign language as a system, widening one's horizon, expanding one's creativity, getting acquainted with different forms of behaviour (which other empirical studies show, cf. Candelier/Hermann-Brennecke 418, 431-432) were not mentioned at all. Obviously, the beginners had no idea of the multidimensional existence of a language and could not imagine its multifaceted ties. Instead, they were predominantly expecting to improve their communicative competence.

Furthermore, the results of the study showed that the students' ideas about their future careers were closely modelled on their own experiences in the English classroom. These had obviously been dominated by grammar and the traditional four skills. Associations with the concepts of language awareness, self-determined learning or intercultural understanding were not mentioned. What could be the reason?

It may well be that most students had only encountered "chalk-and-talk-methods" so that they subconsciously followed the old axiom: "Teachers teach as they were taught and not as they were taught to teach." They obviously had never come across the "post-communicative FLT-methodology" (Wolff 408) or the main points of an educational discourse entailing process-oriented concepts, action learning and learner awareness. Obviously, they had never had the chance to realize the enormous affective and cognitive potential inherent in English as a school subject (cf. Batley, et al. 24-26): interethnic understanding, language awareness and strategy-related language acquisition.

Change of Outlook

At our Institute the study programme for future teachers includes a practical teaching phase in school during the semester on the basis of theoretical courses integrating issues of foreign language acquisition, planning and analysing lessons, and classroom management in order to interrelate theory and classroom practice. The lessons of the students are videotaped, evaluated, and discussed with all the students involved in order to provide them with a critical view of their own achievement in class and arrive at a deeper theoretical understanding to improve their future teaching endeavours. After having thus successfully finished their first encounter with pupils at school, the teacher students are prepared by a particular course on applied linguistics for their four week practical teaching period in an allocated school in Halle or one of their own choice or even abroad. Here they have to cope with all the aspects of the microcosm of school and have to teach at various levels. During their time in school they are regularly tutored and coached by members of *Anglistik und ihre Didaktik*. Student teachers are visited at their schools at least twice. Each lesson they give is videotaped as a basis for analysis, both immediately after class and later as an example from which to work when all the students involved in the practical teaching meet for a final evaluation with regard to issues related to foreign language acquisition research. The successful completion of these two extended practical teaching periods and their theoretical link-up (altogether up to ten weeks) is a prerequisite for graduating from university. According to the answers given on questionnaires and in interviews, first and second term students are still very much inclined to ask for universal teaching help. After their first practical teaching experiences, however, the following comments surfaced on the question: *What do you expect from our study programme "Anglistik und ihre Didaktik"?*

"ideas about how to include new media in English lessons"
"what to do with texts"
"learning how to teach grammar"
"learning how to mark, how to deal with mistakes"
"how to design test papers"
"language games"
"how to deal with beginners' courses"
"how to build up vocabulary in a systematic way"

It is apparent that solely teaching methods and in ten cases methods of learning were expected to be the scope of *Anglistik und ihre Didaktik*:

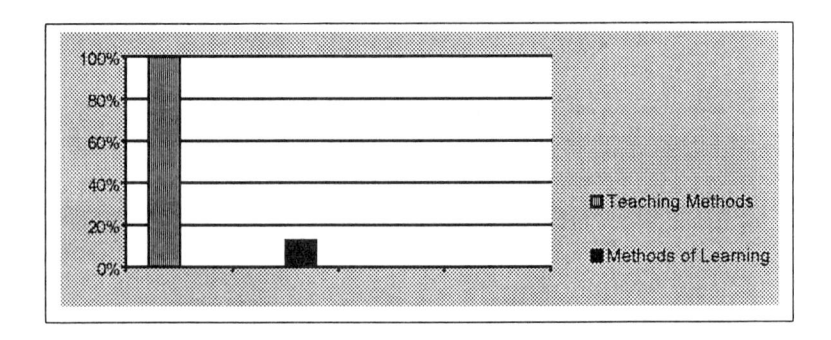

According to the interviews their teaching experiences revealed the following difficulties.

What did you find difficult about teaching at school?
"dealing with 30 pupils at the same time"
"applying motivational techniques in 'difficult' classes"
"differentiate between different levels of proficiency"
"reacting spontaneously and adequately"
"correcting and marking"
"compensating the failure of generalized textbook exercises (pattern drills)"
"picking the adequate method out of a wide range of possibilities"

The table below illustrates the categories into which the students' answers fall:

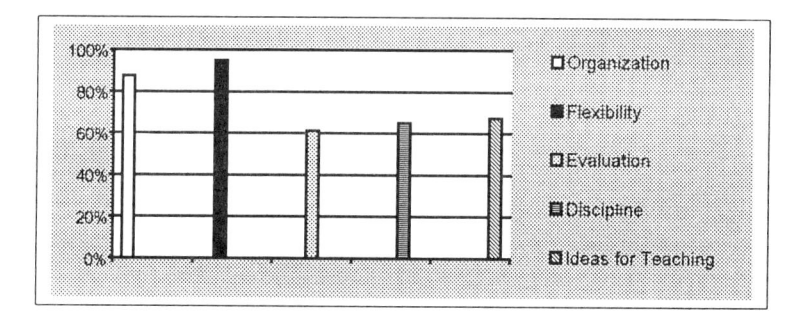

It is only natural that before taking up their studies the students still had only a vague understanding of the subject matter based on their own experiences. All students expected to get to know teaching methods, whereas only 13,7% considered their future addressees (the pupils in class) of any importance. After standing in front of a class for the first time in their lives, the students did no longer overemphasize the demand for teaching methods but stressed the importance of various complex factors related to the organization of classroom interaction, evaluation criteria and flexibility of the teacher. When teaching, student teachers have to face a great number of decisions. In order to be capable of reacting flexibly students need a solid theoretical background to pick from as far as an efficient choice of diagnostic and methodological measures is concerned.

The analysis of videotaped lessons, reports of the students as well as interviews with the students' mentors revealed the following points of friction: finding a suitable topic, the appropriate evaluation of the pupils' performances, teaching within a rigid frame of prescribed topics and exercises, conducting a lively classroom interaction in the target language, using rhetorical means and coping with an intricate web of behaviour. It is difficult for the students to pinpoint the essentials of a chosen topic. Often this is why lessons tend to be crammed and overloaded and too teacher-dominated. In not very many cases the latent potential of a topic was met with adequate methodological structures. More than 40% of the analysed students' lessons turned out to be teacher-centred, textbook-based and only little discussion-oriented. It is also interesting to note that syllabi overemphasize the cognitive side of learning instead of adopting a holistic approach by taking into account the affective and interactive needs of learning.

Pitfalls of Teaching a Class

Learners show different degrees of cognitive and affective development. Knowing one's affective, procedural and declarative potential appears to be one essential prerequisite for a self-determined and flexible integration into a socio-dynamic structure. Student teachers have to respond to this and hit the right level of abstraction regarding academic discourse. A lesson represents a tight canvas of pre-conditions not only brought in by the individual learners. Therefore it is understandable that some students who teach for the first time are afraid of having their authority challenged. Knowing which goals to pursue and giving clear instructions is crucially important for efficient teaching, though not always crowned with success. It needs quite an amount of knowledge, a high level of abstraction and an alert manner to put the appropriate questions and apply adequate teaching aids. To avoid being sometimes distracted by distracting tactics employed by pupils, students struggle to stick to their teaching objectives come what may. To notice inadequate teaching behaviour implies accepting one's own responsibility even personality-wise. Opening oneself up to criticism represents yet another hurdle. Here, the use of video recordings is a helpful medium, as it provides the student teachers with the opportunity to observe themselves in the classroom situation and to discover their strengths and weaknesses as they come to the fore.

At present, one third of the students enrolled at the English Institute study English to become teachers. This implies that they have to overcome the discrepancy between their own experiences as one-time pupils and the challenges of the study programme. This also means that they need not only come to terms with a changing outlook on society but also with their role as mediators between the individual and society.

Today, English as a school subject presents itself as neither reduced to strictly utilitarian purposes nor as a means to acquire general cognitive skills, but has developed into a complex reflection of social requirements: Previously, teachers using a textbook or following a pre-defined syllabus were not forced to make decisions about what to teach at a particular time. The problem in teacher-training now is that, with a task-oriented approach, teachers are not going to be asked to teach any particular language item, but must select tasks according to criteria that up to now have hardly been included in teacher-training: 'conceptual readiness' and 'interest readiness' (Corder 189).

The survey as well as the analysis of the students' lessons based on the theoretical courses offered along with them underline the demand for a teacher study programme fostering flexibility. This implies impacting the student's personality in such a way that what they have learnt in courses on foreign language acquisition must be applied to the actual classroom, so that they are aware of the purpose of in-class activities such as warm-up games, motivational techniques, presentational and organizational skills, rhetorical skills, role-play set-ups as well as discourse strategies, diagnostic measures and the like.

Recent Trends and Their Impact on Education

Trend figures forecast significant changes regarding social codes and their inherent challenges for the individual (cf. Mathia/Salzman 287). This concerns abounding information, globalisation vs. regionalisation, optimised logistics, virtualisation, ageing society, lifelong learning (cf. Batley, et al. 30), learners as experts and re-defining moral values through altered terms of reference (cf. Oxford 144-150). Hence, many parts of society will be forced to face the seemingly contradictory demand for high flexibility paired with high specialization:

> Two seemingly conflicting impulses drive experience today; a focus on creating full, flexible, diverse lives; and a quest for simplicity and control in an ever changing-world. (Mathia/Salzman 404)

Educational discourse increasingly focuses on transparent teaching objectives as a result of a tendency towards self-determined learning, interdisciplinary approaches, content-based instruction, extra-curricular training and differentiation in the classroom. Teachers find themselves confronted with a wide spectrum of individualized conceptions that they must handle with high flexibility and diligent expertise. The capability to change perspectives, to abstract, to compare, to select and to show open-mindedness towards the unknown prepare the ground for an approach to teaching that focuses on diagnosis, problem-solving and close examination rather than on training as transmission (cf. Legutke/Howard 307).

To meet these conditions professional teacher-training tries to come up with an altered conception: concentrating on underlying structures, trying to foster the awareness of the way psychological conditions interact, being able to identify problems in the teaching process and finding adequate problem solving strategies, raising questions and selecting suitable "tailor-made" teaching materials rather than relying on institutional guidelines.

Besides, interdisciplinary thinking and commitment to and awareness of attitudes play a vital role in teaching and influence perception (cf. Hermann, "Reactions"). In the traditional field of study programmes for teachers of English this is rarely a major issue. Therefore our study programme *Anglistik und ihre Didaktik* emphasizes these aspects and establishes a link between theoretical aspects and the actual school situation in guided practical teaching. It serves as the only compulsory connection between university and school within those 4.5 years of studying.

Towards Teaching Awareness

Humans make distinctions based on various concepts of perception that have evolved within their respective cultural background and their language. Such patterns may emerge as linguistic features. The interaction between language, cognition and affect offers the chance to expand cultural understanding in the language classroom. The acquisition of a foreign language may actually expand the personal horizon. Opening up new perspectives as well as increasing sensitivity towards the target language forces the learners to overcome individual barriers and gain a better understanding of attitudes towards "otherness". Furthermore, the ability to communicate in a language other than one's own may decrease subconscious anxieties to approach cultural differences (as empirical studies reveal, cf. Hermann, "Wie 'frei'"; Hermann-Brennecke, "Verunsicherung"). Dealing with different "world views" requires empathy and cognitive insight. Foreign language learning provides both the chance to experiment with languages as well as to enact situations while realizing different cultural modes. Thus, analysing literature in the English language classroom seems to offer a particularly intriguing opportunity to gain a different understanding of other people's convention, modes of behaviour, and ways of thinking. Contrasting different cultural and ideological instances of perception may well contribute to shaping intercultural understanding and identity.

Since teaching depends on all the individuals involved and how they perceive "reality", each lesson is unique. The discrepancy between conscious teaching and formalized methodologies can only be overcome by developing teaching modules focusing on a holistic approach to complex subject matters by employing ideas rather than isolated topics adapted to conventional boundaries.

> Students are usually schooled to acquire knowledge in a linear fashion, structured by chapters in books, days on the syllabus, items to be tested, and curricular requirements to be checked off. By contrast, real-life materials provide a world of knowledge that is non-sequentially organized and that invites relational thinking and hierarchical structuring of the phenomena observed. (Kramsch 200)

A great number of pupils, parents and adult learners expect the teacher to facilitate their individual ways of learning, thereby hoping to get personally addressed and involved.

For this expectation to materialise, it cannot suffice just to be corrected by the teacher who keeps referring to generally accepted rules, patterns, definitions or commonly accepted values. Instead, learners should be taught to become aware of what is taking place while they are learning. Only in this, the fundamentals of critical analysis, problem-oriented reflection, cognitive and affective discovery as well as conscious transfer can be established. Thus, they will be encouraged to take responsibility for their own learning process including self-evaluation. "Learning how to learn" (cf. Batley, et al. 30) requires a teacher who has a thorough scientific understanding of how language acquisition works. This is most likely to be achieved by a systematically intertwined interdisciplinary studies programme at university level, so as to gradually eclipse haphazard and trial-and-error-based teaching endeavours in school.

In this respect, a considerable increase in the level of awareness could be noticed over the last years, something that became apparent in the briefings the students had to write on their practical teaching. A great number of these reports yielded a solid understanding of the affective and cognitive processes taking place in the foreign language teaching classroom.

The reports also showed that though educational parameters vary, teachers should refrain from operating a rigid true-or-false grid and encourage questions in the classroom. They should fuel alternative ways of answering and thinking instead in order to develop a critical sensitivity to and awareness of the relativity of right and wrong. The art of questioning is not as simple as one might think, as one must know a lot in order to put appropriate questions, which link up with already stored pieces of information and are supposed to stimulate discovery learning. It presupposes a profound understanding of the subject, broad background knowledge as well as a highly developed disposable network of cross-references. Questions should be regarded as a teaching goal in their own right rather than a means to an end.

It seems that formulating intentions, setting up teaching objectives, discovering topics and finding suitable ways of teaching can only develop when theoretical knowledge and practical teaching issues become closely interwoven. It is this blend of practical experience and applied theory which prepares future teachers for the prospective challenges of their profession.

Works Cited

Adams, Henry. *Novels: Mont-Saint Michel and Chartres. The Education of Henry Adams: An Autobiography.* [1907] New York: Library of America, 1983.
Batley, Edward, Michel Candelier, Gisela Hermann-Brennecke, and György Szepe. *Language Policies for the Twenty-First Century. Report for UNESCO.* Osnabrück: Universitätsverlag, 1993.
Böse, Maximilian, et.al. *English For You. Englisches Lehrbuch Teil V.* 3rd ed. Berlin: Volk und Wissen, 1987.
Böse, Maximilian, et.al. *English For You. Englisches Lehrbuch Teil VI.* 3rd ed. Berlin: Volk und Wissen, 1988.
Buchbinder, V.A. [Wolf Avramovič], and Wolfgang H. Strauß, eds. *Grundlagen der Methodik des Fremdsprachenunterrichts.* Leipzig: Verlag Enzyklopädie, 1986.
Corder, Pit. "Talking Shop. Pit Corder on Language Teaching and Applied Linguistics." *English Language Teaching Journal* 40 (1986): 185-190.
Elze, Karl. *Die englische Sprache und Literatur in Deutschland.* Dresden 1864.
Gericke, Günther. *English For You. DEFA Dokfilm.* Reg.-Nr. 50. n.d.
Gräf, Gerhard. *English For You. Englisches Lehrbuch Teil I.* 2nd ed. Berlin: Volk und Wissen, 1983.
Candelier, Michel, and Gisela Hermann-Brennecke. "Wahl und Abwahl von Fremdsprachen: Deutsche und französische Schüler und Schülerinnen im Vergleich." *Die Neueren Sprachen* 91 (1992): 416-434.
Hermann, Gisela. "Reactions of Foreign Learners to Atttitude Scales in L1 and L2: An Unexpected Glimpse of the Hidden Self." *Verstehen und Verständigung.* Ed. Christoph Edelhoff, and Christopher Candlin. Bochum: Kamp, 1989. 208-218.
Hermann, Gisela. "Wie 'frei' macht eine Fremdsprache von muttersprachlichen Kognitionen?" *Sprachen – Tor zur Welt.* Ed. Wilfried Brusch, and Irene Scheuermann. Hamburg: Hamburger Beiträge zur Erziehungswissenschaft, 1991. 42-54.
Hermann-Brennecke, Gisela. "Zur Verunsicherung von Wahrnehmungsmustern durch fremde Sprachen." *Interkulturelle Bildung und Sprachen.* Ed. Manfred Erdmenger. Braunschweig: Schmidt, 1992. 35-47.
Kramsch, Claire. *Context and Culture in Language Teaching.* Oxford: OUP, 1993.
Legutke, Michael, and Thomas Hogwart. *Process and Experience in the Language Classroom.* New York: Longman, 1993.

Martin-Luther-Universität Halle-Wittenberg in Halle/Saale. *Personal- und Vorlesungsverzeichnis für das Sommersemester 1948.* Halle (Saale): Ostdeutsche Druckerei und Verlag Otto Jung, 1948.

Mathia, Ira, and Marian Salzman. *Next: Trends for the Near Future.* New York: Woodstock, 1999.

Meinhardt, Margret, et al. *English For You. Englisches Lehrbuch Teil III.* 7th ed. Berlin: Volk und Wissen, 1985.

Meinhardt, Margret et al. *English For You. Englisches Lehrbuch Teil IV.* 7th ed. Berlin: Volk und Wissen, 1987.

Ministerrat der Deutschen Demokratischen Republik; Ministerium für Volksbildung/Ministerium für Hoch- und Fachschulwesen. *Lehrprogramme für die Ausbildung von Diplomlehrern der allgemeinbildenden polytechnischen Oberschulen im Fach Englisch an Universitäten und Hochschulen der DDR.* Berlin: Volk und Wissen, 1982.

Ministerrat der Deutschen Demokratischen Republik; Ministerium für Volksbildung/Ministerium für Hoch- und Fachschulwesen. *Lehrprogramme für die Ausbildung von Diplomlehrern der allgemeinbildenden polytechnischen Oberschulen in der Methodik des Englischunterrichts an Universitäten und Hochschulen der DDR.*. Berlin: Volk und Wissen, 1983.

Ministerrat der Deutschen Demokratischen Republik; Ministerium für Volksbildung/Ministerium für Hoch- und Fachschulwesen. *Studienplan für die Ausbildung von Diplomlehrern der allgemeinbildenden polytechnischen Oberschulen in der Fachkombination Deutsche Sprache und Literatur/Englisch an Universitäten und Hochschulen der DDR.* Berlin: Volk und Wissen, 1982.

Ministerrat der Deutschen Demokratischen Republik; Ministerium für Volksbildung/Ministerium für Hoch- und Fachschulwesen. *Studienplan für die Ausbildung von Diplomlehrern der allgemeinbildenden polytechnischen Oberschulen in der Fachkombination Russisch/Englisch an Universitäten und Hochschulen der DDR.*. Berlin: Volk und Wissen, 1982.

Oxford, Rebecca. *Language Learning Strategies: What Every Teacher Should Know.* Boston: Heinle & Heinle Publishers, 1990.

Schibor, Dorothea. *English For You. Englisches Lehrbuch Teil II.* 3rd ed. Berlin: Volk und Wissen, 1984.

Viëtor, Wilhelm. *Der Sprachunterricht muß umkehren.* [1882] Ed. Konrad Schröder. München: Hueber, 1984.

Wolff, Dieter. "Der Konstruktivismus: Ein neues Paradigma in der Fremdsprachendidaktik?" *Die Neueren Sprachen* 93 (1994): 407-429.

"Every Decoding is Another Encoding":

A Didactic Discovery of David Lodge's *Small World*

Gisela Hermann-Brennecke

Didactic Frame of Reference

The class I taught on *The Analysis of Literature* at the English Department of the University of New Mexico in the Spring Semester of 2001 had as its main objectives to give the students insight into English literature, to introduce them to close reading, and to open a gateway to fiction.

Analyzing fiction is an engaging, creative and dynamic endeavor, because each text consists of multiple layers, which have to be taken off one by one. As the gradual unfolding takes place mental images creep in, images, which are colored by the reader's own stock of experience. These must not necessarily correspond with the pre-dispositions implied by the text, because: "Every Eye sees differently. As the Eye, Such the Object." (Keynes III, 20) "Every thing possible to be believ'd is an image of truth." (Keynes I, 185)

Blake's aphorisms hint at the wide spectrum of possible interpretations that unravels in the attempt to arrive at a single transparent meaning. The insinuated process of discovery can be thrilling, intriguing and awe inspiring.

The Text

With this notion in mind, I decided to choose David Lodge's *Small World* (1984) as the basic text from which to work. It had kept me spellbound when reading it for the first time years ago. Or to put it in Roland Barthes' words:

> Le texte me choisit, par toute une disposition d'écrans invisibles, de chicanes sélectives: le vocabulaire, les références, la lisibilité, etc; et, perdu au milieu du texte (non pas *derrière* lui à façon d'un dieu de machinerie), il y a toujours l'autre, l'auteur. (Barthes 1973, 45)

Well aware of the fact that what had attracted my attention would not forcibly affect other readers in a similar way, there were a number of didactic considerations that persuaded me to give it a try.

In a most entertaining fashion the novel deals with academia, a world which may be personally relevant to students as it forms part of their life on campus. It consists of multiple stories told simultaneously with characters caught up in sequences of events with outlandish climaxes. It abounds with allusions to and parodies of other literary works and provides a plurality of implications and references waiting to be disclosed. It highlights the theme of discovery and entraps the reader in a labyrinth of ambitious quests for love and knowledge. It introduces the reader to a number of linguistic schools and literary theories, which are personified and enacted in a delightfully instructive and prodigiously palpable manner. It interlaces academic and non-academic discourse by having the characters satirically ponder over and comment on what is happening to them in the light of sophisticated and still comprehensible theoretical models. It is a romance, which contains a happy ending for most of the minor characters, but denies this in its major plot: personal desires turn out to be unattainable. This is why the quest must go on.

The Class

The students of my class were between 19 and 50 years old and covered the whole undergraduate range from first to fourth year. Some of them had returned to college after an 18-year hiatus, working in jobs such as air traffic controller, dress designer, archivist, motel manager or homemaker. Except for one person from Toronto, all had moved to New Mexico with their families during infancy or adolescence.

Only two of the nineteen people enrolled took this class out of sheer interest in fiction. For the majority it was mandatory for their English major because they were concentrating on creative or professional writing or because they needed an elective English course to fill their degree requirements as studio art, athletic training or athletic major. Their minors comprised a variety of studies such as aerospace, politics, science, biology, language arts, psychology, philosophy, history, education and music.

Only one member of the class did not know which profession to choose after graduation. The rest of the students envisaged careers as high-school teacher, opera singer, graphic designer, technical writer, athletic trainer, attorney, environmental lawyer, novelist, snowboard instructor, manager, creative writer and elementary school teacher.

Expectations of this course oscillated between "no idea", "nothing much", "no high hopes" and "make it or break it". For some it represented a first scholarly acquaintance with literature since high-school, while for others it was merely another option in a row of literary courses. Two had chosen it because they had attended one of my courses in the preceding fall semester. If it had not been for one non-degree student who as a full-time staff member got free tuition, nobody would have taken this class "just for fun".

In view of this rather heterogeneous array of age, social standing, professional outlook, academic training, and background, it was obvious that this course had to be both thrilling and enjoyable. In order to open the mind to new ways of looking at fiction and to sustain an interest in literature beyond this particular class, the study atmosphere had to be productive and captivating.

The Method

As to the question of how to proceed, it seemed self-evident to model the approach on the narrative codes employed in *Small World*, which may be compared to a voyage of discovery appealing to all senses.

The reader finds himself embarked on a literary venture full of detours, enigmas, postponements, multivalent situations, moments of uncertainty, errors and suspense. He keeps stumbling across ambiguities, paradoxes, polyphonic connotations, oblique allusions, mysterious symbols and obscure intertextualities that arouse his curiosity, make him ponder and linger. Hence, the way the novel is told almost peremptorily requires a similar dilatory analysis.

A further argument speaks in favor of this method of deferral. Though Lodge claims in an interview not "to come down on either side" (Billington 7), his satirical treatment of different positions in the controversy about literary theory is noticeably tailored to "every decoding is another encoding" (*SW* 25), as Morris Zapp, the American professor with strong post-structuralist and deconstructive persuasions declares. Consequently a text can never be "possessed". Remaining radically open to alternative readings, its evasiveness resembles the quest for the Grail.

The methodological paradigm applied to my class reflects this notion in the following way:

First and foremost, the students were asked not to read the whole novel all at once, but successively throughout the semester with chapters assigned over a 16 weeks' schedule with two 75 minutes' teaching periods each. The segmentation of the reading process served the purpose of allowing time for diligently unfolding the various layers of the text, going into their implications in depth, focusing on literary and metafictional allusions, and suggesting interpretations.

Keeping the revelation of the narrative strands thus in a limbo would add to the suspense and at the same time inspire the students' imagination concerning the intertextual bonds criss-crossing the respective chapters.

Secondly, the students were assigned individual research projects, which had to meet three requirements: provide background information about the references, reflect on their occurrence at a particular stage of the novel, and hypothesize their role in the development of plot and subplots. Hence, the task was not limited to getting information about specific works and their writers, genres, literary terms, linguistic and literary theories, but to interlace it with the passage in which it occurred and thereby act as an incentive to their analytical and creative powers, spurring on their cognitive and affective involvement.

Thirdly, each individual research project had to be presented orally in class, which further delayed reaching the end of the novel. The main points and arguments of the presentations had to be outlined on handouts, which were distributed before they were due in order to fuel subsequent discussions. Besides, it was hoped that these abstracts would provide the basic stock of an expanding collection of materials on the analysis of literature, serving not only as a guideline within class but also as a source of reference for future studies.

A fourth element of delay were the papers, which the students had to write during the semester. Three of them were to be conceived according to the level of understanding the analysis had reached so far, critically blending in with the findings of class discussions and individual research projects.

The first paper was about Persse's statement: "'I suppose everyone is looking for his own Grail.' (*SW* 12). Comment on his statement by referring to some of the literary references and describe their relevance to the characters introduced so far." It was due after the analysis of *Part I/One & Two* (*SW* 1-79).

A second one was due almost in the middle of the term after having finished *Part II/One & Two* (*SW* 83-145): "Give an outline of the basic characteristics of literary theories such as *New Criticism, structuralism, Marxism, reader-response criticism, and deconstruction*." This one was assigned as a group paper because I assumed that in spite of a certain class routine that would have set in at this point of the syllabus, the students might still not have got to know each other well enough to feel comfortable and at ease in class. In order to foster community spirit and to intensify their interactive behavior, they had to split into groups of four or five members during class time to plan the structure of the paper. They also had to meet outside of class to coordinate their individual findings and channel them into a joint thesis. Having to share responsibilities reduces the individual study load, but also asks for a meticulous preparation of each contribution so that it is accepted by the whole group. It was hoped that this experience would be encouraging enough to continue with collaborative research on the remaining two papers, which would be written individually.

After the completion of *Part III/One & Two* and *Part IV/Two* of (*SW* 149-270) a third topic was assigned with the title: "Comment on the role of *The Holy Grail* and the *Siege Perilous* in the academic world."

The fourth and final paper "There is no single 'truth'. Discuss the issue of *difference* in *Small World*." was the only one based on the knowledge of the whole novel.

Apart from serving the purpose of postponing the revelation of the end of the novel, the written papers were also intended as a means to clarify the process of interpretation, to provoke alternative findings, to engender new ideas and to critically revise opinions held so far. The process of planning and producing arguments in writing was supposed to foster the intellectual and emotional commitment in such a way that it would be remembered as a painstaking and yet pleasant experience, sufficiently rewarding to impact life-long reading.

The Syllabus

Each section of *Small World* ties in with a plurality of allusions, which are basically available through books of reference. The ones used in this class were *The Norton Anthology of English Literature* (*NA*); *The Oxford Companion to English Literature*; *A Glossary of Literary Terms*; *Princeton Encyclopedia of Poetry and Poetics*; *A Reader's Guide to Contemporary Literary Theory*;

Modern Literary Theory. Other sources considered to be relevant are listed in the survey below. Minor references were either mentioned in passing or interlaced when in demand.

- *Prologue* and *Part I/One* (*SW* 1-57):

Geoffrey Chaucer and *The Canterbury Tales* (especially the "General Prologue" (*NA* 178-198), T.S. Eliot and *The Waste Land*: "The Burial of the Dead" (*NA* 2613-2616); Roland Barthes "Striptease" (1972, 84-87); Perceval and The Grail: Dhira Mahoney *The Grail* (1-41) and Jessie L. Weston *From Ritual to Romance* (1-22); Roman Jacobson and *structuralism*; James Joyce and *Finnegans Wake* and *A Portrait of the Artist as a Young Man*; Charles Sanders Peirce and *semiotics*; Ludovico Ariosto and *Orlando Furioso*; Edmund Spenser and *The Faerie Queene NA* 357-417); John Keats and *The Eve of St. Agnes* (*NA* 1804-1814); Lord Alfred Tennyson's poem "St. Agnes' Eve"(89-90); verse forms such as *limerick* and *haiku*.

- *Part I/Two* (*SW* 58-79):

William Blake and *The Marriage of Heaven and Hell* (*NA* 1378-1388); John Milton and *Paradise Lost* (*NA* 722-853); Victor Shlovsky and *Russian formalism*; Jane Austen; *Ecclesiastes 12*.

- *Part II/One* (*SW* 83-113):

New Criticism and *contextual criticism*; Louis Althusser and *Marxism*; Matthew Arnold and "The Function of Criticism" (*NA* 2073-2078; 2103-2117); Samuel Taylor Coleridge and *Christabel* (*NA* 1573-1575; 1598-1613); Jessie Weston "The Fisher King" (107-129) and Nitze's "The Fisher King in The Grail Romances"; *The Angry Young Men*.

- *Part II/Two* (*SW* 114-145):

Jacques Derrida and deconstruction; hermeneutics; Sigmund Freud and psychoanalytic criticism (including Julia Kristeva); reader-response criticism; narratology; post-structuralism.

- *Part III/One* (*SW* 149-190):

Beowulf (*NA* 23-95); George Bernard Shaw and *Pygmalion*; William Hazlitt and his essay "On Criticism" (vol.8, 215-226); Mary Shelley and *Frankenstein or The Modern Prometheus*; *computational stylistics*.

- *Part III/Two* (*SW* 191-227):

William Butler Yeats and "The Lake Isle of Innisfree" (*NA* 2363-2369), "Politics" (356) and "Into the Twilight" (55); Ferdinand de Saussure; theories of genres: *tragedy, comedy, pastoral, lyric* and *epic*.

- *Part IV/One* (*SW* 231-250):

Thomas Hardy; *imagism*; Lord Alfred Tennyson and *Idylls of the King*: "The Holy Grail"; (388-410); "Scandals of Faith and Gender in Tennyson's Grail Poems" (415-445) and "'Pure Hearts and Clean Hands': The Victorian and the Grail" (447-464) in Dhira Mahoney.

- *Part IV/Two* (*SW* 251-270):

Edmund Spenser "The Bower of Bliss" (*NA* 655-661); Samuel Richardson and *Pamela*; the genres of *romance* and *folklore*; Patricia Parker's *Inescapable Romance*: "Introduction"(3-15) and "Epilogue" (219-243); Northrop Frye's *Anatomy of Criticism*: "The Mythos of Summer: Romance" (186-206); T.S. Eliot's "The Fire Sermon" (*NA* 2619-2623); "T.S. Eliot" (505-523) in Dhira Mahoney.

- *Part IV/Three* (*SW* 271-310):

William Shakespeare: *Romeo and Juliet, Julius Caesar, Othello, King Lear, Pericles, The Merchant of Venice, All's Well that Ends Well, The Comedy of Errors*; Benjamin Lee Whorf and "Language, mind and reality"; *intentional fallacy* (*hermeneutic fallacy*).

- *Part V/One & Two* (*SW* 313-339):

Plot, peripiteia, denouement; Roland Barthes: *Le plaisir du texte*; John Haffenden's *Novelists in Interview*: David Lodge (145-167).

Exemplification of Points of Discovery and Deferral

It is obvious that the entire syllabus cannot be implemented here. In order to illustrate the process of discovery and deferral, the focus will be on *Prologue* and *Part I/One* of *Small World* (1-57). Even this will provide only an exemplary glimpse.

At the beginning of the novel the scene is set to explore the *global campus*, "the only university that really matters", and its buzzing conference life: "A young man in a hurry can see the world by conference hopping."(*SW* 44.) The initial stages are sketched of the passage from ignorance to knowledge: "What is structuralism? Is it a good thing or a bad thing?" (*SW* 14), and from innocence to experience: "Ah, virginity, [...]. What is it? A presence or an absence?" (*SW* 39). Man's never ending quest is introduced: "I suppose everyone is looking for his own Grail." (*SW* 12). But in the tradition of the Grail, the search will be long and hardy, full of tests and challenges, temptations and disappointments. Apart from the chance of attaining it, "It's not just a question of making it [...], there's also keeping it." (*SW* 42), the relativity of it all "Different languages divide up the world differently."(*SW* 23) epitomizes in a "fundamental scepticism about the possibility of achieving certainty about anything" (*SW* 27). This sounds familiar in view of Blake's aphorisms referred to above and is projected onto the reading process:

> The tennis analogy will not do for the activity of reading - it is not a to-and-fro process, but an endless, tantalising leading-on, a flirtation without consummation, or if there is consummation, it is solitary, masturbatory. [...] The reader plays with himself as the text plays upon him, plays upon his curiosity, desire, as a striptease dancer plays upon her audience's curiosity and desire. (SW 26).

The metaphor is taken from Barthes (1972), who argues that the erotic nature of a striptease derives from the ritual, the props, the decor, the whole display of adornment made of furs, fans, feathers, fishnet-stockings, gloves and the like (85). The dance, which is the last barrier to nakedness, represents an entirely artistic element, furnishing the dancers with "the icy indifference of skilful practitioners, haughtily taking refuge in the sureness of their technique: their science clothes them like a garment"(86). Nudity is human and universal, no more and no less than the "*natural* vesture of woman" (85). Hence, looking into the female orifice merely faces us with where we come from, with our own origin. This is why the actual eroticism arises from "the *delay* in the stripping [...] not the stripping itself." (*SW* 26).

As a text is just another object in disguise, the true excitement arises from unveiling it:

> To read is to surrender oneself to an endless displacement of curiosity and desire from one sentence to another, from one action to another, from one level of the text to another. The text unveils itself before us, but never allows itself to be possessed; and instead of striving to posses it we should take pleasure in its teasing. (*SW* 27)

Thus it remains a hermeneutic fallacy to believe that the meaning of the first sixty or so pages of *Small World* can ever be fully recuperated, with or without having read the whole novel. Within the diversity of plot strands that unravels here, let us focus on Persse's quest.

The Spirit of the Season

Similar to the "General Prologue" of *The Canterbury Tales* the novel begins with a *Prologue*. Though its first 12 lines are taken from Chaucer's version, they are not cited in their original Middle English iambic pentameters but integrated as a prose passage in Modern English. Parallel to Chaucer's pilgrims who gather at the Tabard Inn on their way to the shrine of St. Thomas à Becket in Canterbury, scholars assemble at conferences "bent on self-improvement" and on socializing. Thus the canvas is provided for a number of tales told by various "story"-tellers who have come together in an easygoing "felaweshipe"

(*NA* 179, l.26), interchanging and interacting with each other. It is the month of April that "with his shoures soote" (*NA* 178,l.1) animates ("priketh", l.11) man and nature alike.

One page later, however, right at the outset of *Part I/One* the pleasantness of the season seems to have gone: "April is the cruellest month." (*SW* 3) There is apparently nothing "soote" about the snow "crusting the lawns and flowerbeds of the Rummidge campus" hosting a conference (*SW* 3). The grim metamorphosis is conveyed by Persse McGarrigle, a young University lecturer from Limerick. But the words he uses are not his own. On looking down from his dormitory window at the unseasonable layers of white, he silently quotes to himself T. S. Eliot's first line of *The Waste Land* (*NA* 2613). It appears logical that someone, who has written his "Master's dissertation on the poetry of T. S. Eliot" (*SW* 3) literally remembers passages from "The Burial of the Dead", a poem rendering a disillusioned view of a ruined and sterile country after the First World War and resounding with depression, loneliness, and emptiness. Knowing that Eliot had composed it while "recovering from a nervous breakdown in the winter of 1921-22" (*SW* 263) adds to the general tenor of irrational apprehensions and spiritual dryness.

Thus, the chord of merrymaking has subsided before the young scholar has actually started on his pilgrimage into the world of academia. Pure in mind and heart, eager to "improve" himself and to "find out what is going on in the great world of ideas" (*SW* 15), he represents innocence and inexperience, both academically "a conference virgin" (*SW* 18) and sexually "I'm a virgin myself" (*SW* 40). A convinced Catholic (*SW* 48-50), he believes "in premarital chastity" (*SW* 39) and embarks on a quest to win the love of Angelica, a beautiful intellectual: "Will you marry me?" (*SW* 39). She assumes for him the sacred importance of the Holy Grail.

Traditions of the Grail

Persse's conjunction with the Grail seeking knight Sir Perceval is unmistakably established, when he is asked whether Persse is "short for Percival?" He replies: "It could be [...] if you like." His second name McGarrigle, which is derived from old Gaelic *fearadhach* or "manly" (Grenan 225), means "Son of Super-valour" (*SW* 9). If the reader wishes to see it this way, both his names interlace with the earliest extant romance *Li Contes del graal* by Chrétiens de Troyes (*SW* 24), written between 1180 and 1190. "Within fifty years, at least four different writers picked up his narrative and wrote Continuations, developing Perceval's adventures" (Mahoney 3). Generally speaking, all of them deal with his military, chivalric, spiritual, and religious formation and portray him as

> ... the perfectly pure and innocent knight who alone could succeed in the quest for the Holy Grail (a cup or bowl with supernatural powers), which in medieval legend was identified with the chalice that had received Christ's blood at the Crucifixion." (Harks and Hodges 264)

However, the Christian connotations of the quest for the Grail are interspersed with other traditions such as vegetation rituals, fertility ceremonies, life-cults as promulgated by "Miss Weston's book, *From Ritual to Romance*" (*SW* 11). Here the following explanation is offered:

> At its root lies the record, more or less distorted, of an ancient Ritual, having for its ultimate object the initiation into the secret of the sources of Life, physical and spiritual. This ritual, in its lower esoteric form, as affecting the processes of Nature, and physical life, survives to-day, and can be traced all over the world, [...].(191).

With this archetypal view of man's initiation into physical and spiritual life, Persse's quest gains the quality of "a ritual of a Life Cult" (Weston 107). Viewing the Grail as a source of life, its sexual implications are explicitly highlighted by the retired academic Miss Sybil Maiden, who compares the Grail cup with the female symbol of conception and the Grail spear with the phallic symbol (*SW* 12). She also explains that T. S. Eliot was inspired by Miss Weston's book as far as title, plan and "much of the imagery and allusion" of *The Wasteland* is concerned. Besides using the Grail myth as a unifying image, she is convinced that his poem is about his own "fears of impotence and sterility" (*SW* 12).

Her psychoanalytical approach neatly interleaves with yet another legend of the Grail myth. In Celtic folklore the central feature is that of the Fisher King who is maimed, sick and old. His infirmity and lack of virility react disastrously upon his kingdom: It foregoes its reproductive forces and becomes waste. Pagan belief has it that the ruler and the wasteland will be restored to fertility by a youth endowed with special qualities, such as strength, wisdom, humility and purity. The potential healing is referred to by Morris Zapp, who has just confided to Persse that his goal in life is to "be the highest paid Professor of English in the world" before he retires: "The hero cures the king's sterility" (*SW* 42). Whether Persse will be "the hero" or not, who is meant by the king and how his rescue will be achieved – the latter depends on asking the crucial question - is up to speculation at this point of the novel.

This mysteriousness matches the enigmatic nature of the Grail, which is shrouded in mystery itself even on the etymological level. Except for a general consensus on the basic root morpheme *gradalis* there is no etymological certainty to whether the Grail is a cup, a dish or a stone. Possible derivations from "*gradus* ("degree, step"), *cratis* ("wickerwork"), *creta* (fuller's earth) and *cratera/craterus* ("crater") point at the food put into the vessel, at the material of which it was made, and at other words for receptacles in analogy to the secondarily expanded suffix -*alis* (*Encyclopedia*, vol.VI, 90).

Representation and Meaning

The elusiveness and the exclusiveness of the Grail is mirrored in Persse's futile attempt at writing about Angelica in a poem that is shorter than *haiku* (*SW* 17). This Japanese lyric form of 17 syllables in a 5-7-5 pattern emerged back in the 16th century and tries to capture the poet's impression of a natural object or scene viewed at a particular moment. Just like the Grail, Angelica, who is somewhere between reality and artifice, content and form, substance and style, cannot be put into a specific mold. Persse's poetic failure appears to symbolize the volatile relation between *signifiant* and *signifié* as it emerges in the general discussion on *structuralism* (*SW* 22-23).

His lyrical endeavor culminates in a "a one-word poem" in a "huge, wavering script" (*SW* 38), made of the letters of Angelica's name in a trail of footprints on the snow-covered lawn of the Rummidge campus. The differing opinions on whether it should be called "earth poem", "snow poem", "sun poem" or "moon poem" testify to the arbitrariness of representation and meaning and anticipate Angelica's evanescent identity: The next morning she is gone. So is her name, which has melted away (*SW* 41). Like an untouchable phantom the Grail has disappeared from sight.

Its evasiveness surfaces in Persse's rhetorical question: "Was there ever such a girl for disappearing?" (*SW* 45) and thus establishes itself as a pattern of the-nearer-the-more-unattainable-relationship between quester and object.

Earlier in the first chapter Persse quotes the first line of "The Burial of the Dead" "under his breath" for a second time, when he cannot spot Angelica in the lecture-room (*SW* 13). With the fertility rites and the first verse from *The Wasteland* as a foil, the underlying tension between repressed libidinal inclinations and internalized standards of moral propriety can no longer be blinked:

> April is the cruellest month, breeding
> Lilacs out of the dead land, mixing
> Memory and desire, stirring
> Dull roots with spring rain. (*NA* 2613-2614)

Considering the constituents "pierce" and "veil" or "val" of the name "Perceval", the "cruelty" of the conflict between unconscious desires and the gratification of physical urges suggests the semiotic link with *invagination*. This term was coined by Jacques Derrida "to describe the complex relationship between inside and outside in discursive practices" (*SW* 322). Within the first part of the novel it could either make us realize "that we have somehow overshot the goal of our quest" (*SW* 27), or that we are yet again succumbing to the pleasure of "stripping the veils of representation from meaning" (*SW* 28). The cross-reference with the American philosopher Charles Sanders Peirce, another "namesake" of Persse's (*SW* 30), may lead us on even further. Based on features such as inherent similarities, causal relations or social conventions, the founder of *semiotics* distinguished between three classes of signs: *icon, index,* and *symbol*. It is especially the *symbol* or *sign proper* which shows that "the relation between the signifying item and what it signifies is not a natural one, but entirely a matter of social convention" (Abrams 238).

Further semantic entanglements proliferate when Persse's name is interconnected with "The Ballad of Persse O'Reilley" in *Finnegans Wake* (*SW* 9). The first stanza contains already the crucial and conclusive episode:

> Have you heard of one Humpty Dumpty
> How he fell with a roll and a rumble
> And curled up like Lord Olofa Crumple
> By the butt of the Magazine Wall,
> (Chorus) Of the Magazine Wall,
> Hump, helmet and all? (Joyce 1958, 44)

In a plain, repetitive, and impersonal language the catastrophe is driven at throughout the ballad so that the final lines of the last stanza do not really harbor any surprise. They emphasize once more what is already known:

> And not all the king's men nor his horses
> Will resurrect his corpus
> For there's no true spell in Connacht or hell
> (bis) That's able to raise a Cain. (Joyce 1958, 47)

What transpires here is that the border-line between the popular and the sacred, the ridiculous and the sublime, the banal and the divine is extremely thin.

This hovering impression becomes more substantial when a conference colleague obscenely extemporizes on Persse's professional place of provenance, the University of Limerick "*There was a young lecturer from Limerick* [...]" (*SW* 7). As the appeal of a nonsense verse like this lies not so much in the subject matter but in the dexterous finding of suitable rhymes for the most improbable words, "*dip his wick*" as a first try seems to scan best (*SW* 7). Persse seeks to cover his embarrassment about the vulgarity of its colloquial version "screwing" by diverting the attention to the inadequacy of the meter. Though a renewed rhyming effort on the part of the same academic heeds the required dactyl, it turns out to be no less obnoxious in content (*SW* 37). It serves as another example of how difficult it is to mold imagination to external "reality" without having it tainted by and caught up in ambivalence and obscurity.

Entrapment in Romances

The intricate tapestry of opinionated ambiguities, unconscious fixations, and disguised fantasies bears out the essence of a quest-romance:

> Translated into dream terms, the quest-romance is the search of the libido or desiring self for a fulfilment that will deliver it from the anxieties of reality but will still contain that reality. [...] Translated into ritual terms, the quest-romance is the victory of fertility over the wasteland. Fertility means food and drink, bread and wine, body and blood, the union of male and female. (Frye 1969, 193)

Like Morris Zapp in his lecture on "Textuality as Striptease" (*SW* 20), Angelica, who is the romance specialist, compares the pleasure of this "supremely invaginated mode of narrative" (*SW* 322) with the pleasure of watching a striptease: It leads the reader on endlessly and repeatedly postpones the "ultimate revelation which never comes - or, when it does, terminates the pleasure of the text" (*SW* 29). Though there are a few romances with "actual striptease" taking place in them, such as Ludovico Ariosto's *Orlando Furioso*, Edmund Spenser's "The Bower of Bliss", John Keats' *The Eve of St. Agnes*, and Samuel Taylor Coleridge's *Christabel* (*SW* 29), the nudity displayed here wavers between dream and reality, spirituality and physicality, desire and gratification.

Related to Persse they suggest different outcomes of his quest: The long-chased heroine in *Orlando Furioso* is also called Angelica. When the hero finds out that she has married a Moorish youth wounded in battle, he looses all his trust in the love of a good woman and runs wild:

> I am not I the man that erst I was;
> *Orlando*: he is buried and ded.
> His most ungratefull love (ah foolish lasse)
> Hath killd *Orlando* and cut of his head.
> I am his ghost that up and downe must passe,
> In this tormenting hell for ever led,
> To be fearfull sample and a just
> To all such fooles as put in love their trust.
> (*Orlando Furioso*, Book XXIII, v. 102; 262)

His disappointment drives him crazy: "The fourth with rage and not with reason waked, He rents his cloths and runs about starke naked." (Book XXIII, v. 105; 262). In his madness he wreaks havoc on everything and everybody coming his way, without realizing of course, how foolishly and ridiculously he behaves.

Though Edmund Spenser's *The Faerie Queene* is modelled on *Orlando Furioso*, there is hardly a vein of humor running through Sir Gunyon's battle against temptation. This worthy Knight of Temperance resists the alluring charms of "Two naked Damzelles" in the "The Bower of Bliss". Their lascivious bathing in a lake where they "ne car'd to hyde, their dainty parts from vew of any, which them eyde" (Book II, Canto 12, v. 63; *NA* 423) cannot divert him from his virtuous path. Not without the aid of reason, though which is personified by his faithful Palmer. In the light of this model of a "virgin" Persse stands a good chance of sticking to his belief in "premarital chastity" (*SW* 39).

However, this option is pending in John Keats' *The Eve of St. Agnes* (*NA* 1804-1814), a romance which Persse extensively consults and quotes from to find out "whether or not sexual intercourse was taking place" between Madeline and Porphyro (*SW* 46). Legend has it that if a chaste young woman performs the proper ritual, she will dream of her future husband on the evening before 21 January, which is the day of St. Agnes, the patron saint of virgins. Persse's romantic proposal "Be my Madeline, and let me be your Porphyro!" is most pragmatically turned down by Angelica, his adored object of desire: "What, and miss the rest of the conference?"(*SW* 40). Unlike the virgin bride in Tennyson's poem "St. Agnes' Eve", who is united with the Heavenly Bridegroom in complete Christian devotion (Tennyson 89-90), Persse apparently falls victim to an erroneous preconception.

Echoes from the Class

The intertextual analysis of post-structuralist and semiotic notions, the protagonist's name and his background, the Grail and its legends, romances and their purpose as they are sketched here, only gives an approximate picture of the discovery process that took place in class. It cannot pay full tribute to the analysis of *Prologue* and *Part I/One* of *Small World* as it proliferated new vistas of plot strands, obscure ambiguities and surprising intricacies, asking for further disclosure. As the novel was dissected chapter by chapter, it triggered an unflagging interest on the part of the students within the frame of mythology and literary tradition, literary theories and literary terms, linguistic schools and metafictional references listed in the syllabus.

Course Objectives

At the University of New Mexico computerized student evaluations (ICES) are part of the program. This made it easier for me to ask my students for elaborate comments on the didactic frame of reference, both written and orally.

As far as the objectives of the course are concerned, they appear to have been reached on various planes.

- Cognitive progress alongside acquisition of knowledge are reflected in statements like these:

    Both the instructor and the novel opened my mind to new ways of looking at literature. I will now approach the novels I read in much the same way.
    It was interesting to find out that the way I read books (New Criticism) is actually a school of thought, and that others exist.
    I believe that criticism serves a good purpose. However, as a student of literature, I do not want to get caught in the trap of looking at literature in only one particular way.

- Personal involvement and emotional satisfaction, which are prerequisites for efficient and meaningful learning, become evident in comments such as:

    Your class provided a creative and stimulating environment for learning that was truly a joy.
    This class was well worth the time and sacrifice. I wish it could go on so I could learn more about literary analysis.
    I would have liked this class to last at least four semesters!
    The teaching style was "laid back" and open to new ideas. It was also magnificent because even though someone has a Ph.D. this doesn't mean that they have to act pompous or intimidating.

- Growth in self-esteem can be discovered in responses such as the subsequent one:

    My first contact with literature was a few summers ago when I took a poetry class. That wasn't fun. It was real torture. I never did understand anything I was reading and I hate to admit that I tried hard to understand. Your English 250 course gave me hope. I think someday I may actually be able to read a book and understand all of the underlying themes and see the intertextuality. Because of your encouragement, I am going to take "The Bible as Literature" in the fall semester. Of course I'm scared, but I think I can get through it and learn.

- "Learning how to learn", a precondition for life-long learning, surfaces in opinions like these:

    I feel confident with what I learned and I am inspired to continue looking deeper into literature and to continue learning, not only while I am in college but in life in general. This is a valuable lesson and one which I can model to my future students and also to my own two children.

The Text

As for the novel, it was widely acclaimed as "fascinating", "deep", "thoroughly entertaining", "excellent", "humorous", "exciting", "great", "smart", "delightful", "witty", "informative", "educational", "intelligent", and "artful". Only one student thought that it had "too much sex and the sex wasn't even descriptive, such as in 'bodice ripper' novels". Contrary to my original assumption many of the students had encountered the world of academia for the first time. Its positive impact is reflected in this comment:

    I had never bothered to consider the lives of English academia. In fact, I did not even know of their existence in the context of the novel. After *Small World*, I feel that I empathize with the characters. In fact, many of the characters remind me of myself. The novel only served to put a human face on the mysterious lives of college professors.

The idea to choose *Small World* as a basic text from which to work was unanimously approved as an opportunity to be introduced "to fictional and non-fictional texts that I had no idea they existed", to experience "an entertaining and effective approach to the study of the classics", to get acquainted with "many great writers who an English major will eventually read", to encounter "literary works, authors, poets, linguists, and literary genres", to be familiarized with "different schools of literary criticism", to learn "that no one theory is correct", and to get "a feel of intertextuality".

The Method

The method of discovery and deferral met with overall consent. Sifting through the reactions according to the various strategies employed, such as segmented reading of the novel, presentation of individual research and written papers, the following picture emerges:

As far as incremental reading is concerned, only one student was "strongly opposed to the idea", because *Small World* does not "merit the limits. I still do not feel that anticipation of events to come is necessary to enjoy this novel, and it was very frustrating". She realizes, however, that this approach served as "a unifying factor in class discussions". Another student who had initially been skeptical about how such a sequential access to the novel could work, recognized in the course of the semester that "otherwise we could not have covered the wide range of texts and authors". The rest of the class enjoyed this procedure.

Individual Research

The presentation and the discussion of individual research in class were overwhelmingly considered to have been beneficial in various manners: It engaged "us in more productive means of learning than a series of boring lectures;" "I learned more about the subjects I had to research myself;" "the presentations were helpful and informative;" "we gained a good look into the realm of literary writers, theories, concepts and structures all in one course;" "I was able to learn more in a short amount of time;" "the time I spent researching was well spent. I learned a lot about literary reference material and I think that will aid me in my future literature classes."

Apart from the cognitive progress it triggered, the required individual initiative appears to have reinforced the students' self-assertion and social competence: "We as students had to stand on our feet" with the instructor as "a knowledgeable mediator who let us learn and grow within the capabilities of ourselves, but added her expertise to discussions and kept things flowing smoothly;" "the independent nature was very conducive to the productivity of the students;" "the class seemed more like a discussion group, with everyone on the same level;" "class discussions were very deep and intimate. This helped to ease the environment considerably;" "I am a shy person and do not always speak out in class. The presentations enabled me to talk and participate in class discussions."

Written Papers

The written papers obviously met the expected analytical and emotional challenge: "I would rather write a paper than take a test any day;" "the papers that were to be written were very helpful in making you purge yourself of creative ideas and analyses. Isn't that what the study of English is all about?" "Once we had to write about what we had discussed in class, I began to understand how it interconnected;" "the papers helped me with close reading; I felt more certain each time;" "writing is a painstaking task, but it helps to put things into perspective;" "the most beneficial thing about the papers was that it helped me organize my thoughts."

The following paper is included to give an example. It was written after the whole novel had been analyzed. Its topic "There is no single 'truth'. Discuss the issue of diversity in *Small World*." was changed to "To Win Is to Lose the Game" (*SW* 319) by J. Matthew Edwards, who agreed to having his essay inserted here:

> The Yin and Yang of Chinese Dao are believed to represent the opposing forces of nature and mankind. Dao teaches that Yin, the dark, feminine and cold force, is a necessary binary opposite of Yang, the light, active and male force. The Yin and Yang flow in a comfortable symbiosis, they cannot exist independent of

each other. To the Chinese, the interplay between the Yin and Yang engenders life to our wasteland. *Small World* introduces the reader to similar opposing forces. The various literary critical approaches persist through time in the fruitless search of the Grail of textual meaning that will continually elude and perplex us. Yet there cannot be a winner in the tournament of these literary approaches for it is together that their purpose is fulfilled. Like the Yin and Yang, literary theories coexist, giving life, energy and fire to the English language.

T.S. Eliot, the secluded poet whose mental trauma drove him to create what many call *the* poem of the twentieth century, is as enigmatic as his prose.

> What are the roots that clutch, what branches grow
> Out of this stony rubbish? Son of man,
> You cannot say, or guess, for you know only
> A heap of broken images, where the sun beats,
> And the dead tree gives no shelter, the cricket no relief.
> (Eliot 1002)

For the literary critic searching for absolute truth, the stony rubbish of language prevents the successful conclusion of the quest. Words are only a heap of broken images rendering an infinite number of meanings. This is the wasted reality of literary criticism, there are no superior interpretations, no champion will be crowned. There can be no doubt that *The Wasteland* is a majestic poem. For the literary critics, the question is what makes the poem so beautiful. What is Eliot communicating to the reader? The answer to this timeless question lies innately in each of us, within the reader's heart a unique meaning is born. Fortunately, there are no mathematical postulates to bring to poetry, no absolute unquestionable derivation can be calculated. On the contrary, the beauty of literature comes from its obscurities, its simple ability to communicate with our souls.

From Zapp's thrill of *deconstruction* to Morgana's seducing *Marxism*, each player in this tournament for the modern Siege Perilous brings a different approach, Derrida speaks of *différance*, to describe mystical beauty of literature. Morris Zapp lectures across Europe about the complexity of language. To Zapp, language can never be accurately translated, "conversation is like playing tennis with a ball of Krazy Putty that keeps coming back over the net in a different shape". (*SW* 29). Zapp believes that even through the use of the same language, meaning can never be fully understood. Each speaker brings a unique experience to the words and structures of language. The arbitrary morphologies that make up words deviate, however so slightly, in meaning from person to person. In a sense, every speaker has a continually evolving dictionary hardwired into the brain consisting of unique meanings. Therefore, accurately translating any use of language is impossible, from a stranger's passing greeting to the mystery of Eliot's *Wasteland*.

Translating meaning across cultures is an even more daunting task. The Japanese translator Akira Sakazaki, despite tremendous efforts, simply cannot accurately translate phrases like "Bugger me, but I feel like some faggots tonight," (*SW* 105) from Frobisher's *Could Try Harder*. The word "faggot" simply cannot be translated from the standard English-Japanese dictionary. Sakazaki mistakenly identifies the word with homosexual implications; he has never heard of the faggots of the dull English cuisine. This is once more illustrated by Sakazaki's conversation with Persse in a Tokyo *karaoke* bar. As Persse discovers to his amusement, even the titles of Shakespeare's infamous plays must be changed to approach an accurate translation. *Julius Caesar* becomes "Swords of Freedom" and *The Merchant of Venice* mysteriously morphs to "A Strange Affair of the Flesh and the Bosom" (*SW* 294). These titles not only speak of Japanese culture, they illustrate the impractical nature of accurate translations across geographies.

The interpretations of literature will change through the ages. The followers of Christianity fervently look for the return of their Messiah. In this quest, each generation predictably has a new interpretation of passages from the final book of the New Testament, the mysterious prophesies of the Apostle John's *Revelation*. Each generation believes that the book speaks to their time. As time's chariot slowly brings the changing of the seasons, the Christians prepare for the return of the Lord. But just as the second coming is always around the corner, so is the ultimate revelation of the timeless works of literature. Persse's analysis of T.S. Eliot's influence on Shakespeare is not as enigmatic as it appears. Shakespeare's true meaning was lost the moment the ink dried on the original manuscripts nearly 400 years ago. Therefore, Shakespeare brings a different message to every generation and culture. Eliot's numerous references to Shakespeare's works in *The Wasteland* surely influence the way the modern critic reads Shakespeare. Like John's *Revelation*, the interpretations change predictably with time.

The wasteland of *Small World* is that of Arthur Kingfisher, the once esteemed literary critic who, stricken with impotence of mind and body, has fallen from his throne. Kingfisher's creativity has ebbed, his intellectual mind lies in ruins. As in the Grail tradition, the noblest knight without ambition will utter the words of righteousness, bringing water to the barren land. And as the knights of the Round Table competed for the prize, so the modern knights prepare for battle with *New Criticism*, *Structuralism*, *Reception Theory*, *Marxism*, and *Deconstruction*, as metaphoric jousts to unsaddle their competition.

It the cold New York winter, the tournament for the UNESCO chair comes to a climax. The players have all gathered for the competition, leaving the despairing Kingfisher to judge the superior literary theory. The speeches of Swallow, Tardieu, Von Turpitz, Morgana and Zapp all summarize the theories each of them so humorously personifies throughout the novel. But in the tradition of the Grail, these prideful knights cannot sway the modern Fisher King. In the end, the humble Persse brings light to Arthur Kingfisher's darkness, asking the contestants: "What follows if everybody agrees with you?" (*SW* 363) The simplicity of this "valiant knight's" question shocks the contestants, but is the key to curing Kingfisher's impotent mind, who replies:

> You imply, of course, that what matters in the field of critical practice is not truth but difference. If everybody were convinced by your arguments, they would have to do the same as you and then there would be no satisfaction in doing it. To win is to lose the game. (*SW* 319).

In Kingfisher's statement, the reader is suddenly blatantly confronted with the academic moral of *Small World*. The esoteric jargon spewing from the mouths of highly educated academia cannot bring the satisfaction of interpreting meaning for oneself. Just as the Yin and Yang exist in mutual dependence, so the forces of literary criticism function together. The key to solving the mystery is an appreciation of the difference of each unique interpretation. A closed mind will not find the door to understanding.

The conclusion to this study of literary analysis comes from where it began in Lodge's novel, *The Wasteland*. Eliot writes of this *différance* in the final section of *The Wasteland*. Borrowing from Brihadaranyaka Upanishad, Eliot beautifully intertexualizes the story of the three gods who asked the Thunder, their father, for their duty. In response to their question, the thunder speaks the same word, *Da*, to each of his three sons.

> Then spoke the thunder
> Da
> *Datta*: What have we given?
> My friend, blood shaking my heart
> The awful daring of a moment's surrender...
> Da
> *Dayadhvam*: I have heard the key
> Turn in the door once and turn once only
> We think of the key, each in his prison...
> Da
> *Damyata:* The boat responded
> Gaily, to the hand expert with said and oar
> The sea was calm, your heart would have responded
> Gaily, when invited, beating obedient
> To controlling hands. (Eliot 1012)

Just as the thunder's word is interpreted differently by each of his sons, so each reader finds something completely his own in literature. Literature is a dance in darkness, a flirtation with the mysteries that turn the universe. The beauty, emotion, pleasure and lessons from each work lies solely with the reader.

Group Work

Reactions to the paper which the students had to research and to write together, something which a number of them had done for the first time in their lives, varied between "the best experience" and "the weakest point of the syllabus." The following comment shows the crux of the matter: "It is a good idea to collaborate on research, but I think it's a better idea to have everyone write his own paper based on the group's research."

Negative reactions evolved around lack of personal commitment, reluctance to share responsibilities, and failing chemistry between group members: "It shows you that in life there are people who work hard and those who slack off," "the efficiency depends on the members of the group;" "you end up relying too much on others;" "I do not like having others have complete control over the contents of my projects, especially not if the wave-length is not the same."

Positive responses centered on aspects of efficiency, self-assertion, and social ease: "When you gather information, you get more done;" "two hands are better than one;" "in a group you get more out of it;" "it is encouraging and competitive;" "when you are shy this opens you up to others more naturally;" "it is easier to talk with each other;" "I had to accept advise from others, which is difficult for me;" "people have to rely on you, which is helpful;" "the group phase was the best place to have it, because I felt more comfortable in class afterwards."

Hence, the pendulum swung between "any time" and "make it optional" as far as putting the results into a joint paper is concerned, mentioning inherent dangers such as "becoming too dependent on one person," " one person ending up doing the bulk of the work" or "not feeling well enough represented."

Almost everybody agreed on the opinion "to do the research for a paper together, but write individually," something that was actually done by two groups who continued working together in preparation for the last two papers.

Recommendations

Asked to make suggestions on how to improve the syllabus, most of the students wanted it to stay the way it was. The following proposals speak for a didactic sensitivity, which deserves further contemplation:

- Make the students keep a notebook with two sections on *Literature* and *Theory* and check regularly to ensure getting back fast to the information accumulated in class.
- Insert a multiple-choice test in mid semester to verify that the students have key criticism points in hand.
- Develop a time chart to illustrate the convergence of literary works, worldwide events and theories.
- Spend more time on each literary theory.
- Replace one of the topics for the written papers by having the students apply the literary theories to a short text or to a poem and evaluate it in every manner we discussed.

One student put her finger on a problem, which I had painfully noticed while we were analyzing *Prologue* and *Part I/One* of *Small World* in class:

> Any criticism I can offer to this course would be to say that we focused a bit too much on the first chapter of the book, where we should have moved on a bit earlier. I realize there were a lot of individual research topics to be covered right away, but by the time the second paper rolled around - the group paper - I feel that we did not have as much time as we should have had to completely *understand* what we were writing on.

This is a real teaser, which surfaced yet again on a different plane, when it came to portraying the voyage of discovery as it had taken place in class. The entire process had to be considerably extracted and narrowed down to fit the present purpose.

But the quest will not only go on in this respect alone. What seems to have worked with this class must not necessarily affect others in a similar way: "Every decoding is another encoding" (*SW* 25).

Works Cited

Abrams, Meyer Howard. *A Glossary of Literary Terms.* 5th ed. New York: Holt, Rinehart & Winston, 1988.
Barthes, Roland. *Le plaisir du texte.* Paris: Éditions du Seuil, 1973.
---. *Mythologies.* Trans. Annette Lavers. New York: Hill and Wang, 1972.
---. "Style and Its Image." *Literary Style: A Symposium.* Ed. and (in part) trans. Seymour Chatman. London: OUP, 1971. 3-15.
Billington, Michael. "Leading Three Lives." *New York Times Book Review* 17 March 1985: 7.
Blake, William. *The Poems of William Blake.* Ed. David V. Erdman. London: Longman, 1971.
Bradbury, Malcolm. *My Strange Quest for Mensonge.* Trans. David Lodge. London: André Deutsch, 1987.
Chaucer, Geoffrey. *Canterbury Tales.* London: Dent, 1958.
Coleridge, Samuel Taylor. *The Portable Coleridge.* Ed. Ivor A. Richards. New York: Viking, 1950.
Derrida, Jacques. "Structure, Sign, and Play in the Discourse of Human Sciences." Trans. Bernard Vannier and Gerald Kamber. *The Structuralist Controversy: The Languages of Criticism and the Sciences of Man.* Ed. Richard Macksey and Eugenio Donato. Baltimore, MD: John Hopkins UP, 1972. 247-265.
Eliot, Thomas Stearns. "The Wasteland." *The Norton Anthology of Poetry.* Ed. Arthur Eastman, et al. New York: Norton, 1970. 1001-1012.
Encyclopedia of Religion. Ed. Mircea Eliade. New York: McMillan, 1987.
Frye, Northrop. *Anatomy of Criticism. Four Essays.* 9th ed. New York: Atheneum, 1969.
---. *Fearful Symmetry: A Study of William Blake.* Princeton, NJ: Princeton UP, 1947.
Grenan, Ida. *The Dictionary of Irish Family Names.* Boulder, CO: Robert Rinehart Publ., 1997.
Haffenden, John. *Novelists in Interview.* London: Methuen, 1985.
Harks, Patrick, and Flavia Hodges. *A Dictionary of First Names.* Oxford: OUP, 1990.
Hazlitt, William. "On Criticism." *The Complete Works of William Hazlitt in Twenty-OneVolumes.* Ed. Percival P. Howe. Vol. 8. London: Dent, 1930-1934. 214-226.
Joyce, James. *A Portrait of the Artist as a Young Man.* 8th ed. New York: Viking, 1959.
---, *Finnegans Wake.* 8th ed. New York: Viking, 1958.
Jefferson, Ann, and David Robey, eds. *Modern Literary Theory: A Comparative Introduction.* Totowa, NJ: Barnes & Noble, 1984.
Keats, John. *The Complete Poems.* New York: Modern Library, 1994.
Keynes, Geoffrey, ed. *The Writings of William Blake.* 3 vols. London: OUP, 1905.
Lodge, David. *Small World.* Harmondsworth: Penguin, 1984.
---. *After Bakhtin: Essays on Fiction and Criticism.* London: Routledge, 1990.

Mahoney, Dhira B. *The Grail: A Casebook*. New York: Garland, 2000.
Milton, John. *Paradise Lost*. Ed. Alastair Fowler. 2nd ed.London: Longman, 1998.
Nitze, William A. "The Fisher King In The Grail Romances." *PMLA* 29:3 (1909): 365-418.
New American Standard Bible. Life Application Study Bible. Grand Rapids, MI: Zondervan Publishing House, 2000.
Norton Anthology of English Literature. Ed. Meyer H. Abrams and Stephen Greenblatt. 7th ed. New York: Norton, 2001.
Orlando Furioso; by Ludovico Ariosto. Trans. Sir John Harington.[1591] Ed. Robert McNulty. Oxford: Clarendon, 1972.
Oxford Companion to English Literature. Ed. Margaret Drabble. 5th ed. Oxford: OUP 1985.
Parker, Patricia A. *Inescapable Romance: Studies in the Poetics of a Mode*. Princeton, NJ: Princeton UP, 1979.
Princeton Encyclopedia of Poetry and Poetics. Ed. Alex Preminger, Frank J. Warnke, and O.B.Hardison, Jr. Princeton, NJ: Princeton UP, 1965.
Selden, Raman. *A Reader's Guide to Contemporary Literary Theory*. Brighton: Harvester, 1986.
Shakespeare, William. *The Tempest*. Ed. Robert Langbaum. New York: New American Library, 1964.
---. *The Complete Works of William Shakespeare*. Ed. Charlotte Porter and Helen A. Clarke. New York: Fred de Fau, 1903.
Shaw, Bernard. *Pygmalion*. Bernard Shaw. *Complete Plays, with Prefaces*. 2 vols. Vol. 1. New York: Dodd, Mead & Co., 1962. 189-295.
Shelley, Mary. *Frankenstein; or The Modern Prometheus*. Johanna E. Smith, ed. *Case Studies in Contemporary Criticism*. Boston: Bedford Books of St. Martin's Press, 1992. 19-85.
Skovmand, Michael, and Steffen Skovmand, eds. *The Angry Young Men: Osborne, Sillitoe, Wain, Braine, Amis*. Tryk [Copenhagen]: Akademisk Forlag, 1975.
Southam, B. C. *A Student's Guide to the Selected Poems of T.S. Eliot*. London: Faber & Faber, 1974.
Spenser, Edmund. *The Faerie Queene*. 2 vols. London: Dent, 1952.
Richardson, Samuel. *Pamela*. London: Dent, 1938.
Tennyson, Alfred. *Poems of Tennyson*. Ed. Jerome H. Buckley. Cambridge, MA.: Riverside Press, 1958.
Weston, Jessie L. *From Ritual to Romance*. Mineola,NY: Dover, 1997.
Whorf, Benjamin Lee. "Language, Mind and Reality." *Language, Thought and Reality: Selected Writings of Benjamin Lee Whorf*. Ed. John B. Carroll. Cambridge, MA: MIT Press, 1956. 246-270.
Yeats, William Butler. *The Poems*. Ed. Richard J. Finneran. 2nd ed. New York: Scribner, 1997.

Contributors

Eva Boesenberg, currently Assistant Professor for *American Studies*, is the author of *Gender – Voice – Vernacular: The Formation of Female Subjectivity in Hurston, Morrison, and Walker*, as well as articles on Charlotte Perkins Gilman, slave narratives, African American women's literature, the 1990's masculinity crisis, and basketball. She studied English, German, and Indology at the Albrecht-Ludwig-University Freiburg and the University of Massachusetts, doing research at Cornell University and Harvard University as well. She is presently working on a *Habilitation* titled *Money and Gender in the American Novel*.

Gisela Hermann-Brennecke, Prof. Dr., has taught and researched at different universities in Germany and abroad, most recently at the Department of English Language and Literature at the University of New Mexico. She joined the faculty of the English Institute in 1995. Her publications appeared in German, English and French, and include studies on empirical issues related to foreign language acquisition and attitude formation, on the interdependence of language and thought, and on literary topics.

Annemarie Hindorf, Dr. phil., has been working at the English Institute since 1971. From 1978 to 1979 she worked as a lector in German at the University of Newcastle upon Tyne. She qualified in the field of English linguistics with with a doctoral thesis on *The Syntactical Use of the English Verbal Noun in* –ing. Main fields of work and research: English Phonetics and Phonology, History of the English Language, Old English, Middle English.

Olaf Jäkel, Dr. phil., assistant professor of English linguistics at the Martin-Luther-University Halle-Wittenberg since 1998. Before that, assistant teacher in North-England, DFG-research scholarship at the Graduate College of Cognitive Science and lecturer at the University of Hamburg as well as school teacher of English and Philosophy. Numerous articles in English and German, in particular on issues in cognitive linguistics, lexicology, and semantics. Book publications include *Metaphern in abstrakten Diskurs-Domänen* (1997), *Sokratisches Textgespräch* (2001).

Wolf Kindermann is professor of American literature at the English Institute since 1994. Books on Faulkner and on critical assessements of the American Enlightenment in the writings of Benjamin Rush, Crèvecoeur, and Charles Brockden Brown. Articles on Poe, Simms, O'Neill, W.E.B. DuBois, Afro-Caribbean, South African, and Asian-American writers, King Philip's War, and the interdependence of painting and fiction in early 19th-century America.

Andreas Marschollek was assistant lecturer at the English Institute and worked on his dissertation "Cognitive and Affective Flexibility through Foreign Languages at Primary Level: An Empirical Study" between 1996 and 2000. Now he is assistant lecturer at Erfurt University.

Hans-Dieter Metzger teaches British Studies. He studied Photography and Printing Methods (Dipl. Ing., Staatsexamen) at FH Cologne and the University of Darmstadt, and Modern History and Philosophy (M.A., Dr. phil., Habilitation, PD) at the University of Darmstadt. His publications include *Thomas Hobbes und die Englische Revolution, 1640-1660* (1991), *Religious Thinking and National Identities* (2000), "Heiden, Juden oder Teufel? Puritanische Indianermission in Massachusetts." *Geschichte und Gesellschaft* 27 (2001), and *Protestantische Ethik und christliches Gemeinwesen* (forthcoming).

Jürgen Meyer, M.A., studied English and German literature at the universities of Göttingen and Freiburg between 1988 and 1995. Until 1996 he worked in two projects of the Special Research Project 321 *Transitions and Tensions Between Literacy and Orality* at Freiburg. From 1997 until 2000 he was funded by the post-graduate college on *Theory of Literature and Communications* (Konstanz Univ.), completing his doctoral thesis on *Allegorien des Wissens: Flann O'Briens "The Third Policeman" und Friedrich Dürrenmatts "Durcheinandertal" als 'ironische Kosmographien'*. Since April 2000 he teaches English literature as assistant professor at the English Institute.

Werner Plehn, Dr. phil. Habil., Privatdozent, has been a member of staff at the English Institute since 1972. He studied English and Russian and worked as a lecturer of German at the universities of Newcastle upon Tyne and Leeds in 1977-78 and in 1980-82 respectively. He qualified in the field of linguistics. His doctoral thesis deals with *The Social Vocabulary in Charles Dickens' Works* and his Habilitation explores *Linguistic Reflections* *of Social Liberty in 18th Century England.* Main fields of work and research: Sociolinguistics, Varieties of English, Semantics, General Linguistics.

Dietmar Schneider has been linked with the English Institute since his student days, later as a lecturer and senior lecturer, and since 1998 as a Privatdozent in the Linguistics and English Language section. His special interests are English grammar and lexicology, text linguistics and pragmatics as well as the history of the English language. He was a lector in German at the University of Newcastle upon Tyne and a post-doctoral research fellow at the University of Edinburgh. Recent publications include "Werbung in der Politik – eine linguistische Analyse britischer Wahlprogramme 1997" (co-author Franka Marx) in *Profile von Sprachmustern, Texten und Sprechern des Englischen.* Ed. S. Ehrhardt, et al. Aachen: Shaker, 2001. 81-140.

Hans-Dieter Schöne has been working at the English Institute since 1968, mainly in the ELT section. In 1983 he obtained a doctorate form Martin-Luther-University. For one year (1985/86) he taught German at the University of Newcastle upon Tyne. Since 1991 he is the coordinator of the ELT division. His research interests include grammar, discourse analysis, and corpus linguistics.

Julia Semmer studied English, German language and literature, German as a foreign language, and Education at Martin-Luther-University and at the University of Newcastle upon Tyne. After qualifying as a teacher of English and German and giving classes at various public and private institutions she returned to the English Institute as a member of staff. She offers courses on foreign language acquisition, intercultural studies, and literature. These courses serve as a basis for teacher students during their practical teaching phase in school, which is an integral part of the study programme for future English teachers.

Angela Senst teaches American literature at the English Institute. She studied at Purdue University and at the University of Göttingen, where she received degrees in history, American, English, and Russian literature and culture. In her research she focuses on American literature of the 20th century and comparative literature. She is currently completing her Ph.D. dissertation on Robert Frost and T.S. Eliot.

Dirk Thormann studied English, Biology, German as a foreign language, and Education at Martin-Luther-University. After graduation he taught at the Waldorf School in Halle and at various public and private institutions. He joined the English Institute in 1999 where he has been offering courses on foreign language acquisition, psycholinguistic aspects of foreign language teaching, and classroom management. His research interests focus on learner autonomy and curriculum design.

Sabine Volk-Birke, professor of English literature at Halle since 2000. She previously taught at Bamberg University, and was a guest professor at the universities of Jena and Vienna. She has written books on R.S. Thomas, *Chaucer and Medieval Preaching*, and co-edited a volume on Literacy and Orality in Medieval England. She has published articles on Ford Madox Ford, Shelley, Richardson, Virginia Woolf, Henryson's *Testament of Cresseid*, Jane Austen, Sidney's *Arcadia*, on the motif of "death-in-life" in modern English poetry, and on Shakespeare in Germany in the 19th century.

Hallenser Studien zur Anglistik und Amerikanistik

herausgegeben am Institut für Anglistik und Amerikanistik (Martin-Luther-Universität Halle-Wittenberg)

Martin Meyer; Gabriele Spengemann; Wolf Kindermann (Hrsg.)
Tangenten: Literatur & Geschichte
Die Hallenser Studien zur Anglistik und Amerikanistik wollen an die Tradition des Dialogs unter den inzwischen vielfältig verzweigten Teilgebieten eines einstmals einheitlichen Faches anknüpfen, wie sie durch den Hallenser Anglisten Hans Weyhe und seine Kollegen gepflegt wurde.
Der vorliegende erste Band der Reihe ist dem Weyhe-Schüler Martin Schulze gewidmet, dessen Werdegang und Tätigkeit als Hochschullehrer die vielschichtigen Entwicklungen des Faches im Schatten des Ost-West-Konfliktes spiegelt, und dessen Initiative die Hallenser Anglistik die Chance eines Neubeginns verdankt.
Die hier versammelten Beiträge zur englischen und amerikanischen Literatur, zu Geschichte, Sprachwissenschaft und Bildungspolitik eint trotz aller Vielfalt der Blick auf die Wechselbeziehungen zwischen europäischer und amerikanischer Kulturtradition sowie das Bemühen um den Dialog zwischen den philologischen und den historisch-sozialwissenschaftlichen Disziplinen.
Bd. 1, 1996, 278 S., 48,80 DM, br., ISBN 3-8258-2907-3

Wolf Kindermann (Hrsg.)
Entwicklungslinien: 120 Jahre Anglistik in Halle
Das Institut für Anglistik und Amerikanistik an der Martin-Luther-Universität in Halle und Wittenberg feierte im Jahr 1996 sein 120jähriges Bestehen. Als erstes rein englisches Seminar in deutschen Landen kann es auf eine lange Tradition der anglistischen Forschung und Lehre, vor allem auf dem Gebiet von Sprachwissenschaft und Sprachgeschichte, zurückblicken. Namhafte Fachgelehrte, unter ihnen Friedrich E. Elze, Max Förster, Max Deutschbein, Hans Weyhe und Otto Ritter, haben die Geschichte der Hallenser Anglistik mit geprägt. Heute steht das Institut vor einem Neubeginn, der sich aber auch den Entwicklungslinien der Hallenser Anglistik verpflichtet fühlen muß.
Der vorliegende Band soll durch Forschungsergebnisse und Arbeitsproben von Mitarbeitern und Gästen des Instituts die thematische Vielfalt des Neubeginns dokumentieren. Er umfaßt neben einem kurzen Überblick zur Institutsgeschichte Beiträge zur Realismusproblematik in der englischen Literatur des 18. Jahrhunderts, zu H.G. Wells, zur anglo-irischen (Yeats, Joyce, Heaney und Friel) und zur amerikanischen Literatur (Poe, Hemingway und Heller, Zora Neale Hurston und Alice Walker). Ferner finden sich sprachwissenschaftliche Beiträge zu den "Anglo-Saxon Wills", zum Verhältnis von Sprache und Ideologie bei Burke und Paine, zu "Intertextuality in Press Correspondence", zum "Pendel des sprachlichen Handelns" sowie ein Beitrag zum Stellenwert von Einstellungen im Fremdsprachenunterricht.
Bd. 2, 1997, 240 S., 49,80 DM, br., ISBN 3-8258-3304-6

Pamela Winchester
Indian Myth and White History
Bd. 3, 1997, 240 S., 48,80 DM, br., ISBN 3-8258-3446-8

Gisela Hermann-Brennecke; Wilhelm Geisler (Hrsg.)
Zur Theorie der Praxis & Praxis der Theorie des Fremdsprachenerwerbs
Der Band thematisiert die reziproke Einheit empirisch orientierter Theorie und theoriegeleiteter Praxis fremdsprachendidaktischer Fragestellungen. Während sich Theorie als Ergebnis und Prozeß der Fremdsprachenforschung im Wechselspiel mit und an der fremdsprachlichen Unterrichtspraxis als ihrem Gegenstand ausrichtet, liefert die Praxis die Basis, von der Theorie überhaupt erst ihre Impulse empfängt. Beides geschieht immer unter der Prämisse, die eigenen Voraussetzungen, Bedingungen und Grenzen unter Einbeziehung des Verhältnisses zu anderen Bezugswissenschaften kritisch zu hinterfragen.
Die hier vorgelegten Beiträge behandeln verschiedene Aspekte des Theorie-Praxis-Bezugs, eine Thematik, die die Forschung und Lehre von Wolfgang Butzkamm, dem zu Ehren dieser Sammelband erscheint, wie ein roter Faden durchzieht. So stehen neben wissenschaftstheoretischen, paralinguistischen, quantenphysikalischen, empirischen und mentalistischen Reflexionen auch solche zum Umgang mit Literatur, Bilingualismus, Mehrsprachigkeit, gesprochener Sprache und ihrer Kontextualisierung aus suggestopädischer Sicht. Gleichwertig und reziprok.
Bd. 4, 1998, 292 S., 49,80 DM, br., ISBN 3-8258-3840-4

Gisela Hermann-Brennecke (Hrsg.)
Frühes schulisches Fremdsprachenlernen zwischen Empirie & Theorie
Die hier versammelten Beiträge behandeln Zugriffe auf frühes schulisches Fremdsprachenlernen in verschiedenen europäischen Ländern, in der russischen Föderation sowie in den USA und berichten von den dabei gesammelten Erfahrungen. Sie wollen zu weiteren Forschungsaktivitäten anregen und dadurch zu bildungspolitischen Entscheidungspro-

LIT Verlag Münster – Hamburg – Berlin – London
Grevener Str. 179 48159 Münster
Tel.: 0251 – 23 50 91 – Fax: 0251 – 23 19 72
e-Mail: lit@lit-verlag.de – http://www.lit-verlag.de

Preise: unv. PE

zessen beitragen.
The present collection of articles deals with various approaches to foreign language learning at primary school in different European countries, in the Russian Federation and in the USA. The results presented want to stimulate further research activities and to contribute to processes of educational decision making.
Bd. 5, 1999, 216 S., 49,80 DM, br., ISBN 3-8258-4351-3

Martina Ghosh-Schellhorn (ed.)
Writing Women Across Borders and Categories
Generally held to be rigid, borders and categories are nonetheless expanded when those bounded by the demarcations of hegemony, challenge its strictures. Significant instances of this constructive transgression can be found in the women's writing with which this collection of essays by international critics engages. Whereas in travel writing by women (Sarah Hobson, Dervla Murphy, Jan Morris) 'transgression' is seen to have settled into a familiar strategy, in autobiography (Ann Fanshawe, Margaret Cavendish, Christine Brooke-Rose), cultural analysis (Virginia Woolf, Marianna Torgovnick, Donna Haraway), and fiction (Michelle Cliff, Jeanette Winterson, Ellen Galford, Fiona Cooper), women have succeeded in creating an innovative space for themselves.
Bd. 6, 2000, 176 S., 39,80 DM, pb., ISBN 3-8258-4639-3

Claudia Franken
Gertrude Stein, Writer and Thinker
Gertrude Stein, Writer and Thinker, "presents the first sensible overview which includes a demonstration of the 'content' which may be found in each of Stein's presumably 'abstract' key works" (Robert Bartlett Haas, Foreword).
This study offers a guided commentary on the *about* and the "literariness" of her works which helps the reader to understand and appreciate her writing and thinking. Exploring Stein's figures of thought within the context of the philosophies of William James and A. N. Whitehead and considering the aesthetic and ethical significance of texts of all phases and genres of her writing, this commentary convinces us that Stein was indeed one of the 20th century's most original and complex authors.
Bd. 7, 2000, 400 S., 49,80 DM, pb., ISBN 3-8258-4761-6

Angela Kuhk
Vielstimmige Welt
Die Werke St. John de Crèvecœurs in deutscher Sprache
"Das Werk hat unter den Händen des Teutschen Übersetzers noch gewonnen." Die europaweite Begeisterung für die Werke Crèvecœurs äußerte sich auch in einer Flut an deutschen Übersetzungen: Zwischen 1782 und 1802 entstanden mehr als 30 Schriften, die auf die Zeilen des berühmten "Amerikanischen Landmanns" zurückgingen. Erstmals erfolgt hier eine bibliographische Erfassung und eine chronologische Vorstellung dieser Texte wie auch der Rezeptionsdokumente.
Ausführliche Übersetzungsanalysen zu den Themen Indianer, Quäker, Sklaverei, deutsche Einwanderer, Walfang, Flora und Fauna liefern neue Beiträge zum deutschen Amerikabild im ausgehenden 18. Jahrhundert und erlauben einen detaillierten Einblick in die vielstimmige Welt Crèvecœurs.
Bd. 8, 2001, 480 S., 49,80 DM, br., ISBN 3-8258-4882-5

Erlanger Studien zur Anglistik und Amerikanistik
herausgegeben von
Rudolf Freiburg und Dieter Meindl

Rudolf Freiburg; Jan Schnitker (Hrsg.)
"Do you consider yourself a postmodern author?"
Interviews with Contemporary English Writers
Bd. 1, 1999, 248 S., 39,80 DM, br., ISBN 3-8258-4395-5

Hannah Jacobmeyer
Märchen und Romanzen in der zeitgenössischen englischen Literatur
Im Zentrum einer vielfach konstatierten Renaissance des "Wunderbaren" in der Kultur des ausgehenden 20. Jahrhunderts stehen die Formen und Strukturen von Märchen und Romanze. Gelten sie uns einerseits als Merkmale einer prämodernen Narrativik, so sind sie andererseits zu Konstanten von Literatur geworden, die sich durch das Jahrhunderte bis in die sogenannte postmoderne Literatur hinein nachweisen lassen. Anhand ausgewählter zeitgenössischer Texte der englischen Literatur zeigt die Autorin, wie Märchen und Romanzen fortleben - aber auch, wo sie sich überschneiden und auf welche Weise sie in eine endlose, intertextuelle "Echokammer" eingebunden werden. Romanzenmuster erlauben zudem, Einsicht in die Gemeinsamkeiten hoher und "trivialer" Literatur zu nehmen. Autoren der detailliert analysierten Märchen und Romanzen sind u. a. Salman Rushdie, A. S. Byatt, Graham Swift, Angela Carter und Barbara Cartland.
Bd. 2, 2000, 224 S., 68,80 DM, br., ISBN 3-8258-4686-5

LIT Verlag Münster – Hamburg – Berlin – London
Grevener Str. 179 48159 Münster
Tel.: 0251 – 23 50 91 – Fax: 0251 – 23 19 72
e-Mail: lit@lit-verlag.de – http://www.lit-verlag.de
Preise: unv. PE